# Documents
## of
# Christian Worship

## DESCRIPTIVE AND
## INTERPRETIVE SOURCES

## James F. White

T&T CLARK INTERNATIONAL
*A Continuum imprint*
LONDON • NEW YORK

Originally published in the United States of America by
Westminster/John Knox Press

This edition published under licence from
Westminster/John Knox Press by

T&T Clark
A Continuum Imprint
The Tower Building
11 York Road
London SE1 7NX

Acknowledgments will be found on pages 249–250

First Published 1992
Reprinted 2003, 2004
ISBN 0 567 29218 5


British Library Cataloguing in Publication Data

A catalogue record for this book
is available from the British Library


Printed and bound in Great Britain by
Antony Rowe Ltd
Chippenham Wiltshire

*In grateful memory of
Mark Searle,
1941–1992,
scholar, colleague, friend*

# Contents

List of Tables   viii

List of Plates   ix

Preface   xi

Abbreviations   xiii

I.   The Teaching of Christian Worship   1

II.   Time as Communication   17

III.   Space as Communication   41

IV.   Daily Public Prayer   75

V.   The Service of the Word   100

VI.   Sacraments in General   119

VII.   Christian Initiation   145

VIII.   The Eucharist   180

IX.   Occasional Services   214

Glossary   239

Acknowledgments   249

Index of Authors and Documents   251

Index of Subjects   255

# Tables

1. The Classical Liturgical Families,
   Sixth Century to Present                                    6

2. The Protestant Traditions of Worship,
   Sixteenth Century to Present                                7

3. The Classical Liturgical Families, c. 600 A.D.             8

4. The Protestant Traditions of Worship, c. 1600 A.D.         9

5. Early Documents and Writers on Christian Worship          10

6. The Jewish Calendar                                       22

7. Division of Original Unitive Commemorations               24

8. Cycles of the Liturgical Year
   According to the Common Calendar                           39

9. Patterns of Daily Prayer                                  77

10. Verbal and Conceptual Progression of Baptism            157

11. The Ceremonies of the Baptismal Initiation              161

12. Principal Eucharistic Rites, 1521–1571                  200

Chronology                                                   11

# Plates

Chapter I. The Divinity School, Oxford, from Thomas Richman, *An Attempt to Discriminate the Styles of Architecture in England from the Conquest to the Reformation*. London: John Henry Parker, 1848.

Chapter II. Christian Martyrs, frontispiece of John Foxe, *Book of Martyrs; or, A History of the Lives, Sufferings, and Triumphant Deaths, of Many of the Primitive as Well as Protestant Martyrs*. New York: Charles K. Moore, 1842.

Chapter III. Seal of the Cambridge Camden Society, frontispiece of *A Hand-Book of English Ecclesiology*. London: Joseph Masters, 1847.

Chapter IV. The Church at Prayer, plate from *Hierurgia Anglicana: or Documents and Extracts Illustrative of the Ritual of the Church in England after the Reformation*. London: J. G. F. & J. Rivington; J. Masters, 1848.

Chapter V. The Service of the Word, title page of Anthony Sparrow, *A Rationale upon the Book of Common-Prayer of the Church of England*. London: T. Garthwait, 1664.

Chapter VI. Brass effigy of Edmund Assheton (died 1522), Middleton Church, Lancashire, in Charles Boutell, *The Monumental Brasses of England*. London: George Bell, 1849.

Chapter VII. River baptism, title page of anonymous tract, *The Practical Uses of Baptism*. Philadelphia: American Baptist Publication Society, c. 1850.

Chapter VIII. North end celebration, frontispiece of Charles Wheatly, *A Rational Illustration of the Book of Common Prayer*, third edition, London: A. Bettesworth, W. & J. Innys, & C. Rivington, 1720.

Chapter IX. Burial, plate from *The Book of Common Prayer*. Oxford: Bartlett & Newman, 1814.

# Preface

Most of my lifetime has been devoted to teaching Christian worship or to preparing others to do the same. I feel great empathy with the moving words with which H. A. Reinhold concluded his 1956 *Autobiography:* "When I had first ventured out, the road was narrow and the wayfarers few; . . . The road is wider now." When I began teaching Christian worship in 1959, the wayfarers were still comparatively few; today the North American Academy of Liturgy alone numbers nearly four hundred members, and there are many other laborers in the same vineyard. The road is much wider now.

In recent years I have given much thought to what materials I wish I could put in the hands of students of Christian worship. This book is the result of those reflections. It began as a series of documents I collected and/or translated for my students during two decades of teaching at Perkins School of Theology. Now I find my doctoral students and graduates are requesting permission to use the same collections with their students. It seems time to provide them with something better. I have tried to let my imagination range as far as I could in order to develop a better format and to discover a wider range of materials not readily available or, in some cases, never before accessible. To the two hundred verbal documents, I have added various maps, diagrams, bibliographies, a chronology, a glossary, and visual illustrations. I have tried to reach beyond conventional verbal documents and to provide materials particularly pertinent to the worship of North American Christians.

I think it is exciting for students to have direct access to verbal and visual documents so they can see for themselves. My teaching method has been to exegete texts in class and to answer questions. Thus I have not added introductions, expecting the instructor will do this. Of course, some of the sources speak for themselves; others—such as the debate whether or not *Didache* 9–10 refers to the eucharist—require extensive interpretation.

The historical documents reflect in most cases worldviews that marginalize many people and would not be acceptable today. However, it would be historically inaccurate to impose modern sensitivities on ancient documents, and so they speak for themselves, if not for us.

For the most part, I have avoided reproducing liturgical texts in favor of descriptive or interpretive documents. Several excellent collections of liturgies are readily available, especially Bard Thompson, *Liturgies of the Western Church*, and R. C. D. Jasper and G. J. Cuming, *Prayers of the Eucharist: Early and Reformed*. For those who read other languages, A. Hänggi and I. Pahl, *Prex Eucharistica*, and I. Pahl, *Coena Domini I*, are highly useful. The chief exception on liturgical texts has been the reproduction of considerable portions of the *Apostolic Tradition*, attributed to Hippolytus. Descriptive or interpretive documents often tell us much more than do the words uttered in worship because such sources indicate those things an observer considered worth noting or how he or she understood the meaning of what the Christian community did.

In most cases, I have used the best available English translation; in others, where none existed or seemed satisfactory, I have made my own. In every instance, I have indicated the source from which permission was given or signified the text from which I translated. I am happy to thank Dr. Susan J. White for taking most of the photographs.

The arrangement I have followed is to trace significant structures of worship through the course of their development. This enables the reader to see issues and practices develop without having to sort out all the contemporary problems, both related and unrelated. This will make it easier for those who also use as a textbook my *Introduction to Christian Worship* (rev. ed., 1990). The books complement each other.

I am grateful for the careful assistance of Nancy Kegler, Sherry Reichold, and Cheryl Reed in producing a clean manuscript.

I owe much to my students and colleagues who have frequently been my teachers. The comments of Grant S. Sperry-White, John K. Brooks-Leonard, Paul F. Bradshaw, and Robert F. Taft, S.J., have contributed much to improving the clarity and accuracy of this book.

Above all, I hope this book will strengthen the ministry of those fellow wayfarers who are engaged in teaching and studying the forms and meaning of Christian worship.

J. F. W.

*University of Notre Dame*
*June 15, 1992*

# Abbreviations

ACC    *Alcuin Club Collections*

ACW    *Ancient Christian Writers*

ANF    *Ante-Nicene Fathers*

ASB    *Alternative Service Book*

BCP    *Book of Common Prayer*

BEM    *Baptism, Eucharist and Ministry*

CSL    *Constitution on the Sacred Liturgy*

FC    *Fathers of the Church*

HBS    *Henry Bradshaw Society*

LBW    *Lutheran Book of Worship*

LCC    *Library of Christian Classics*

LW    *Luther's Works*

NPNF    *Nicene and Post-Nicene Fathers*

PG    *Patrologia Graeca*

PL    *Patrologia Latina*

UMH    *United Methodist Hymnal*

# CHAPTER I

# The Teaching of
# Christian Worship

Learning how to worship is an essential part of becoming a Christian. In
the heroic age of Christianity, being permitted to worship at the eucharist with the Christian community was a sign of one's final initiation
into the faith. It was preceded by months or even years of preparation
before one was deemed ready for this step of full acceptance by the
community. The same is no less true today although usually less dra-
matic. Christian children are trained in the worship tradition of their
parents (or sponsors) by being brought to worship week after week,
year after year. From a very early age they become conscious of what
Christians do in worship and how they do it. The same is true of those
of a more mature age who come to Christianity by conversion. They,
too, must be taught what Christians do in worship in order to become
part of the community.

If learning to worship is essential to becoming a Christian, then the teaching of Christian worship is a major part of ministry to new Christians. Making disciples involves much teaching of Christian worship. This ministry involves all Christians, lay and ordained. It does not mean that one has to be a liturgical scholar to engage in this ministry, but it does imply a basic familiarity with the practices and beliefs underlying Christian worship. A method of organizing one's knowledge about these communal experiences is necessary for teaching Christian worship in a clear and accurate pattern. The careful organization of information about worship is a high priority for effective communication of such knowledge.

In this chapter, we shall make a few basic comments on the organization of our knowledge and experience of worship, give a few graphic means for the presentation of this information, and provide a bibliography of general books on Christian worship.

## The Organization of Liturgical Pedagogy

It is customary to divide our knowledge about Christian worship into three rather general areas: biblical and historical, theological, and practical or pastoral. Obviously these overlap at many points: for example, when one examines the shape and meaning of baptism in the fourth century (history and theology). What makes the study of worship most interesting is how often theory and practice intersect. Purely historical scholarship has reshaped the way we actually do many things in worship today such as recent reforms in the structure of the eucharist (history and practice). Theology and practice also go hand in hand. One cannot discuss the theology of the wedding service without finding implications for how it is to be performed (theology and practice).

The biblical and historical witness is essential in the teaching of worship simply because it explains how we came to do what we now do. The search for the origins of Christian worship helps us to understand better the sources of much that we still do, such as the mixing of water and wine in the eucharist. But traditions develop as they mature, and it is important to know why changes were made. In a sense, the study of biblical and historical sources is a means of self-understanding so we know what factors formed us to be as we now are and to act as we do.

At the same time, it is necessary to raise theological questions about the meaning of what we do. This can take various forms: the theology of worship in general, theology of proclamation (dealing especially with preaching), and theology of the sacraments (usually called "sacramental theology," although the latter term is capable of a much broader interpretation). In addition, there is liturgical theology, which uses Christian worship as a source for theological reflection.[1]

It is also essential to be concerned about the actual practice of worship so it can lead to the fullest and deepest level of active participation on the part of worshipers. One can speak of pastoral liturgy with a threefold concern about the quality of planning, preparing for, and conducting worship. Each of these three stages involves important practical concerns. To prepare for an Ash Wednesday service, one must plan for the imposition of ashes, see to it that the ashes are secured in advance, and conduct the service so that this act communicates in depth. A more theoretical approach to the practical aspects of worship is found in the discipline of ritual studies, which often expands beyond the scope of Christian worship.

One soon realizes that much of the work of teaching Christian worship is a matter of inculcating basic vocabulary. Some terms are in common use: pulpit, Christmas, hymn. Others are a bit more esoteric: epiclesis, concomitance, antiphon. But each relates to a practice or concept that is important for developing a deeper knowledge of Christian worship. Tests on the meaning of basic terms are often good means for gauging familiarity with the practices and ideas they represent. Until one develops a basic liturgical vocabulary, it is difficult to converse on the subject. One writer has called this "liturgical literacy."[2] He happened to choose more than 650 terms as "essential" while concentrating on the Roman Catholic tradition. Several liturgical dictionaries are listed in the bibliography at the end of this chapter.

Of course, worship is not an abstraction. It can only be fully understood by doing it, although at times it may be useful to detach oneself enough to observe it in a fairly objective fashion. Robert Frost speaks of a scientist who catches, chloroforms, and mounts a butterfly in order to study it, only to discover that he no longer has a real butterfly. Christian worship has to be experienced to be understood, and this cannot be done in laboratory or library but only in church. Only by participating can we understand what it is Christians do in worship.

However, it is advisable deliberately to broaden one's contacts with

---

[1]Geoffrey Wainwright, *Doxology* (New York: Oxford University Press, 1980), is a pioneering work in this field.

[2]Dennis C. Smolarski, *Liturgical Literacy* (New York: Paulist Press, 1990).

worshiping communities beyond those with whom one is immediately familiar. Latin Rite Roman Catholics certainly should worship with Eastern Rite Catholics such as Ukranians or Melkites; Episcopalians need to worship with both Evangelicals and Anglo-Catholics in order to comprehend just their own Anglican tradition. This requires systematic effort. Often the yellow pages of the telephone book will categorize churches by denominations, and it is comparatively easy to figure out what worshiping traditions are present in any area. (See Table 2.) One may need to remember that Presbyterians, the Christian Reformed Church, and the Reformed Church in America all share in the Reformed tradition. The largest number of American denominations stem from the Frontier tradition. Churches whose denominational names include such terms as Lutheran, Methodist, or Pentecostal belong to the respective traditions called by those terms. Anabaptists are present as Mennonites, and Quakers as the Society of Friends or simply Friends. All Western Christians will learn much from worshiping with churches usually listed as "Eastern Orthodox." Christians are often welcome at Jewish synagogues or temples and will learn much from these encounters.

Visits to unfamiliar worshiping traditions will be enhanced if one learns to look for much more than what words are said and sung. It is important to have some structure to remind one to look for such items as: who the people are (age, race, sex), what roles each group plays (including ministers and choir), what is the architectural setting of worship, what visual arts are present, how people arrive and leave, what actions happen (such as offering, receiving communion, baptism, etc.), what leadership roles are apparent (usher, reader, presider), who sings and how, the use or disuse of printed materials, and how strangers are treated. One soon realizes that much more is done in worship than is said. Sometimes it is helpful to imagine oneself as a pagan who comes to worship just out of curiosity to see what Christians do. And many Christians might be surprised to see what their worship looks like to others. We may discover some self-contradictory non-verbal statements: for example, do we profess inclusivity and exclude children from any significant role? Eyes to observe may be opened wide in astonishment.

The broader our experience of Christian worship is and the more we reflect on it, the better we are able to teach others and to help them appropriate for themselves its richness and depth. This is certainly an important ministry in bringing people to newness of life in Christ. Our hope is that the documents that follow will put readers in direct contact with the Christian community's experience of public worship over the course of two millennia. And then they will be better equipped to pass this tradition on to others.

## Graphic Presentations

The tables, maps, and chronology that follow are greatly simplified. They are meant to help one visualize relations in time and space of the chief items of importance. In order to do this, it is necessary to concentrate on essentials and to omit all else.

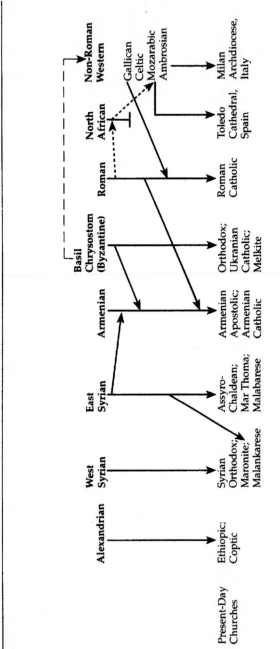

The Classical Liturgical Families
Sixth Century to Present

Table 1

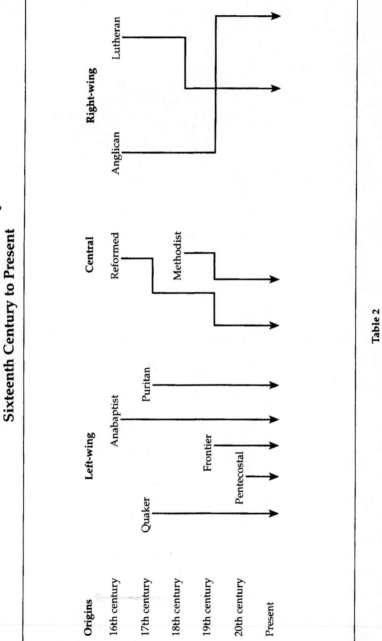

The Protestant Traditions of Worship
Sixteenth Century to Present

Table 2

## The Classical Liturgical Families, c. 600 A.D.

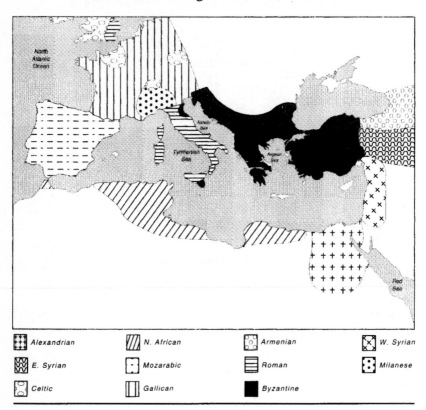

| | | | |
|---|---|---|---|
| Alexandrian | N. African | Armenian | W. Syrian |
| E. Syrian | Mozarabic | Roman | Milanese |
| Celtic | Gallican | Byzantine | |

**Table 3**

## The Protestant Traditions of Worship, c. 1600 A.D.

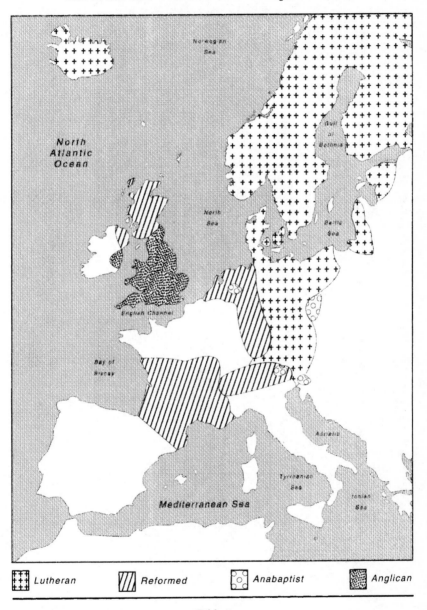

Lutheran    Reformed    Anabaptist    Anglican

Table 4

# Early Documents and Writers on Christian Worship

| | N. Africa | Egypt | Jerusalem | Syria | Asia Minor | Rome | Milan |
|---|---|---|---|---|---|---|---|
| 1st century | | | | Didache | | 1 Clement | |
| 2nd century | | Clement of Alexandria | | Ignatius Barnabas | Pliny | Justin Martyr | |
| 3rd century | Tertullian Cyprian | Origen | | Didascalia | | Apostolic Tradition | |
| 4th century | Augustine | Apostolic Church Order Canons of Hippolytus Sarapion | Cyril Egeria | Apostolic Constitutions Epitome | Basil Chrysostom Theodore Testamentum Domini | Jerome | Ambrose |
| 5th century | | | | | | | Cassian (Marseilles) |
| 6th century | | | | | | Benedict Gregory I | |

Table 5

## Chronology

| Century | Liturgical Documents/Writers | Church Events/ Persons | World Events/ Persons |
|---|---|---|---|
| 1st | *Didache*<br>*First Clement* | N.T., 50–135 A.D.<br>Neronian persecution | fall of Jerusalem, 70 |
| 2nd | *Letter of Pliny*<br>Irenaeus<br>Polycarp<br>Ignatius<br>Justin Martyr<br>Clement of Alexandria<br>*Epistle of Barnabas* | spread of church<br>   around Mediterranean<br><br>sporadic persecution | |
| 3rd | Tertullian<br>*Apostolic Tradition*<br>monastic origins<br>Origen (c. 185–c. 254)<br>Cyprian (d. 258)<br>*Didascalia* | monastic origins<br>empire-wide<br>   persecutions | |
| 4th | *Apostolic Church Order*<br>Sarapion<br>Cyril of Jerusalem<br>   (c. 315–86)<br>Egeria<br>*Apostolic Constitutions*<br>Eusebius of Caesarea<br>*Epitome*<br>Basil (c. 330–79)<br>Chrysostom (c. 347–407)<br>Theodore of Mopsuestia<br>   (c. 350–428)<br>Ambrose (c. 339–97)<br>Jerome (c. 342–420)<br>Augustine (354–430)<br>*Testamentum Domini* | conversion of<br>   Constantine, 312<br>Council of Nicaea, 325<br>Trinitarian controversies<br>Council of<br>   Constantinople, 381<br><br><br><br><br><br>gradual conversion of<br>   northern tribes | Christianity made<br>   legal, then official<br><br>division of empire<br><br><br><br><br><br><br>barbarian invasions |
| 5th | *Canons of Hippolytus*<br>Cassian (c. 360–435) | Christological<br>   controversies<br>Council of Ephesus, 431<br>Council of Chalcedon,<br>   451 | fall of Rome, 455 |
| 6th | Benedict of Nursia<br>   (c. 480–c. 550)<br>Gregory I (590–604) | organization of<br>   Western monasticism | |
| 7th | *Ordo Romanus*<br>   *Primus*<br>sacramentaries | | spread of Islam |

## Chronology (cont.)

| Century | Liturgical Documents/Writers | Church Events/ Persons | World Events/ Persons |
|---|---|---|---|
| 8th | Hadrianum sent to Charlemagne | John of Damascus (c. 675–c. 749) Iconoclastic controversy Council of Nicaea, 787 Bede (c. 673–735) | |
| 9th | supplement added Benedict of Aniane (c. 750–821) Ratramnus (d. 868) Paschasius Radbertus (c. 790–865) | | Charlemagne crowned, 800 learning revived |
| 10th | | low ebb of Rome and papacy Cluniac monastic reforms | |
| 11th | Berengarius (c. 999–1088) Lanfranc (c. 1005–89) | schism East and West, 1054 Anselm (1033–1109) Gregory VII (1073–85) Crusades begin | emperor intervenes in Rome |
| 12th | Suger (c. 1081–1151) Hugh of St. Victor (c. 1096–1141) Peter Lombard (1095–1159) | invention of gothic Cistercian monastic reforms | |
| 13th | Innocent III (1198–1216) Thomas Aquinas (c. 1225–74) | Francis of Assisi (1181–1226) scholastic theology mendicant orders Fourth Lateran Council, 1215 Crusades end | |
| 14th | John Wycliffe (c. 1329–84) | Avignon papacy 1309–77 split of papacy, 1378–1417 | |
| 15th | *Decree for Armenians,* 1438 | John Huss burned, 1415 Council of Basel, 1431–49 | fall of Constantinople, 1453 invention of printing Columbus reaches America, 1492 |

## Chronology (cont.)

| Century | Liturgical Documents/Writers | Church Events/ Persons | World Events/ Persons |
|---|---|---|---|
| 16th | Martin Luther (1483–1546) Ulrich Zwingli (1484–1531) Martin Bucer (1491–1551) Menno Simons (1496–1561) John Calvin (1509–64) John Knox (1514–72) Thomas Cranmer (1489–1556) revised Roman books, 1568–1614 Thomas Cartwright (1535–1603) | Erasmus (c. 1466–1536) Reformation begun, 1517 founding of Jesuits, 1540 Council of Trent (1545–63) missions expand Bible translations *Schleitheim Confession,* 1527 Marburg Colloquy, 1529 | colonization of Latin America defeat of Spanish Armada, 1588 reign of Elizabeth I, 1558–1603 |
| 17th | *Millenary Petition,* 1603 Westminster *Directory,* 1645 Robert Barclay's *Apology,* 1676 Christopher Wren (1632–1723) | age of baroque art Puritan ascendancy Quakers originate age of Jansenism | colonization of North America Isaac Newton (1642–1727) |
| 18th | John Wesley (1703–91) *Sunday Service,* 1784 American BCP, 1789 J. S. Bach (1685–1750) | latitudinarianism Synod of Pistoia, 1786 Febronianism Immanuel Kant (1724–1804) | age of enlightenment American Revolution French Revolution |
| 19th | Charles G. Finney (1792–1875) John Nevin (1803–86) Alexander Campbell (1788–1866) Prosper Guéranger (1805–75) A. W. N. Pugin (1812–52) | scientific study of Bible Christianizing of American frontier Oxford Movement worldwide missions Pius IX (1846–78) | Charles Darwin (1809–82) Karl Marx (1818–83) age of reform abolition of slavery women's rights |
| 20th | Fanny Crosby (1825–1915) Pius X (1903–14) Lambert Beauduin (1873–1960) *Mediator Dei,* 1947 BEM, 1982 revised R.C. rites LBW, 1978 BCP, 1979 ASB, 1980 UMH, 1989 | Pentecostal churches anti-modernism liturgical movement Vatican II, 1962–65 Karl Barth (1886–1968) Karl Rahner (1904–84) Faith and Order, 1927 World Council of Churches, 1948 | World War I World War II atomic age, 1945 space age, 1957 Korean War Vietnam War Iraq War |

## Select Bibliography of General Books on Christian Worship

*Alcuin Club Collections*. London: SPCK/Alcuin Club, 1897–    (currently 70 vols.).

Alcuin/GROW Liturgical Studies. Bramcote, Notts.: Grove Books, 1987– (currently 20 vols.).

Baumstark, Anton. *Comparative Liturgy*. London: A. R. Mowbray, 1958.

Bishop, Edmund. *Liturgica Historica*. Oxford: Clarendon Press, 1918.

Bradshaw, Paul F. *A Bibliography of Recent Liturgical Studies*. Runcorn: Alcuin Club, 1989.

Brunner, Peter. *Worship in the Name of Jesus*. St. Louis: Concordia Publishing House, 1968.

Casel, Odo. *The Mystery of Christian Worship*. Westminster, Md.: Newman Press, 1962.

Clarke, W. K. L., and Charles Harris. *Liturgy and Worship*. London: SPCK, 1932.

Dalmais, I. H. *Introduction to the Liturgy*. London: Geoffrey Chapman, 1961.

Davies, J. G., ed. *The New Westminster Dictionary of Liturgy and Worship*. Philadelphia: Westminster Press, 1986.

Duffy, Regis. *Real Presence*. San Francisco: Harper & Row, 1982.

Fink, Peter E., ed. *The New Dictionary of Sacramental Worship*. Collegeville, Minn.: Liturgical Press, 1990.

Forrester, Duncan; James I. H. McDonald; and Gian Tellini. *Encounter with God*. Edinburgh: T. & T. Clark, 1983.

Garrett, T. S. *Christian Worship*. London: Oxford University Press, 1961.

*Grove Liturgical Studies*. 48 vols. Bramcote, Notts.: Grove Books, 1975–1986.

Hardman, Oscar. *A History of Christian Worship*. London: University of London Press, 1948.

Hatchett, Marion J. *Sanctifying Life, Time, and Space*. New York: Seabury Press, 1976.

Hislop, D. H. *Our Heritage in Public Worship*. Edinburgh: T. & T. Clark, 1935.

Hoffman, Lawrence A. *The Art of Public Prayer*. Washington: Pastoral Press, 1988.

Hoon, Paul W. *The Integrity of Worship*. Nashville: Abingdon Press, 1971.

Jones, Cheslyn, Geoffrey Wainwright, Edward Yarnold, and Paul Bradshaw, eds. *The Study of Liturgy*. Revised edition. New York: Oxford University Press, 1992.

Jones, Ilion T. *A Historical Approach to Evangelical Worship*. Nashville: Abingdon Press, 1954.

Jungmann, J. A. *Pastoral Liturgy*. New York: Herder & Herder, 1962.

Kavanagh, Aidan. *On Liturgical Theology*. New York: Pueblo Publishing House, 1984.

Klauser, Theodor. *A Short History of the Western Liturgy*. Second edition. Oxford: Oxford University Press, 1979.

Lebon, Jean. *How to Understand the Liturgy*. London: SCM Press, 1987.

*Leiturgia: Handbuch des evangelischen-Gottesdienst.* 5 vols. Kassel: Johannes Stauda-Verlag, 1954–1970.

Lercaro, Giacomo. *A Small Liturgical Dictionary.* London: Burns & Oates, 1959.

Martimort, A. G., ed. *The Church at Prayer.* 4 vols. New ed. Collegeville: Liturgical Press, 1986–1988.

Maxwell, William D. *History of Christian Worship.* Grand Rapids: Baker Book House, 1982.

McClain, William B. *Come Sunday: The Liturgy of Zion.* Nashville: Abingdon Press, 1990.

Micklem, Nathaniel. *Christian Worship.* Oxford: Oxford University Press, 1936.

Miller, John H. *Fundamentals of the Liturgy.* Notre Dame: Fides Publishers, 1959.

Peil, Rudolf. *A Handbook of the Liturgy.* Freiburg: Herder, 1960.

Podhradsky, Gerhard. *New Dictionary of the Liturgy.* Staten Island: Alba House, 1966.

Procter-Smith, Marjorie, *In Her Own Rite.* Nashville: Abingdon Press, 1990.

Reed, Luther D. *Worship: A Study of Corporate Devotion.* Philadelphia: Fortress Press, 1959.

Saliers, Don E. *Worship and Spirituality.* Philadelphia: Westminster Press, 1984.

Schmemann, Alexander. *Introduction to Liturgical Theology.* London: Faith Press, 1966.

Schmidt, Hermann A. P. *Introductio in Liturgiam Occidentalem.* Rome: Herder, 1960.

Searle, Mark. *Sunday Morning: A Time for Worship.* Collegeville, Minn.: Liturgical Press, 1982.

Segler, Franklin. *Christian Worship.* Nashville: Broadman Press, 1967.

Senn, Frank C., ed. *Protestant Spiritual Traditions.* New York: Paulist Press, 1986.

Shepherd, Massey H., Jr., ed. *Worship in Scripture and Tradition.* New York: Oxford University Press, 1963.

Spielmann, Richard M. *History of Christian Worship.* New York: Seabury Press, 1966.

Steuart, Benedict. *The Development of Christian Worship.* London: Longmans, 1953.

Taft, Robert. *Beyond East and West: Problems of Liturgical Understanding.* Washington, D.C.: Pastoral Press, 1984.

Talley, Thomas J. *Worship Reforming Tradition.* Washington, D.C.: Pastoral Press, 1990.

Thompson, Bard. *A Bibliography of Christian Worship.* Metuchen, N.J.: ATLA and Scarecrow Press, 1989.

Underhill, Evelyn. *Worship.* London: Nisbet & Co., 1936.

Verheul, Ambrosius. *Introduction to the Liturgy.* London: Burns & Oates, 1968.

Von Allmen, J.-J. *Worship: Its Theology and Practice.* New York: Oxford University Press, 1965.

Webber, Robert E. *Worship Old and New.* Grand Rapids: Zondervan Publishing House, 1982.

Wegman, Herman. *Christian Worship in East and West.* New York: Pueblo Publishing Co., 1985.

White, James F. *Introduction to Christian Worship.* Rev. ed. Nashville: Abingdon Press, 1990.

# CHAPTER II

# Time as Communication

## I. THE CHRISTIAN DAY
### A. The liturgical day begins at nightfall.
1. Scripture: Genesis 1:5.

> And there was evening and there was morning, the first day.

### B. The day is divided by times of prayer.
See documents in chapter IV, "Daily Public Prayer."

## II. THE CHRISTIAN WEEK
### A. The resurrection marks the beginning of a new week.
2. Scripture: Mark 16:1–2 (see also Matt. 28:1; Luke 24:1; John 20:1).

> When the sabbath was over, . . . very early on the first day of the week, when the sun had risen, they went to the tomb.

### B. Hints of the observance of the first day as the occasion for Christian worship appear in the New Testament.
3. Scripture.

*a.* 1 Corinthians 16:2.
> On the first day of every week, each of you is to put aside and save whatever extra you earn, so that collections need not be taken when I come.

*b.* Acts 20:7, 11.
> On the first day of the week, when we met to break bread, Paul . . . continued speaking until midnight. . . . Then Paul went upstairs, and after he had broken bread and eaten, he continued to converse with them until dawn; then he left [Troas].

*c.* Revelation 1:10.
> I was in the spirit on the Lord's day [*kyriakē hēmera*], and I heard behind me a loud voice like a trumpet.

### C. References to Sunday become more common in the second century.
4. Pliny the Younger, *Letter 10* (c. 112). Trans. Henry Bettenson, *Documents of the Christian Church* (New York: Oxford University Press, 1947), p. 6.

> On an appointed day, they had been accustomed to meet before daybreak [*stato die ante lucem*], and to recite a hymn antiphonally to Christ, as to a god.

5. *The Didache,* XIV (late first or early second century). Trans. Cyril C. Richardson, LCC, I, 178.

> On every Lord's Day—his special day [*kyriakēn de kyriou*]—come together and break bread and give thanks, first confessing your sins so that your sacrifice may be pure.

6. *The Epistle of Barnabas*, XV, 8–9 (late first or early second century). Trans. Kirsopp Lake, *Apostolic Fathers* (Cambridge: Harvard University Press, 1965), I, 395–396.

> The present sabbaths are not acceptable to me, but that which I have made, in which I will give rest to all things and make the beginning of an eighth day, that is the beginning of another world. Wherefore we also celebrate with gladness the eighth day in which Jesus also rose from the dead, and was made manifest, and ascended into Heaven.

7. Ignatius, *To the Magnesians*, IX (c. 115). Trans. Cyril C. Richardson, LCC, I, 96.

> Those, then, who lived by ancient practices arrived at a new hope. They ceased to keep the Sabbath and lived by the Lord's Day [*kyriakēn*] on which our life as well as theirs shone forth, thanks to Him and his death, though some deny this.

8. Justin Martyr, *First Apology*, LXVII (c. 155). Trans. Edward Rochie Hardy, LCC, I, 287–288.

> We all hold this common gathering on Sunday [*hēliou hēmeran*], since it is the first day, on which God transforming darkness and matter made the universe, and Jesus Christ our Saviour rose from the dead on the same day. For they crucified him on the day before Saturday, and on the day after Saturday, he appeared to his apostles and disciples and taught them these things which I have passed on to you also for your serious consideration.

### D. In 321 Sunday is recognized as the day of rest by imperial decree.

9. *Codex Justinianus*, III, xii, 3 (321). Trans. Henry Bettenson, *Documents of the Christian Church* (New York: Oxford University Press, 1947), p. 27.

> Constantine to Elpidius. All judges, city-people and craftsmen shall rest on the venerable day of the Sun. But countrymen may without hindrance attend to agriculture, since it often happens that this is the most suitable day for sowing grain or planting vines, so that the opportunity afforded by divine providence may not be lost, for the right season is of short duration. 7 March 321.

### E. Wednesdays and Fridays become fast days.
10. Scripture: Luke 18:11–12.

> The Pharisee, standing by himself, was praying thus, "God, I thank you that I am not like other people: thieves, rogues, adulterers, or even like this tax collector. I fast twice a week; I give a tenth of all my income."

11. *Didache*, VIII (late first or early second century). Trans. Cyril C. Richardson, LCC, I, 174.

> Your fasts must not be identical with those of the hypocrites. They fast on Mondays and Thursdays; but you should fast on Wednesdays and Fridays.

12. *Apostolic Constitutions*, VII, 23 (c. 375). Trans. James Donaldson, ANF, VII, 469.

> But do you . . . fast . . . on the fourth day of the week, and on the day of Preparation, because on the fourth day the condemnation went out against the Lord, Judas then promising to betray him for money; and you must fast on the day of Preparation, because on that day the Lord suffered the death of the cross under Pontius Pilate.

### F. Saturday retains a quasi-liturgical significance.
13. Tertullian, *On Prayer*, XXIII (c. 205). Trans. S. Thelwall, ANF, III, 689.

> In the mater of *kneeling* also prayer is subject to diversity of observance, through the fact of some few who abstain from kneeling on the Sabbath. . . . We, however (just as we have received), only on the day of the Lord's Resurrection ought to not only guard against kneeling, but [also against] every posture and office of solicitude.

14. *Apostolic Constitutions*, VII, 23 (c. 375). Trans. James Donaldson, ANF, VII, 469.

> But keep the Sabbath and the Lord's day festival; because the former is the memorial of the creation, the latter of the resurrection. But there is one only Sabbath to be observed by you in the whole

year, which is that of our Lord's burial, on which men ought to keep a fast, but not a festival. For inasmuch as the Creator was then under the earth, the sorrow for Him is more forcible than the joy of the creation; for the Creator is more honorable by nature and dignity than His own creatures.

## III. THE CHRISTIAN YEAR
### A. The Pascha is central for Judaism and Christianity.
15. Scripture.

a. Exodus 12:6–8.
> You shall keep it [the lamb] until the fourteenth day of this month; then the whole assembled congregation of Israel shall slaughter it at twilight. They shall take some of the blood and put it on the two doorposts and the lintel of the houses in which they eat it. They shall eat the lamb that same night; they shall eat it roasted over the fire with unleavened bread and bitter herbs.

b. 1 Corinthians 5:7–8.
> Clean out the old yeast so that you may be a new batch, as you really are unleavened. For our paschal lamb, Christ, has been sacrificed. Therefore, let us celebrate the festival, not with the old yeast, the yeast of malice and evil, but with the unleavened bread of sincerity and truth.

### B. Third-century documents show elaboration of the Christian Pascha.
See chapter VII, "Christian Initiation," document 7, section 20, beginning at the words, "Those who are to be baptized . . . " and chapter VIII, "The Eucharist," document 6, section 21.

16. Tertullian, *On Baptism*, XIX (c. 205). Trans. S. Thelwall, ANF, III, 678.

> The Passover [Pascha] affords a more than usually solemn day for baptism; when, withal, the Lord's passion in which we are baptized, was completed. Nor will it be incongruous to interpret figuratively the fact that, when the Lord was about to celebrate the last Passover, He said to the disciples who were sent to make preparation, "Ye will meet a man bearing water." He points out the place for celebrating the Passover by the sign of water.

## The Jewish Calendar

| Roman | Jewish | Theological Cycles | Agriculture | Holiday | Theological Cycles | Historical |
|---|---|---|---|---|---|---|
| February | Shevat | | mature trees | Tu B'Shevat | human action | Antiochene persecution |
| March | Adar | redemption | spring buds | Purim | | |
| April | Nisan | | | Passover | God's action | Exodus |
| May | Iyyar | | | Omer | | |
| June | Sivan | revelation | summer harvest | Shavuot (Pentecost) | | giving of Torah/ wilderness wandering |
| July | Tammuz | | | | | |
| August | Av | | summer heat | Three Weeks · Tisha B'Av | | Temple destruction |
| September | Elul | | | Selihot | creation | kingdom |
| | Tishri | | | Rosh Hashanah (New Year) | repentance | |
| | | | | Yom Kippur (Atonement) | redemption | eschaton |
| October | | creation: shelter | fall harvest | Sukkot (Booths) | | redemption/ wilderness wandering |
| | | creation: Torah | | Simhat Torah | | reception of Torah |
| November | Marheshvan | | | | | |
| December | Kislev | | | Hanukkah | | rabbinic light |
| January | Tevet | | | | | |

Table 6. By permission of Roger Brooks.

17. *Didascalia Apostolorum*, XXI (mid-third century). Trans. R. Hugh Connolly, *Didascalia Apostolorum* (Oxford: Clarendon Press, 1969), p. 190.

> Especially incumbent on you therefore is the fast of the Friday and of the Sabbath; and likewise the vigil and watching of the Sabbath, and the reading of the Scriptures, and psalms, and prayer and intercession for them that have sinned, and the expectation and hope of the resurrection of our Lord Jesus, until the third hour in the night after the Sabbath. And then offer your oblations; and thereafter eat and make good cheer, and rejoice and be glad, because that the earnest of our resurrection, Christ, is risen.

**C. The Quartodeciman controversy rages over whether Easter should always be observed on Sunday or on the same day of the week as the Jewish Passover.**
18. Eusebius, *The History of the Church*, V, 23–24 (323). Trans. G. A. Williamson, *The History of the Church* (Baltimore: Penguin Books, 1965), pp. 229–230.

> It was at that stage [late second century] that a controversy of great significance took place, because all the Asian dioceses thought that in accordance with ancient tradition they ought to observe the fourteenth day of the lunar month [Nisan] as the beginning of the Paschal festival—the day on which the Jews had been commanded to sacrifice the lamb: on that day, no matter which day of the week it might be, they must without fail bring the fast to an end. But nowhere else in the world was it customary to arrange their celebrations in that way: in accordance with apostolic tradition, they preserved the view which still prevails, that it was improper to end the fast on any day other than that of our Saviour's resurrection. So synods and conferences of bishops were convened, and without a dissentient voice, drew up a decree of the Church, in the form of letters addressed to Christians everywhere, that never on any day other than the Lord's Day should the mystery of the Lord's resurrection from the dead be celebrated, and that on that day alone we should observe the end of the Paschal fast.

**D. The Pascha (like Epiphany and Pentecost) splits into a series of separate commemorations during the fourth century.**

## Division of Original Unitive Commemorations

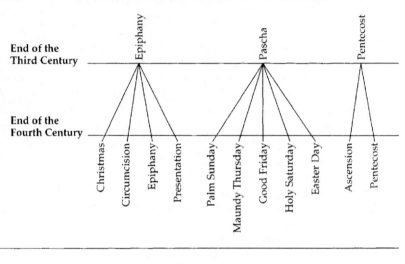

Table 7

19. Egeria, *Travels*, XXX–XXXVIII (c. 384). Trans. John Wilkinson, *Egeria's Travels* (London: SPCK, 1971), pp. 132–138.

> Sunday is the beginning of the Easter week or, as they call it here [Jerusalem], "The Great Week." . . . [Sunday] the bishop and all the people rise from their places, and start off on foot down from the summit of the Mount of Olives. All the people go before him with psalms and antiphons, all the time repeating, "Blessed is he that cometh in the name of the Lord." . . .
>
> Wednesday is exactly like Monday and Tuesday . . . but at night . . . a presbyter . . . reads the passage about Judas Iscariot going to the Jews and fixing what they must pay him to betray the Lord. The people groan and lament at this reading in a way that would make you weep to hear them. . . .
>
> Thursday . . . everyone receives Communion. . . . When the cocks begin to crow, everyone leaves the Imbomon [place of the ascension], and comes down with singing to the place where the Lord prayed. . . . From there all of them, including the smallest children, now go down with singing and conduct the bishop to Gethsemane. . . .

[Friday] The Bishop's chair is placed on Golgotha Behind the Cross (the cross there now), and he takes his seat. A table is placed before him with a cloth on it, and the deacons stand round, and there is brought to him a gold and silver box containing the holy Wood of the Cross. It is opened, and the Wood of the Cross and the Title [inscription] are taken out and placed on the table. . . . all the people, catechumens as well as faithful, come up one by one to the table. They stoop down over it, kiss the Wood, and move on.

Saturday . . . they keep their paschal vigil like us.

20. Augustine, *Letter 55: to Januarius* (c. 400). Trans. Wilfrid Parsons, FC, XII, 279, 283.

Note, therefore, the three sacred days of His Crucifixion, Burial and Resurrection. . . .

Since it is clear from the Gospel on what days the Lord was crucified and rested in the tomb and rose again, there is added, through the councils of the fathers, the requirement of retaining those same days, and the whole Christian world is convinced that the pasch should be celebrated in that way.

### E. A period of preparation develops for those to be baptized at Easter and eventually is applied to all Christians.

21. Hippolytus, *Apostolic Tradition*, XX (c. 217). Trans. Geoffrey J. Cuming, *Hippolytus: A Text for Students* (Bramcote: Grove Books, 1976), p. 17.

And when those who are to receive baptism are chosen, let their life be examined: have they lived good lives when they were catechumens? Have they honoured the widows? Have they visited the sick? Have they done every kind of good work? And when those who brought them bear witness to each "He has," let them hear the gospel.

From the time that they were set apart, let hands be laid on them daily while they are exorcized. And when the day of their baptism approaches, the bishop shall exorcize each one of them, in order that he may know whether he is pure. And if anyone is not good or not pure, let him be put aside, because he has not heard the word with faith, for it is impossible that the Alien should hide himself for ever.

Those who are to be baptized should be instructed to bathe and wash themselves on the Thursday. . . . Those who are to receive baptism shall fast on the Friday. On the Saturday those who are to receive baptism shall be gathered in one place at the bishop's decision.

22. Council of Nicaea, *Canon V* (325). Trans. Henry R. Percival, NPNF, 2nd series, XIV, 13.

And let these synods be held, the one before Lent [literally the forty] (that the pure Gift may be offered to God after all bitterness has been put away), and let the second be held about autumn.

23. Cyril of Jerusalem, *Procatechesis*, IV (c. 350). Trans. William Telfer, LCC, IV, 68.

You have a long period of grace, forty days for repentance. You have plenty of time to discard and wash thoroughly your soul's apparel, and so to clothe yourself and come back. . . . For though the water will receive you, the Holy Spirit will not.

24. Augustine, *Letter 55: to Januarius* (c. 400). Trans. Wilfrid Parsons, FC, XII, 283–284.

The forty-day fast of Lent draws its authority from the Old Testament, from the fasts of Moses and Elias, and from the Gospel, because the Lord fasted that many days, showing that the Gospel is not at variance with the Law and the Prophets. . . . In what part of the year, then, could the observance of Lent be more appropriately instituted than that adjoining, so to speak, and touching on the Lord's Passion?

**F. Pentecost, the great fifty days following Easter, culminates in the Day of Pentecost.**
25. Scripture.

*a.* Leviticus 23:15–16.
And from the day after the sabbath, from the day on which you bring the sheaf of the elevation offering, you shall count off seven weeks; they shall be complete. You shall count until the day after the seventh sabbath, fifty days; then you shall present an offering of new grain to the LORD.

*b.* 2 Corinthians 3:7–8.

Now if the ministry of death, chiseled in letters on stone tablets, came in glory so that the people of Israel could not gaze at Moses' face because of the glory of his face, a glory now set aside, how much more will the ministry of the Spirit come in glory?

*c.* Acts 1:8–9.

"But you will receive power when the Holy Spirit has come upon you; and you will be my witnesses in Jerusalem, in all Judea and Samaria, and to the ends of the earth." When he had said this, as they were watching, he was lifted up, and a cloud took him out of their sight.

*d.* Acts 2:1–4.

When the day of Pentecost had come, they were all together in one place. And suddenly from heaven there came a sound like the rush of a violent wind, and it filled the entire house where they were sitting. Divided tongues, as of fire, appeared among them, and a tongue rested on each of them. All of them were filled with the Holy Spirit and began to speak in other languages, as the Spirit gave them ability.

26. Tertullian.

*a. On Baptism,* XIX (c. 205). Trans. S. Thelwall, ANF, III, 678.

After that [the Pascha], Pentecost is a most joyous space for conferring baptisms; wherein, too, the resurrection of the Lord was repeatedly proved among the disciples, and the hope of the advent of the Lord indirectly pointed to, in that, at that time, when he had been received back into the heavens, the angels told the apostles that "He would so come, as He had withal ascended into the heavens"; at Pentecost, of course. But, moreover, when Jeremiah says, "And I will gather them together from the extremities of the land in the feast-day," he signifies the day of the Passover and of the Pentecost which is properly a "feast-day."

*b. De Corona,* III (c. 211). Trans. S. Thelwall, ANF, III, 94.

As often as the anniversary [of a death] comes round, we make offerings for the dead as birthday honours. We count fasting or kneeling in worship on the Lord's day to be unlawful. We rejoice in the same privilege also from Easter to Pentecost.

**27.** Augustine, *Letter 55: to Januarius* (c. 400). Trans. Wilfrid Parsons, FC, XII, 284–285.

These days after the Lord's Resurrection form a period, not of labor, but of peace and joy. That is why there is no fasting and we pray standing, which is a sign of resurrection. This practice is observed at the altar on all Sundays, and the Alleluia is sung, to indicate that our future occupation is to be no other than the praise of God. . . .

Easter and Pentecost are feasts with the strongest Scriptural authority. The observance of forty days before Easter rests on the decree of the Church, and by the same authority the eight days of the neophytes [newly baptized who underwent eight days of instruction after Easter] are distinguished from other days, so that the eighth harmonizes with the first.

**28.** *Testament of Our Lord*, II, 12 (fourth century). Trans. Grant Sperry-White from I. E. Rahmani, *Testamentum Domini Nostri Jesu Christi* (Mainz, 1899), pp. 134–135.

[At or in] Pentecost let no one fast or kneel. For they are days of rest and joy. Let those who carry the burdens of labor refresh themselves a little in the days of Pentecost, and on every Sunday.

**29.** Eusebius, *Life of Constantine*, IV, 64 (c. 338). Trans. E. C. Richardson, NPNF, 2nd series, I, 557.

All these events occurred during a most important festival, I mean the august and holy solemnity of Pentecost, which is distinguished by a period of seven weeks, and sealed with that one day on which the holy Scriptures attest the ascension of our common Saviour into heaven, and the descent of the Holy Spirit among men.

**G. By the end of the fourth century, Ascension is distinct from the Day of Pentecost.**

**30.** *Apostolic Constitutions*, V, 19 (c. 375). Trans. James Donaldson, ANF, VII, 447–448.

And again, from the first Lord's day count forty days, from the Lord's day till the fifth day of the week, and celebrate the feast of

the ascension of the Lord, whereon He finished all His dispensation and constitution, and returned to that God and Father that
sent Him, and sat down at the right hand of power, and remains
there until His enemies are put under His feet; who also will come
at the consummation of the world with power and great glory, to
judge the quick and the dead, and to recompense to every one
according to his works.

## H. The Manifestation of God in Jesus Christ or Epiphany commemorates Jesus' baptism and first sign.

31. Scripture.

*a.* John 1:5.
> The light shines [*phainei*] in the darkness, and the darkness did not
> overcome it.

*b.* John 1:9.
> The true light, which enlightens everyone, was coming into the
> world.

*c.* John 1:32–34 (see also Matt. 3:1–17; Mark 1:4–11; Luke 3:21–22).
> And John testified, "I saw the Spirit descending from heaven like a
> dove, and it remained on him. I myself did not know him, but the
> one who sent me to baptize with water said to me, 'He on whom
> you see the Spirit descend and remain is the one who baptizes
> with the Holy Spirit.' And I myself have seen and have testified
> that this is the Son of God."

*d.* John 2:11.
> Jesus did this, the first of his signs, in Cana of Galilee, and re-
> vealed [*ephanerōsen*] his glory and his disciples believed in him.

*e.* 1 Timothy 3:16.
> He was revealed [*ephanerōthē*] in flesh,
>> vindicated in spirit,
>>> seen by angels,
>> proclaimed among Gentiles,
>>> believed in throughout the world,
>>>> taken up in glory.

32. Clement of Alexandria, *Miscellanies*, I, 21 (c. 200). Trans. William Wilson, ANF, II, 333.

> And the followers of Basilides [a Gnostic] hold the day of his [Jesus'] baptism as a festival, spending the night before in readings.
>
> And they say it was the fifteenth year of Tiberius Caesar, the fifteenth day of the month Tubi; and some that it was the eleventh [January 6] of the same month.

33. John Chrysostom.

*a. Sermon Preached at Antioch, January 6, 387.* Trans. from *Opera Omnia* (Paris: Gaume, 1834), II, 436.

> But why is it not the day on which he was born, but the day on which he was baptized, that is called Epiphany? For this is the day on which he was baptized, and made holy the nature of the waters. . . . Why then is this day called Epiphany? Because it was not when he was born that he became manifest to all, but when he was baptized; for up to this day he was unknown to the multitudes.

*b. Sermon Preached on December 20, 386.* Trans. from *Opera Omnia* (Paris: Gaume, 1834), I, 608.

> For if Christ had not been born into flesh, He would not have been baptized, which is the Theophany [Orthodox term for Epiphany], He would not have been crucified [some texts add: and would not have risen] which is the Pascha, He would not have sent down the Spirit, which is the Pentecost.

34. Cassian, *Conferences*, X, 2 (c. 428). Trans. E. C. S. Gibson, NPNF, 2nd series, XI, 401.

> In the country of Egypt this custom is by ancient tradition observed that—when Epiphany is past, which the priests of that province regard as the time, both for our Lord's baptism and also of His birth in the flesh, and so celebrate the commemoration of either mystery not separately as in the Western provinces but on the single festival of this day—letters are sent from the Bishop of Alexandria through all the Churches of Egypt, by which the beginning of Lent and the day of Easter are pointed out not only in all the cities but also in the monasteries.

### I. Christmas apparently originates in Rome about 330 A.D.

35. *Philocalian Martyrology* (c. 354). Line included in a list of commemorations. Trans. from A. Allan McArthur, *The Evolution of the Christian Year* (London: SCM Press, 1953), p. 42.

> [December 25] The birth of Christ in Bethlehem of Judea.

36. John Chrysostom, *Sermon Preached at Antioch, December 25, 386.* Trans. Albert D. Alexander, cited by McArthur, ibid., pp. 49–50.

> And moreover it is not yet the tenth year since this day has become clearly known to us. . . . And so this day too, which has been known from of old to the inhabitants of the West and has now been brought to us, not many years ago, has developed so quickly and has manifestily proved so fruitful. . . . And the star brought the Magi from the East.

37. *Apostolic Constitutions,* VIII, 33 (c. 375). Trans. James Donaldson, ANF, VII, 495.

> Let them [slaves] rest on the festival of His birth, because on it the unexpected favour was granted to men, that Jesus Christ, the Logos of God, should be born of the Virgin Mary, for the salvation of the world. Let them rest on the feast of the Epiphany, because on it a manifestation took place of the divinity of Christ, for the Father bore testimony to him at the baptism; and the Paraclete, in the form of a dove, pointed out to the bystanders Him to whom testimony was borne.

### J. The advent of Advent comes as preparation for Epiphany.

38. Council of Saragossa (380). Trans. from A. Allan McArthur, *The Evolution of the Christian Year* (London: SCM Press, 1953), p. 56.

> From December 17 until the day of Epiphany, which is January 6, it is not permitted to be absent from church.

### K. The feasts of saints populate and eventually overrun the calendar.

39. *The Martyrdom of Polycarp,* XVIII (c. 156). Trans. Massey H. Shepherd, Jr., LCC, I, 156.

So we later took up his bones, more precious than costly stones and more valuable than gold, and laid them away in a suitable place. There the Lord will permit us, so far as possible, to gather together in joy and gladness to celebrate the day of his martyrdom as a birthday, in memory of those athletes who have gone before, and to train and make ready those who are to come hereafter.

## IV. MEDIEVAL ELABORATION OF THE SANCTORAL AND TEMPORAL CYCLES
**A. Innocent III (pope 1198–1216) gives the first full rationale for the sequence of colors followed in Rome.**
40. Innocent III, *Concerning the Holy Mystery of the Altar*, LXV (c. 1195). Trans. from PL, CCXVII, 799–802.

There are four principal colors by which the Roman Church distinguishes vestments according to the proper sacred days: white, red, black, and green. In the laws of garments, four colors had been appointed (Ex. 28): gold and violet, purple and scarlet. White is worn in vestments for feasts of confessors and virgins, red in solemnities of apostles and martyrs. Hence the bride says in the Song of Songs: "My beloved is fair and ruddy, chosen from thousands" (Song of Solomon 5). White is used for confessors and virgins, red for martyrs and apostles. Such are the flowers, roses and lilies of the valley.

*White* garb is used in festivals of confessors and virgins because of completeness and innocence. For those belonging to him of Nazareth are made white and they walk always in white with him: "They are virgins and follow wherever the Lamb goes" (Rev. 14). On account of this, white is used in the solemnities following [births of Christ and John the Baptist, Epiphany, Presentation, Maundy Thursday, Easter, Ascension, and at the consecration of a bishop or a church], certainly in the solemnities of the angels, of whose brightness God asked Lucifer: "Where were you when the morning stars praised me?" (Job 38). . . .

*Red*, on the other hand, is used in vestments for the feasts of the apostles and martyrs, on account of the blood of their suffering which they shed for Christ. For "they are those who have come through great tribulation, and have washed their garments in the blood of the Lamb" (Rev. 7). It is used in the feast of the cross, through which Christ poured out his blood for us, hence the Prophet: "Why is your clothing red, as one who treads grapes in a winepress?" (Isa. 63). Or in the feast of the cross it is better to use white when it is not the feast of the passion but of the discovery or the exaltation.

In Pentecost the fervor of the Holy Spirit appeared over the apostles in tongues of fire. "There appeared to them scattered tongues as of fire seated on each of them" (Acts 2). The prophet says: "He sent fire from heaven into my bones" (Lam. 1). For the martyrdoms of the apostles Peter and Paul, red may be used; however, for the conversion (of Paul) and the chair (of Peter) white is used. Likewise for the birth of St. John (the Baptist), white may be used; for his beheading, however, red is used. When the feast is celebrated of someone who was both martyr and virgin, martyrdom takes preference over virginity, since it is the most perfect sign of love, wherefore Truth says: "Greater love no one can have, than that he should lay down his life for his friends" (John 15). On account of which in the commemoration of All Saints at certain times red garments are used; others, indeed, such as the Roman curia, use white, not so much of themselves but because the Church says of this feast, that the saints, according to the Apocalypse of John (ch. 7), stand "before the Lamb, clothed in white robes with palms in their hands."

*Black* vestments are used in days of affliction and abstinence, for sins and for the dead. Black is used during Advent until the vigil of the Nativity and from Septuagesima to Easter eve. The bride ironically says in the Song of Songs: "I am black, but beautiful, daughters of Jerusalem, like the tents of Kedar, as the tent-curtains of Shalmah. Do not despise me, who may be dark, because the sun has discolored me" (Song of Solomon 1).

For Holy Innocents some use black; others contend red garments ought to be used. This is on account of sorrow, because " a voice is heard in Ramah with much lamenting and wailing, Rachel weeping for her children and not wishing to be consoled, because they no longer are" (Jer. 31). Because of this, songs of joy are not sung and a golden miter is not worn. This is on account of martyrdom, commemorating which the Church says: "Under the throne of

God the saints cry out: Vindicate our blood which is shed, our
God" (Luke 18; Rev. 6). Because of this sorrow, silent is the joy of
songs, the miter which is worn is not decorated with gold, but on
account of the martyrs red vestments are used. Today we use violet on the Fourth Sunday of Lent because of joy which the gold
rose signifies. The Roman pontifex carries a miter decorated with
gold cloth, but on account of the abstinence of black, at the same
time violet vestments are used.

It remains that in weekdays and common days *green* vestments
may be used, since green is the color intermediate between white,
black, and red. This color is expressed when it is said: "Henna
with nard, nard and saffron" (Song of Solomon 4).

To these four, others are related: to red the color of scarlet, to black
violet, to green saffron. A few use rose for martyrs, scarlet for
confessors, and white for virgins.


## V. REFORMATION PRUNING OF THE CALENDAR
### A. Luther retains a simplified liturgical year in Wittenberg.
41. Martin Luther.

*a. Formula Missae* (1523). Trans. Paul Zeller Strodach, LW, LIII, 23.
But we at Wittenberg intend to observe only the Lord's days and
the festivals of the Lord. We think that all the feasts of the saints
should be abrogated, or if anything in them deserves it, it should
be brought into the Sunday sermon. We regard the feasts of Purification and Annunciation as feasts of Christ, even as Epiphany and
Circumcision. Instead of the feasts of St. Stephen and of St. John
the Evangelist, we are pleased to use the office of the Nativity. The
feasts of the Holy Cross shall be anathema. Let others act according to their own conscience or in consideration of the weakness of
some—whatever the Spirit may suggest.

*b. German Mass* (1526). Trans. Augustus Steimle, LW, LIII, 68, 90.
For the Epistles and Gospels we have retained the customary division according to the church year, because we do not find anything especially reprehensible in this use. . . . We . . . have no
objection to others who take up the complete books of the evange-
lists [continuous reading]. . . .

But on the festivals, such as Christmas, Easter, Pentecost, St. Michael's, Purification, and the like, we must continue to use Latin until we have enough German songs. This work is just beginning. . . .

Lent, Palm Sunday, and Holy Week shall be retained, not to force anyone to fast, but to preserve the Passion history and the Gospels appointed for that season. This, however, does not include the Lenten veil, throwing of palms, veiling of pictures, and whatever else there is of such tomfoolery. . . . Holy Week shall be like any other week save that the Passion history [shall] be explained every day for an hour . . . and that the sacrament [shall] be given to everyone who desires it.

## B. The Church of England provides propers for the temporal cycle and only for New Testament saints.

42. *The Booke of the Common Prayer* (1549). Bracketed items disappear in 1552 title. *The First and Second Prayer Books of Edward VI* (London: J. M. Dent & Sons, 1910), pp. 32–211 (spelling modernized).

> *The [introts,] collects, epistles, and gospels, to be used at the celebration of the Lord's Supper and Holy Communion through the Year: [with Proper Psalms and Lessons for Divers Feasts and Days.]*
> The first Sunday in Advent . . . [second, third, fourth]
> Christmas Day; At Matins; At the First Communion; At the Second Communion
> St. Stephen's Day
> St. John Evangelist's Day
> The Innocents' Day
> The Sunday after Christmas Day
> The Circumcision of Christ
> The Epiphany
> The first Sunday after the Epiphany . . . [second, third, fourth, fifth]
> The Sunday called Septuagesima
> The Sunday called Sexagesima
> The Sunday called Quinquagesima
> The First day of Lent, commonly called Ash-Wednesday
> The first Sunday in Lent . . . [second, third, fourth, fifth]
> The Sunday next before Easter
> Monday before Easter . . . [Tuesday, Wednesday, Thursday]

On Good Friday
Easter Eve
Easter Day
Monday in Easter Week . . . [Tuesday]
The first Sunday after Easter . . . [second, third, fourth, fifth]
The Ascension Day
The Sunday after the Ascension
Whitsunday
Monday in Whitsun week . . . [Tuesday]
Trinity Sunday
First Sunday after Trinity Sunday [ . . . Twenty-fifth]
St. Andrew's Day
St. Thomas the Apostle
The Conversion of Saint Paul
The Purification of Saint Mary the Virgin
Saint Mathias' Day
The Annunciation of the Virgin Mary
Saint Mark's Day
Saint Philip and James
Saint Barnabas, Apostle
Saint John Baptist
Saint Peter's Day
Saint Mary Magdalene
Saint James the Apostle
Saint Bartholomew
Saint Matthew
Saint Michael and All Angels
Saint Luke Evangelist
Simon and Jude, Apostles
All Saints

## C. The Church of Scotland is more thorough.

43. "The Book of Discipline" (1560). In *John Knox's History of the Reformation in Scotland* (London: Thomas Nelson & Sons, 1949), II, 281.

We understand whatsoever men, by laws, councils, or constitutions have imposed upon the conscience of men, without the expressed commandment of God's Word; such as vows of chastity, forswearing of marriage, binding of men and women to several and disguised apparels, to the superstitious observation of fasting days, difference of meat for conscience sake, prayer for the dead, and keeping of holy days of certain saints commanded by man, such as be all those that the Papists have invented, as the feasts, as they term them, of apostles, martyrs, virgins, of Christmas, circumcision, epiphany, purification, and other fond feasts of our Lady. Which things, because in God's Scriptures they neither have commandment nor assurance, we judge utterly to be abolished from this realm; affirming farther, that the obstinate maintainers and teachers of such abominations ought not to escape the punishment of the civil magistrate.

## D. The Puritans focus on the Lord's Day and on responding to God's present actions.

44. *A Directory for the Publique Worship of God, Throughout the Three Kingdoms of England, Scotland, and Ireland . . .* [Westminster *Directory*] (London: 1644 [1645]). Copy in University Library, Cambridge, pp. 56, 85.

The Lord's day ought to be so remembred beforehand, as that all worldly businesse of our ordinary Callings may be so ordered, and so timely and seasonably laid aside, as they may not be impediments to the due sanctifying of the Day when it comes.

The whole Day is to be celebrated as holy to the Lord, both in publique and private, as being the Christian Sabbath. To which end, it is requisite, that there be a holy cessation, or resting all the day, from all unnecessary labours; and an abstaining, not onely from all sports and pastimes, but also from all worldly words and thoughts. . . .

There is no Day commanded in Scripture to be kept holy under the Gospell, but the Lord's Day, which is the Christian Sabbath.

Festivall days, vulgarly called Holy daies, having no warrant in the Word of God, are not to be continued.

Neverthelesse, it is lawfull and necessary upon speciall emergent occasions, to separate a day or daies for Publique Fasting or Thanksgiving, as the severall eminent and extraordinary dispensations of Gods providence shall administer cause and opportunity to his people.

## E. John Wesley's calendar takes a pragmatic approach.
45. John Wesley.

*a.* Letter bound with *The Sunday Service,* dated September 9, 1784. *John Wesley's Sunday Service* (Nashville: United Methodist Publishing House, 1984), n.p.

> Most of the holy-days (so called) are omitted, as at present answering no valuable end.

*b.* "The Collects, Epistles, and Gospels to be used throughout the Year," from *The Sunday Service of the Methodists in North America* (London, 1784), pp. 27–124.

> The First Sunday in Advent . . . [Second, Third, Fourth]
> The Nativity of our Lord, or the Birth-day of CHRIST, commonly called Christmas-day
> The First Sunday after Christmas . . . [Second to Fifteenth]
> The Sunday next before Easter
> GOOD-FRIDAY
> EASTER-DAY
> The First Sunday after Easter . . . [Second to Fifth]
> The Ascension-day
> Sunday after Ascension-day
> WHIT-SUNDAY
> TRINITY-SUNDAY
> First Sunday after Trinity . . . [Second to Twenty-fifth Sunday after Trinity]

# Cycles of the Liturgical Year According to the Common Calendar

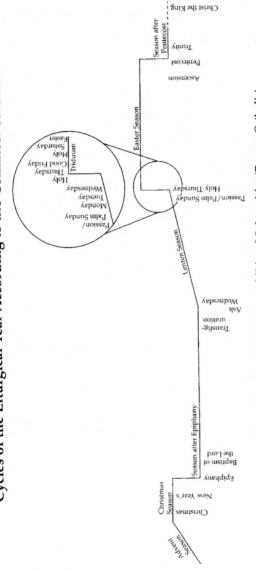

**Special Days (Common Calendar)**
Presentation (February 2)
Annunciation (March 25)
Visitation (May 31)
Holy Cross (September 14)
All Saints (November 1 or first Sunday in November)
Thanksgiving Day (Canada: October 8–14; U.S.A.: November 22–28)

**Additional Solemnities (Roman Catholic)**
Mary, Mother of God (January 1)
Joseph, Husband of Mary (March 19)
Corpus Christi (May or June)
Sacred Heart (May, June, or July)
Birth of John the Baptist (June 24)
Peter and Paul, Apostles (June 29)
Assumption (August 15)
Immaculate Conception (December 8)

**Table 8**

## Select Bibliography on Time as Communication

Adam, Adolf. *The Liturgical Year*. New York: Pueblo Publishing Co., 1981.

Brown, Peter. *The Cult of the Saints: Its Rise and Function in Latin Christianity*. Chicago: University of Chicago Press, 1981.

*Common Lectionary: The Lectionary Proposed by the Consultation on Common Texts*. New York: Church Hymnal Corporation, 1983.

Guéranger, Prosper. *The Liturgical Year*. 12 vols. Dublin: James Duffy, 1867–1890.

Hickman, Hoyt L.; Don E. Saliers; Laurence Hull Stookey; and James F. White. *The New Handbook of the Christian Year*. Nashville: Abingdon Press, 1992.

Jewett, Paul K. *The Lord's Day*. Grand Rapids: Wm. B. Eerdmans Publishing Co., 1971.

Joint Liturgical Group. *A Four-Year Lectionary*. Norwich, England: Canterbury Press, 1990.

McArthur, A. Allan. *The Evolution of the Christian Year*. London: SCM Press, 1953.

Martimort, A. G.; I. H. Dalmais; P. Jounel. *The Church at Prayer*, Vol. IV: *The Liturgy and Time*. New ed. Collegeville, Minn.: Liturgical Press, 1986.

Nocent, Adrian. *The Liturgical Year*. Collegeville, Minn.: Liturgical Press, 1977. 4 vols.

Parsch, Pius. *The Church's Year of Grace*. 5 vols. Collegeville, Minn.: Liturgical Press, 1963–1965.

Pfatteicher, Philip E. *Festivals and Commemorations*. Minneapolis: Augsburg Publishing House, 1980.

Rordorf, Willy. *Sunday*. Philadelphia: Westminster Press, 1968.

Seidenspinner, Clarence. *Great Protestant Festivals*. New York: Henry Schuman, 1952.

Taft, Robert. *Beyond East and West*. Washington, D.C.: Pastoral Press, 1984.

Talley, Thomas J. *The Origins of the Liturgical Year*. New York: Pueblo Publishing Co., 1986.

Vos, Wiebe, and Geoffrey Wainwright, eds. *Liturgical Time*. Rotterdam: Liturgical Ecumenical Center Trust, 1982.

# CHAPTER III

# Space as Communication

## I. THE VOCABULARY OF LITURGICAL SPACES, LITURGICAL CENTERS, AND LITURGICAL ARRANGEMENTS
A. Churches are divided into distinct spaces for different liturgical functions.

1. *Gathering space*, here as enclosed exterior space. St. Francis de Sales Roman Catholic Church, Muskegon, Michigan, c. 1970.

2. *Movement space*, in this case, the entire interior of a Shaker meetinghouse. From Shirley, Massachusetts, now at Hancock, Massachusetts, 1793.

3. *Congregational space,* most of the space in this Quaker meetinghouse. Jordans, Buckinghamshire, England, 1688.

4. *Choir space,* located in this case beside congregational space. St. Paul's Episcopal Cathedral, Burlington, Vermont, c. 1980.

5. *Baptismal space*, here at the entrances. First United Methodist Church, Holland, Michigan, c. 1980.

6. *Altar-table space* encompassed by congregational space. Immaculate Conception Roman Catholic Cathedral, Burlington, Vermont, c. 1980.

## B. Various furnishings serve the worshiping community as liturgical centers.

*7. Baptismal fonts or pools.*

a. Medieval English font.

b. Baptist. Tewkesbury, England, mid-seventeenth century.

c.  Pools for immersion of infants and adults. St. Elizabeth Seton Roman Catholic Church, Carmel, Indiana, c. 1985.

8. *Pulpits, lecterns, and reading desks.*

a.  Equal desks for preaching and prayer as requested by George Herbert. Leighton Bromswold, England, early seventeenth century.

b. Pompion Hill Episcopal Chapel, near Huger, South Carolina, 1763.

c. Burke Hollow, Vermont, 1825. Originally Methodist.

9. *Altar-tables.*

a. Medieval altar-table, modern frontal. Lincoln Cathedral, England.

b. Village Chapel, Roman Catholic, Chimayo, New Mexico, mid-nineteenth century.

c. Priory Chapel, Benson, Vermont, c. 1955.

10. *Presider's chair.*

a. The nineteenth-century legacy. Presbyterian Church, Mosquitoville, Vermont, 1825.

b. St. Procopius Abbey Church, Lisle, Illinois, c. 1975.

## C. A variety of liturgical arrangements reflects the diversity of Christian worship.

Churches can best be analyzed as to liturgical function through the use of simple diagrams. We use here the following code for liturgical spaces: "G" for gathering space; parallel lines indicate choir space; dotted lines suggest the outline of a balcony; a jagged line indicates a movable partition. The liturgical centers are indicated by "A" for altar-table, "B" for baptismal font or pool, "P" for pulpit, "L" for lectern, and "D" for prayer desk. The diagrams that follow are schematic only and are not to scale.

## II. THE DIVERSITY OF LITURGICAL ARRANGEMENTS
### A. Two dominant building types have developed: longitudinal (generally preferred in the West) and central (favored by the East and in the Reformation era).

11. *Longitudinal:* Roman basilica. St. Lawrence outside the Walls, Rome, fourth to thirteenth centuries. Photos: Alinari/Art Resource, New York.

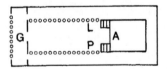

12. *Central:* Eastern Orthodox domed nave with iconostasis dividing congregational space from altar-table space. Holy Trinity Monastery Church, Jordanville, New York, c. 1930. Photos courtesy of Holy Trinity Monastery.

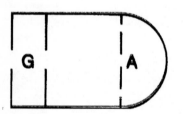

**B. The medieval West saw the development of a variety of types of churches to serve different liturgical purposes.**

13. *Cathedrals* were the church of a bishop and often enclosed vast space for important public functions. Lincoln Cathedral, largely thirteenth and four-teenth centuries.

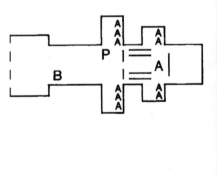

14. *Monastic churches* provided for the worship of religious communities. Worship focused on the daily office, usually sung antiphonally in choir stalls.

a. Selby Abbey (Benedictine), twelfth to fourteenth centuries.

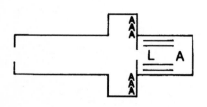

b. Westminster Abbey (Benedictine),
tenth to eighteenth centuries.
Photo: Paul F. Bradshaw

15. *Collegiate churches* sheltered the worship of special communities, religious or academic. Magdalene College Chapel, Cambridge, fifteenth century. Exterior photo: Paul F. Bradshaw.

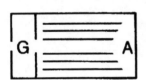

16. *Baptisteries* were built as separate buildings in some countries. Baptistery in Grado, Italy, sixth century, with a font from the tenth or eleventh century. Photos: S. Anita Stauffer.

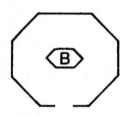

17. *Parish churches* dotted the landscape and cities and provided the usual place of worship for most people.
a. Interior, showing division of space by roodscreens. English medieval parish church.

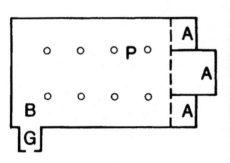

b. Exterior, Parish Church, Lower Slaughter, fourteenth to fifteenth centuries.

## C. Each Protestant tradition developed one or more characterisitc liturgical arrangements.

18. Ebenezer *Lutheran* Church, Jerusalem, Georgia, 1769.

19. *Reformed* Church, Fort Herkimer, New York, 1767 (altered and enlarged 1812).

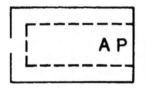

20. *Anabaptist.* Yellow Creek Mennonite Meetinghouse, near Goshen, Indiana, nineteenth century.

21. *Anglican* church as arranged for worship in the eighteenth century. St. Mary's Church, Whitby, Yorkshire.

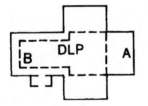

22. *Anglican* church after the Catholic Revival. All Saints' Episcopal Church, Peterborough, New Hampshire, c. 1920.

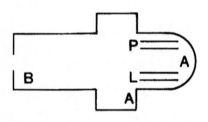

23. *Puritan.* Rockingham Meetinghouse, Rockingham, Vermont, 1787.

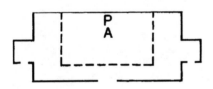

24. *Quaker.* Third Haven Meetinghouse, Easton, Maryland, 1682.

25. *Methodist*. The New Room, Bristol, England, 1739.

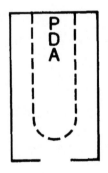

26a. *Frontier:* Camp meeting. Frontispiece from B. W. Gorham, *Camp Meeting Manual* (Boston, 1854). Diagram shows stand, or speakers' platform, with altar area in front of it, ladies' seats on left, gentlemen's seats on right.

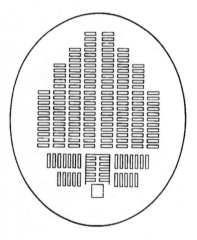

26b. Camp meeting enclosed. Billy Sunday Tabernacle, Winona Lake, Indiana, 1920–1921.

27. *Frontier* today. First Baptist Church, Asheville, North Carolina, 1927.

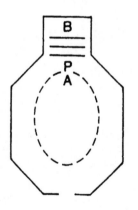

28. *Pentecostal.* United Pentecostal Church, South Bend, Indiana, c. 1980.

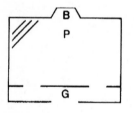

**D. The Central building type has reasserted itself in some recent churches.**

29. *Roman Catholic.* Church of St. John the Evangelist, Hopkins, Minnesota, c. 1970. Photos: Larry Ginzske; Editor: Bro. William Woeger, F.S.C.

30. Trinity *Lutheran* Seminary Chapel, Columbus, Ohio, c. 1980.

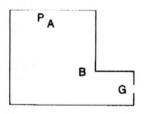

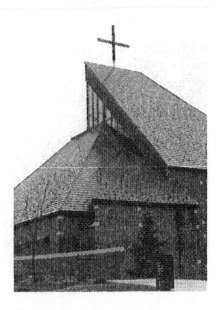

## II. LITERARY DOCUMENTS

### A. Abbot Suger (c. 1081–1151) invents gothic in transforming a mystical theology of light into the glass and stone walls of the Abbey Church of St. Denis near Paris, 1140.

1. Abbot Suger, Inscriptions on the west doors and east end (1140 and 1144), *De Administratione*, XXVII–XXVIII. Trans. Erwin Panofsky, *Abbot Suger on the Abbey Church of St.-Denis and Its Art Treasures*, 2nd ed. (Princeton: Princeton University Press, 1979), pp. 47, 49, 51.

Bright is the noble work; but, being nobly bright,
   the work
Should brighten the minds, so that they may travel,
   through the true lights,
To the True Light where Christ is the true door.
In what manner it be inherent in this world the golden
   door defines:
The dull mind rises to truth through that which is
   material
And, in seeing the light, is resurrected from its former
   submission. . . .


The year was the One Thousand, One Hundred, Forty and
Fourth of the Word when [this structure] was
   consecrated. . . .


Once the new rear part is joined to the part in front,
The church shines with its middle part brightened.
For bright is that which is brightly coupled with the
   bright,
And bright is the noble edifice which is pervaded by the
   new light;
Which stands enlarged in our time,
I, who was Suger, being the leader while it was being
   accomplished.

### B. Sir Christopher Wren (1632–1723) defines the "auditory" church for Anglican worship after designing scores of them himself.

2. Sir Christopher Wren, *Letter* (1708). Stephen Wren, *Parentalia: or, Memoirs of the Family of the Wrens* (London: 1750), pp. 320–321.

The Churches therefore must be large: but still, in our reformed Religion, it should seem vain to make a *Parish-church* larger than that all who are present can both hear and see. The *Romanists*, indeed, may build larger Churches, it is enough if they hear the Murmur of the Mass, and see the Elevation of the Host, but ours are to be fitted for Auditories. I can hardly think it practicable to make a single Room so capacious, with Pews and Galleries, as to hold above 2,000 Persons, and all to hear the Service, and both to hear distinctly, and see the Preacher. . . .

Concerning the placing of the Pulpit, I shall observe—A moderate Voice may be heard 50 Feet distant before the Preacher, 30 Feet on each Side, and 20 behind the Pulpit, and not this, unless the Pronunciation be distinct and equal, without losing the Voice at the Last Word of the Sentence, which is commonly emphatical, and if obscured spoils the whole Sense. A *French* Man is heard further than an *English* Preacher, because he raises his Voice, and not sinks his last Words.

### C. Augustus Welby Northmore Pugin (1812–1852) rediscovers gothic as the only true "Christian architecture" and promotes the gothic revival.

3. A. Welby Pugin, *Contrasts: or, A Parallel between the Noble Edifices of the Middle Ages, And Corresponding Buildings of the Present Day; Shewing the Present Decay of Taste*, 2nd ed. (Edinburgh: John Grant, 1889), pp. 1–3, 7 (originally published in 1836 and 1841).

On comparing the Architectural Works of the last three centuries with those of the Middle Ages, the wonderful superiority of the latter must strike every attentive observer; and the mind is naturally led to reflect on the causes which have wrought this mighty change, and to endeavour to trace the fall of Architectural taste, from the period of its first decline to the present day; and this will form the subject of the following pages.

It will be readily admitted, that the great test of Architectural beauty is the fitness of the design to the purpose for which it is intended, and that the style of a building should so correspond with its use that the spectator may at once perceive the purpose for which it was erected. . . .

Pointed [gothic] or Christian Architecture has far higher claims on our admiration than mere beauty or antiquity; the former may be regarded as a matter of opinion,—the latter, in the abstract, is no proof of excellence, but in it alone we find *the faith of Christianity embodied, and its practices illustrated.* . . .

Christian art was the natural result of the progress of Catholic feeling and devotion; and its decay was consequent on that of the faith itself; and all revived classic buildings, whether erected in Catholic or Protestant countries, are evidences of a lamentable departure from true Catholic principles and feelings.

## D. The modern era rediscovers essentials.

4. [Robert Hovda], Bishops' Committee on the Liturgy, *Environment and Art in Catholic Worship* (Washington: United States Catholic Conference, 1978), pp. 11, 18, 25.

### a. The Experience of Mystery

12. The experience of mystery which liturgy offers is found in its God-consciousness and God-centeredness. This involves a certain beneficial tension with the demands of hospitality, requiring a manner and an environment which invite contemplation (seeing beyond the face of the person or the thing, a sense of the holy, the numinous, mystery). A simple and attractive beauty in everything that is used or done in liturgy is the most effective invitation to this kind of experience. One should be able to sense something special (and nothing trivial) in everything that is seen and heard, touched and smelled, and tasted in liturgy. . . .

### b. The Assembly of Believers

28. Among the symbols with which liturgy deals, none is more important than this assembly of believers. It is common to use the same name to speak of the building in which those persons worship, but that use is misleading. In the words of ancient Christians, the building used for worship is called *domus ecclesiae,* the house of the Church. . . .

### c. Primary Demand: The Assembly

42. The norm for designing liturgical space is the assembly and its liturgies. The building or cover enclosing the architectural space is a shelter or "skin" for a liturgical action. It does not have to "look

like" anything else, past or present. Its integrity, simplicity and beauty, its physical location and landscaping should take into account the neighborhood, city and area in which it is built.

## Select Bibliography on Space as Communication

Bishops' Committee on the Liturgy. *Environment and Art in Catholic Worship.* Washington, D.C.: United States Catholic Conference, 1978.

Bruggink, Donald J., and Carl H. Droppers. *Christ and Architecture.* Grand Rapids: Wm. B. Eerdmans Publishing Co., 1965.

————. *When Faith Takes Form.* Grand Rapids: Wm. B. Eerdmans Publishing Co., 1971.

Debuyst, Frédéric. *Modern Architecture and Christian Celebration.* Richmond: John Knox Press, 1968.

Hammond, Peter. *Liturgy and Architecture.* New York: Columbia University Press, 1961.

————, ed. *Towards a Church Architecture.* London: Architectural Press, 1962.

Hayes, Bartlett. *Tradition Becomes Innovation: Modern Religious Architecture in America.* New York: Pilgrim Press, 1983.

Huffman, Walter C., and S. Anita Stauffer. *Where We Worship.* Minneapolis: Augsburg Publishing House, 1987.

Mauck, Marchita. *Shaping a House for the Church.* Chicago: Liturgy Training Publicatons, 1990.

Reidel, Scott R. *Acoustics in the Worship Space.* St. Louis: Concordia Publishing House, 1986.

Sovik, Edward A. *Architecture for Worship.* Minneapolis: Augsburg Publishing House, 1973.

White, James F. *Protestant Worship and Church Architecture.* New York: Oxford University Press, 1964.

————, and Susan J. White. *Church Architecture: Building and Renovating for Christian Worship.* Nashville: Abingdon Press, 1988.

# CHAPTER IV

# Daily Public Prayer

## I. PRAYERS OF PRIVATE DEVOTION
**A. Biblical texts suggested patterns of daily prayer to early Christians.**

1. Scripture.

*a.* Exodus 29:38–39.

Now this is what you shall offer on the altar: two lambs a year old regularly each day. One lamb you shall offer in the morning, and the other lamb you shall offer in the evening.

*b.* Psalm 55:17.
>  Evening and morning and at noon
>  I utter my complaint and moan,
>  and he will hear my voice.

*c.* Psalm 119:62, 164.
>  At midnight I rise to praise you,
>  because of your righteous ordinances. . . .
>  Seven times a day I praise you
>  for your righteous ordinances.

*d.* Psalm 141:2.
>  Let my prayer be counted as
>  incense before you,
>  and the lifting up of my hands
>  as an evening sacrifice.

*e.* Daniel 6:10.
>  Daniel . . . continued to go to his house, which had windows in its upper room open toward Jerusalem, and to get down on his knees three times a day to pray to his God and praise him, just as he had done previously.

*f.* Acts 2:15; 10:9; 3:1; 16:25.
>  [Pentecost] Indeed, these are not drunk, as you suppose, for it is only nine o'clock in the morning. . . .
>
>  About noon the next day, as they were on their journey and approaching the city [Caesarea], Peter went up on the roof to pray. . . .
>
>  One day Peter and John were going up to the temple at the hour of prayer, at three o'clock in the afternoon. . . .
>
>  About midnight Paul and Silas were praying and singing hymns to God, and the prisoners were listening to them [at Philippi].

*g.* 1 Thessalonians 5:17.
>  Pray without ceasing.

## Patterns of Daily Prayer

| | Private Prayer | | People's Office | | Monastic | | Reformation | | Modern | |
|---|---|---|---|---|---|---|---|---|---|---|
| | Tertullian | Hippolytus | Apostolic Constitutions | Egeria | Basil | Benedict | Luther | BCP | Lutheran BCP | Roman Catholic |
| M | | | | | | | | | | (Office of Readings variable times) |
| 3 | | Cockcrow | (Sunday Vigil) | (Sunday Vigil) | Before Dawn | Nocturns | | | | |
| 6 | Morning | Morning | Morning | Dawn | Morning | Lauds Prime | Matins | Matins (Morning Prayer) | Morning Prayer | Lauds |
| 9 | Third | Third | | | Third | Terce | | | | |
| N | Sixth | Sixth | | Midday | Sixth | Sext | | | Noonday (BCP) | Middle Hour |
| 3 | Ninth | Ninth | | Afternoon | Ninth | None | | | | |
| 6 | Evening | Evening | Evening | Lychnicon | After Work | Vespers | Vespers | Evensong (Evening Prayer) | Evening Prayer | Vespers |
| 9 | | Bedtime Night-time | | | Nightfall | Compline | | | Compline | Compline |
| M | | Midnight | | | Midnight | | | | | |

Table 9

## B. Disciplines for times of prayer develop early.

2. *Didache*, VIII (late first or early second century). Trans. Cyril C. Richardson, LCC, I, 174.

> You must not pray like the hypocrites, but "pray as follows" as the Lord bids us in his gospel:
>
> "Our Father in heaven, hallowed be your name; your Kingdom come; your will be done on earth as it is in heaven; give us today our bread for the morrow; and forgive us our debts as we forgive our debtors. And do not lead us into temptation, but save us from the evil one, for yours is the power and the glory forever."
>
> You should pray in this way three times a day.

3. Clement of Alexandria, *Stromata or Miscellanies*, VII, 7 (c. 200). Trans. William Wilson, ANF, II, 534.

> Prayer is, then, to speak more boldly, converse with God. Though whispering, consequently, and not opening the lips, we speak in silence, yet we cry inwardly. For God hears continually all the inward converse. So also we raise the head and lift the hands to heaven, and set the feet in motion at the closing utterance of the prayer, following the eagerness of the spirit directed towards the intellectual essence; and endeavouring to abstract the body from the earth, along with the discourse, raising the soul aloft, winged with longing for better things, we compel it to advance to the region of holiness, magnanimously despising the chain of the flesh. . . .
>
> Now, if some assign definite hours for prayer—as, for example, the third, and sixth, and ninth—yet the Gnostic [here, true Christian] prays throughout his whole life, endeavouring by prayer to have fellowship with God. And, briefly, having reached to this, he leaves behind him all that is of no service, as having now received the perfection of the man that acts by love.

4. Tertullian.

a. *On Fasting*, X (c. 210). Trans. S. Thelwell, ANF, IV, 108.

> Peter at the *sixth* hour had, for the sake of taking food, gone up first on the roof to pray; so that the *sixth* hour of the day may

rather be made the limit to this duty which (in Peter's case) was apparently to finish that duty, after prayer. Further: since in the self-same commentary of Luke the *third* hour demonstrated as an hour of prayer, about which hour it was that they who had received the initiatory gift of the Holy Spirit were held for drunkards; and the *sixth*, at which Peter went up on the roof; and the *ninth*, at which they entered the temple: why should we not understand that with absolutely perfect indifference, we must pray always, and everywhere, and at every time yet still that these three hours, as being more marked in things human—(hours) which divide the day, which distinguish businesses, which re-echo in the public ear—have likewise ever been of special solemnity in divine prayers? A persuasion which is sanctioned also by the corroborative fact of Daniel praying thrice in the day.

*b. On Prayer*, XXV–XXVI (c. 200). Trans. S. Thelwell, ANF, III, 690.

It may be granted a good thing to establish some definite presumption, which may both add stringency to the admonition to pray, and may, as it were be a law, tear us out from our businesses unto such a duty; so that—what we read to have been observed by Daniel also, in accordance (of course) with Israel's discipline—we pray at least not less than thrice in the day, debtors as we are to Three—Father, Son, and Holy Spirit: of course in addition to our regular prayers which are due, without any admonition, on the entrance of light and of night. But withal, it becomes believers not to take food, and not to go to the bath, before interposing a prayer; for the refreshments and nourishments of the spirit are to be held prior to those of the flesh, and things heavenly prior to things earthly.

You will not dismiss a brother who has entered your house without prayer.—"Have you seen," says *Scripture*, "a brother? You have seen your Lord";—especially "a stranger," lest perhaps he be "an angel." But again, when received yourself by brethren, you will not make earthly refreshments prior to heavenly, for your faith will forthwith be judged. Or else how will you—according to the precept—say, "Peace to this *house*," unless you exchange mutual peace with them who are *in* the house?

## C. By the third century, seven daily hours for prayer are commended to devout Christians.

5. Hippolytus, *Apostolic Tradition*, XLI (c. 217). Trans. Geoffrey J. Cum-

ing, *Hippolytus: A Text for Students* (Bramcote, Notts.: Grove Books, 1976), pp. 29–31.

> Let every faithful man and woman, when they have risen from sleep *in the morning*, before they touch any work at all, wash their hands and pray to God, and so go to their work. . . .

> And if you are at home, pray at the *third hour* and bless God. But if you are somewhere else at that moment, pray to God in your heart. For at that hour Christ was nailed to the tree. For this reason also in the Old (Testament) the Law prescribed that the shewbread should be offered continually as a type of the body and blood of Christ; and the slaughter of the lamb without reason is this type of the perfect lamb. For Christ is the shepherd, and also the bread which came down from heaven.

> Pray likewise at the time of the *sixth hour*. For when Christ was nailed to the wood of the cross, the day was divided, and darkness fell. And so at that hour let them pray a powerful prayer, imitating the voice of him who prayed and made all creation dark for the unbelieving Jews.

> And at the *ninth hour* let them pray also a great prayer and a great blessing, to know the way in which the soul of the righteous blesses God who does not lie, who remembered his saints and sent his word to give them light. For at that hour Christ was pierced in his side and poured out water and blood; giving light to the rest of time of the day, he brought it to evening. Then, in beginning to sleep and making the beginning of another day, he fulfilled the type of the resurrection.

> *Pray before your body rests* on the bed. Rise about *midnight*, wash your hands with water, and pray. If your wife is present also, pray both together; if she is not yet among the faithful, go apart into another room and pray, and go back to bed again. Do not be lazy about praying. He who is bound in the marriage-bond is not de- filed. . . .

> For the elders who gave us the tradition taught us that at that hour all creation is still for a moment, to praise the Lord; stars, trees, waters stop for an instant, and all the host of angels (which) min-

isters to him praises God with the souls of the righteous in this hour. That is why believers should take good care to pray at this hour.

Bearing witness to this, the Lord says thus, "Lo, about midnight a shout was made of men saying, Lo, the bridegroom comes; rise to meet him." And he goes on, saying "Watch therefore, for you know not at what hour he comes."

And likewise rise about *cockcrow*, and pray. For at that hour, as the cock crew, the children of Israel denied Christ, whom we know by faith, our eyes looking towards that day in the hope of eternal light at the resurrection of the dead.

And if you act so, all you faithful, and remember these things, and teach them in your turn, and encourage the catechumens, you will not be able to be tempted or to perish, since you have Christ always in memory.

6.  Origen, *On Prayer*, XII, 2 (c. 233). Trans. John Ernest Leonard Oulton, LCC, II, 261–262.

That man "prays without ceasing" (virtuous deeds or commandments fulfilled being included as part of prayer) who combines with the prayer the needful deeds and the prayer with the fitting actions. For thus alone can we accept "pray without ceasing" as a practicable saying, if we speak of the whole life of the saint as one great unbroken prayer: of which prayer that which is commonly called prayer is a part. This ought to be engaged in not less than three times every day, as is clear from the case of Daniel, who when great danger hung over him "prayed three times a day." . . . The final one is indicated in the words "the lifting up of my hands as the evening sacrifice" (Ps. 141:2). Indeed we shall not fittingly pass even the night time without this prayer: for David says, "At midnight did I rise to give thanks unto thee for the judgments of thy righteousness" (Ps. 119:62); and "Paul," as is stated in the Acts of the Apostles, "about midnight" in company with "Silas," at Philippi, "was praying and singing hymns unto God," so that even the "prisoners listened to them."

7. Cyprian, *On the Lord's Prayer*, XXXIV (c. 251). Trans. Roy J. Deferrari, *Saint Cyprian's Treatises*, FC, XXXVI, 157.

> Now in celebrating prayer we find that the three boys with Daniel strong in the faith and victorious in captivity observed the third, the sixth, and the ninth hours, namely for a sacrament of the Trinity. . . . Having determined upon these spaces of hours in a spiritual sense a long time ago, the worshippers of God were subject to them as the established and lawful times for prayer.

8. Chrysostom, *Homily 26 on the Acts of the Apostles* (c. 400). Trans. J. Walker, J. Sheppard, and H. Browne, NPNF, XI, 172–173.

> Not for this was the night made, that we should sleep all through it and be idle. . . . [At night] Sleep hath invaded and defeated nature: it is the image of death, the image of the end of all things. . . . All this is enough to arouse the soul, and lead it to reflect on the end of all things.

> Here indeed my discourse is for both men and women. Bend thy knees, send forth groans, beseech thy Master to be merciful: He is more moved by prayers in the night, when thou makest the time for rest a time for mourning. . . . After such vigils come sweet slumbers and wondrous revelations. Do this, thou also the man, not the woman only. Let thy house be a Church, consisting of men and women. . . . If thou hast children wake up them also, and let thy house altogether become a Church through the night: but if they be tender, and cannot endure the watching, let them stay for the first or second prayer, and then send them to rest: only stir up thyself, establish thyself in the habit.

## II.  THE PEOPLE'S OFFICE
### A.  The people's office or cathedral office becomes an important daily form of public worship after persecution ends.
9. Hippolytus, *Apostolic Tradition*, XXXIX, XLI (c. 217). Trans. Geoffrey J. Cuming, *Hippolytus: A Text for Students* (Bramcote, Notts.: Grove Books, 1976), pp. 28–29.

The deacons and priests shall assemble daily at the place which the bishop appoints for them. Let the deacons not fail to assemble at all times, unless illness hinders them. When all have assembled, let them teach those who are in the church, and in this way, when they have prayed, let each one go to the work which falls to him. . . .

But if instruction in the word of God is given, each one should choose to go to that place, reckoning in his heart that it is God whom he hears in the instructor.

For he who prays in the church will be able to pass by the wickedness of the day. . . . Therefore let each one be diligent in coming to the church, the place where the holy Spirit flourishes. If there is a day when there is no instruction, let each one, when he is at home, take up a holy book and read in it sufficiently what seems to him to bring profit.

10. Eusebius of Caesarea, *Commentary on Psalm 64:10* (c. 337). Trans. from PG, XXIII, 640.

> Rightly, it is no ordinary sign of the power of God, that throughout the whole world, in the churches of God, hymns, praises, and truly divine delights are offered to God at the morning going forth of the sun and at evening time. For indeed, the delights of God are the hymns poured forth everywhere on earth in his Church, both morning and evening. On account of which it is said somewhere: "May my praise be pleasing to him"; again, "the lifting of my hands as an evening sacrifice," and "may my prayer be as incense in your sight." And so these delights turn out to be a sign of the Savior.

## B. Morning and evening public prayer for all the people become common, plus a vigil Saturday night.

11. *Apostolic Constitutions,* II, 59; VIII, 34, 35 (c. 375). Trans. James Donaldson, ANF, VII, 422–423, 496.

> When thou instructest the people, O bishop, command and exhort them to come constantly to church morning and evening every day, and by no means to forsake it on any account, but to assemble together continually; neither to diminish the Church by withdrawing themselves, and causing the body of Christ to be without its member. For it is not only spoken concerning the priests, but let every one of the laity hearken to it as concerning himself, considering that it is said by the Lord: "He that is not with me is against me, and he that gathereth not with me scattereth abroad" [Matt. 12:30]. Do not you therefore scatter yourselves abroad, who are

the members of Christ, by not assembling together, since you have
Christ your head, according to His promise, present, and commu-
nicating to you. Be not careless of yourselves, neither deprive your
Saviour of His own members, neither divide His body nor disperse
His members, neither prefer the occasions of this life to the word
of God; but assemble yourselves together every day, morning and
evening, singing psalms and praying in the Lord's house: in
the morning saying the sixty-[third] Psalm, and in the evening the
hundred and forty-[first], but principally on the Sabbath-day. And
on the day of our Lord's resurrection, which is the Lord's day, meet
more diligently, sending praise to God that made the universe by
Jesus, and sent Him to us, and condescended to let Him suffer, and
raised Him from the dead. Otherwise what apology will he make
to God who does not assemble on that day to hear the saving word
concerning the resurrection, on which we pray thrice standing in
memory of Him who arose in three days, in which is performed
the reading of the prophets, the preaching of the Gospel, the oblation of the sacrifice, the gift of the holy food? . . .

If it be not possible to assemble either in the church or in a house,
let every one by himself sing, and read, and pray, or two or three
together. For "where two or three are gathered together in my
name, there am I in the midst of them" [Matt. 18:20]. Let not one of
the faithful pray with a catechumen, no, not in the house: for it is
not reasonable that he who is admitted should be polluted with one
not admitted. Let not one of the godly pray with an heretic, no, not
in the house. For "what fellowship hath light with darkness?" . . .

I James, the brother of Christ according to the flesh, but His servant as the only begotten God, and one appointed bishop of Jerusalem by the Lord Himself, and the Apostles, do ordain thus:
When it is evening, thou, O bishop, shalt assemble the church;
and after the repetition of the psalm at the lighting up the lights,
the deacon shall bid prayers for the catechumens, the
energumens, the illuminated, and the penitents, as we have formerly said. But after the dismission of these, the deacon shall say:
So many as are of the faithful, let us pray to the Lord.

12. John Chrysostom, *Baptismal Instructions*, XVII–XVIII (388). Trans.
Paul W. Harkins, *St. John Chrysostom: Baptismal Instructions*, ACW,
XXXI, 126–127.

And I urge you to show great zeal by gathering here in the church at dawn to make your prayers and confessions to the God of all things, and to thank Him for the gifts He has already given. Beseech Him to deign to lend you from now on His powerful aid in guarding this treasure; strengthened with this aid, let each one leave the church to take up his daily tasks, one hastening to work with his hands, another hurrying to his military post, and still another to his post in the government. However, let each one approach his daily task with fear and anguish, and spend his working hours in the knowledge that at evening he should return here to the church, render an account to the Master of his whole day, and beg forgiveness for his falls. . . .

This is the reason why each evening we must beg pardon from the Master for all these faults. This is why we must flee to the loving-kindness of God and make our appeal to Him. Then we must spend the hours of the night soberly, and in this way meet the confessions of the dawn. If each of us manages his own life in this way, he will be able to cross the sea of this life without danger and to deserve the loving-kindness of the Master. And when the hour for gathering in church summons him, let him hold this gathering and all spiritual things in higher regard than anything else. In this way we shall manage the goods we have in our hands and keep them secure.

## C. The holy places in Jerusalem provide locations for daily worship of monks and virgins, lay people, and clergy, each with different roles.

13. Egeria, *Pilgrimage of Egeria*, XXIV–XXV (c. 384). Trans. John Wilkinson, *Egeria's Travels*, (London: SPCK, 1971), pp. 123–126.

Loving sisters, I am sure it will interest you to know about the daily services they have in the holy places, and I must tell you about them. All the doors of the Anastasis [place of the resurrection] are opened before cock-crow each day, and the *"monazontes and parthenae"* [monks and virgins], as they call them here, come in, and also some lay men and women, at least those who are willing to wake at such an early hour. From then until daybreak they join in singing the refrains to the hymns, psalms, and antiphons. There is a prayer between each of the hymns, since there are two or three presbyters and deacons each day by rota, who are there with the monazontes and say the prayers between all the hymns and antiphons.

As soon as *dawn* comes, they start the Morning Hymns, and the bishop with his clergy comes and joins them. He goes straight into the cave [the tomb], and inside the screen he first says the Prayer for All (mentioning any names he wishes) and blesses the catechumens, and then another prayer and blesses the faithful. Then he comes outside the screen, and everyone comes up to kiss his hand. He blesses them one by one, and goes out, and by the time the dismissal takes place it is already day.

Again *at midday* everyone comes into the Anastasis and says psalms and antiphons until a message is sent to the bishop. Again he enters, and, without taking his seat, goes straight inside the screen in the Anastasis (which is to say into the cave where he went in the early morning), and again, after a prayer, he blesses the faithful and comes outside the screen, and again they come to kiss his hand.

At *three o'clock* they do once more what they did at midday, but at *four o'clock* they have *Lychnicon*, as they call it, or in our language, Lucernare. All the people congregate once more in the Anastasis, and the lamps and candles are all lit, which makes it very bright. The fire is brought not from outside, but from the cave—inside the screen—where a lamp is always burning night and day. For some time they have the Lucernare psalms and antiphons; then they send for the bishop, who enters and sits in the chief seat. The presbyters also come and sit in their places, and the hymns and antiphons go on. Then, when they have finished singing everything which is appointed, the bishop rises and goes in front of the screen (i.e., the cave). One of the deacons makes the normal commemoration of individuals, and each time he mentions a name a large group of boys responds, *Kyrie eleison* (in our language, "Lord, have mercy"). Their voices are very loud. As soon as the deacon has done his part, the bishop says a prayer and prays the Prayer for All. Up to this point the faithful and the catechumens are praying together, but now the deacon calls every catechumen to stand where he is and bow his head, and the bishop says the blessing over the catechumens from his place. There is another prayer, after which the deacon calls for all the faithful to bow their head, and the bishop says the blessing over the faithful from his place. Thus the dismissal takes place at the Anastasis, and they all come up one by one to kiss the bishop's hand.

Then, singing hymns, they take the bishop from the Anastasis to the Cross, and everyone goes with him. On arrival he says one prayer and blesses the catechumens, then another and blesses the faithful. Then again the bishop and all the people go Behind the Cross, and do there what they did Before the Cross; and in both places they come to kiss the bishop's hand, as they did in the Anastasis. Great glass lanterns are burning everywhere, and there are many candles in front of the Anastasis, and also Before and Behind the Cross. By the end of all this it is dusk. So these are the services held every weekday at the Cross and at the Anastasis.

But on the seventh day, *the Lord's Day*, there gather in the court-yard *before cock-crow* all the people, as many as can get in, as if it was Easter. The courtyard is the "basilica" beside the Anastasis, that is to say, out of doors, and lamps have been hung there for them. Those who are afraid they may not arrive in time for cock-crow come early, and sit waiting there singing hymns and anti-phons, and they have prayers between, since there are always presbyters and deacons there ready for the vigil, because so many people collect there, and it is not usual to open the holy places before cock-crow.

Soon the first cock crows, and at that the bishop enters, and goes into the cave in the Anastasis. The doors are all opened, and all the people come into the Anastasis, which is already ablaze with lamps. When they are inside, a psalm is said by one of the presby-ters, with everyone responding, and it is followed by a prayer; then a psalm is said by one of the deacons, and other prayer; then a third psalm is said by one of the clergy, a third prayer, and the Commemoration of All. After these three psalms and prayers they take censers into the cave of the Anastasis, so that the whole Anastasis basilica is filled with the smell. Then the bishop, stand-ing inside the screen, takes the Gospel book and goes to the door, where he himself reads the account of the Lord's resurrection. At the beginning of the reading the whole assembly groans and la-ments at all that the Lord underwent for us, and the way they weep would move even the hardest heart to tears. When the Gospel is finished, the bishop comes out, and is taken with singing to the Cross, and they all go with him. They have one psalm there and a prayer, then he blesses the people, and that is the dismissal. As the bishop goes out, everyone comes to kiss his hand.

Then straight away the bishop retires to his house, and all the monazontes go back into the Anastasis to sing psalms and antiphons until daybreak. There are prayers between all these psalms and antiphons, and presbyters and deacons take their turn every day at the Anastasis to keep vigil with the people. Some lay men and women like to stay on there till daybreak, but others prefer to go home again to bed for some sleep. . . .

Except on the special days, which we shall be describing below, this order is observed on every day of the year. What I found most impressive about all this was that the psalms and antiphons they use are always appropriate, whether at night, in the early morning, at the day prayers at midday or three o'clock, or at Lucernare. Everything is suitable, appropriate, and relevant to what is being done.

## III. THE MONASTIC OFFICE
### A. Egyptian monastics set a pattern of an evening and early morning office with twelve psalms at each as established by high authority.
14. Cassian, *Institutes*, II, 3, 5–6 (c. 420). Trans. Edgar C. S. Gibson, NPNF, 2nd series, XI, 205, 207.

And so throughout the whole of Egypt and the Thebaid, where monasteries are not founded at the fancy of every man who renounces the world, but through a succession of fathers and their traditions last even to the present day, or are founded so to last, in these we have noticed that a prescribed system of prayers is observed in their evening assemblies and nocturnal vigils. . . .

As they were going to celebrate their daily rites and prayers, one rose up in the midst to chant the Psalms to the Lord. And while they were all sitting (as is still the custom in Egypt), with their minds intently fixed on the words of the chanter, when he had sung eleven Psalms, separated by prayers introduced between them, verse after verse being evenly enunciated, he finished the twelfth with a response of Alleluia, and then, by his sudden disappearance from the eyes of all, put an end at once to their discussion and their service.

Whereupon the venerable assembly of the Fathers understood that by Divine Providence a general rule had been fixed for the congregations of the brethren through the angel's direction, and so decreed that this number should be preserved both in their evening and in their nocturnal services; and when they added to these two lessons, one from the Old and one from the New Testament, they added them simply as extras and of their own appointment, only for those who liked, and who were eager to gain by constant study a mind well stored with Holy Scripture. But on Saturday and Sunday they read them both from the New Testament; viz., one from the Epistles or the Acts of the Apostles, and one from the Gospel. And this also those do whose concern is the reading and the recollection of the Scriptures, from Easter to Whitsuntide.

## B. The East develops a cycle of eight daily offices in the fourth century.
15. Basil, *The Long Rules*, XXXVII (358–364). Trans. M. Monica Wagner, *Saint Basil: Ascetical Works*, FC, IX, 309–310.

Prayers are recited *early in the morning* so that the first movements of the soul and the mind may be consecrated to God and that we may take up no other consideration before we have been cheered and heartened by the thought of God, as it is written: "I remembered God and was delighted" and that the body may not busy itself with tasks before we have fulfilled the words: "To thee will I pray, O Lord; in the morning thou shalt hear my voice. In the morning I will stand before thee and will see" [Ps. 5:3]. Again *at the third hour* the brethren must assemble and betake themselves to prayer, even if they may have dispersed to their various employments. Recalling to mind the gift of the Spirit bestowed upon the Apostles at this third hour, all should worship together, so that they also may become worthy to receive the gift of sanctity, and they should implore the guidance of the Holy Spirit and His instruction in what is good and useful. . . .

But, if some, perhaps, are not in attendance because the nature or place of their work keeps them at too great a distance, they are strictly obliged to carry out wherever they are, with promptitude, all that is prescribed for common observance, for "where there are two or three gathered together in my name," says the Lord, "there am I in the midst of them" [Matt. 18:20]. It is also our judgment that prayer is necessary *at the sixth hour*, in imitation of the saints who say: "Evening and morning and at noon I will speak and declare; and he shall hear my voice" [Ps. 55:17]. And so that we may be saved from invasion and the noonday Devil, at this time, also, the [ninety-first] Psalm will be recited. The *ninth hour*, however, was appointed as a compulsory time for prayer by the Apostles themselves in the Acts where it is related that "Peter and John went up to the temple at the ninth hour of prayer." *When the day's work is ended*, thanksgiving should be offered for what has been granted us or for what we have done rightly therein and confession made of our omissions whether voluntary or involuntary, or of a secret fault, if we chance to have committed any in words or deeds, or in the heart itself; for by prayer we propitiate God for all our misdemeanors. The examination of our past actions is a great help toward not falling into like faults again; wherefore the Psalmist says: "the things you say in your hearts, be sorry for them upon your beds" [4:4].

Again, *at nightfall*, we must ask that our rest be sinless and untroubled by dreams. At this hour, also, the ninetieth Psalm should be recited. Paul and Silas, furthermore, have handed down to us the practice of compulsory prayer at *midnight*, as the history of the Acts declares: "And at midnight Paul and Silas praised God." The Psalmist also says: "I rose at midnight to give praise to thee for the judgments of thy justifications" [119:62]. Then, too, we *must anticipate the dawn* by prayer, so that the day may not find us in slumber and in bed.

## C. The Western pattern of eight daily monastic offices is fixed by St. Benedict in the sixth century.

16. Benedict of Nursia, *The Rule*, VIII, XVI, XVIII (c. 530). Trans. Owen Chadwick, LCC, XII, 304–305, 307, 309.

In the winter time, that is from the first of November until Easter, having regard to different circumstances, they shall rise at 2 o'clock in the morning, that they may have time to rest till after midnight, and the time of digestion is past. What time remains after the office is done, they may use in studying the psalms and lessons if they do not yet know them thoroughly.

From Easter to the first of November, they shall so arrange the night office as to leave a very short interval after it (so that the brothers may go out for the needs of nature) and then begin Lauds at break of day. . . .

"Seven times a day have I praised thee," said the prophet [Ps. 119:164]. We shall perform this consecrated number of seven if we offer prayer (the duty of our profession) at the hours of Lauds, Prime, Terce, Sext, None, Vespers, and Compline. It was of these day hours that he said: "Seven times a day have I praised thee." Elsewhere the same prophet makes mention of the night office, "at midnight I rose to confess to thee." At these times, therefore, let us render praise to our creator "for the judgments of his justice"—that is, Lauds, Prime, Terce, Sext, None, Vespers, Compline: and let us rise at night to confess to him. . . .

These are the arrangements for the psalmody at the day offices. The remaining psalms are to be distributed equally among the seven night offices, dividing the longer psalms and always assigning twelve for each night.

Notwithstanding, we hereby declare that if anyone does not approve of the present distribution of psalms, he may appoint otherwise, if he thinks better: provided he takes care that the whole psalter, of a hundred and fifty psalms, be sung every week, and that they begin it again at the night office each Sunday. It is a mean devotion if monks should in a week sing less than the whole Psalter with the usual canticles. We read that our holy fathers bravely recited the Psalter in a single day; God grant that we, their degenerate sons, may do the like in seven.

## IV. REFORMATION DEVELOPMENTS
**A. The only familiar pattern for public services, by this time in the West, is the monastic office, which several reformers adapt.**
17. Martin Luther.

*a. Formula Missae* (1523). Trans. by Paul Zeller Strodach and Ulrich S. Leupold, LW, LIII, 37–39.

As for the other days which are called weekdays, I see nothing that we cannot put up with, provided the [weekday] masses be discontinued. For Matins with its three lessons, the [minor] hours, Vespers, and Compline *de tempore* consist—with the exception of the propers for the Saints' days—of nothing but divine words of Scripture. And it is seemly, nay necessary, that the boys should get accustomed to reading and hearing the Psalms and lessons from the Holy Scripture. If anything should be changed, the bishop may reduce the great length [of the services] according to his own judgment so that three Psalms may be sung for Matins and three for Vespers with one or two responsories. These matters are best left to the discretion of the bishop. He should choose the best of the responsories and antiphons and appoint them from Sunday to Sunday throughout the week, taking care lest the people should either be bored by too much repetition of the same or confused by too many changes in the chants and lessons. The whole Psalter, Psalm by Psalm, should remain in use, and the entire Scripture, lesson by lesson, should continue to be read to the people. But we must take care—as I have elsewhere explained—lest the people sing only with their lips, like sounding pipes or harps [1 Cor. 14:7], and without understanding. Daily lessons must therefore be appointed, one in the morning from the New or Old Testament, another for Vespers from the other Testament with an exposition in the vernacular. That this rite is an ancient one is proven by both the custom itself and by the words *homilia* in Matins and *capitulum* in Vespers and in the other [canonical] hours, namely, that the Christians as often as they gathered together read something and then had it interpreted in the vernacular in the manner Paul describes in I Corinthians 14 [:26–27]. But when evil times came and there was a lack of prophets and interpreters, all that was left after the lessons and *capitula* was the response, "Thanks be to God." And then, in place of the interpretation, lessons, Psalms, hymns, and other things were added in boring repetition. Although the hymns and the *Te Deum laudamus* at least confirm the same thing as the *Deo gratias*, namely, that after the exposition and homilies they used to praise God and give thanks for the revealed truth of his words. That is the kind of vernacular songs I should like us to have.

*b. The German Mass* (1526). Translated by Augustus Steimle and Ulrich S. Leupold, LW, LIII, 89–90.

This is what I have to say concerning the daily service and instruction in the Word of God, which serves primarily to train the young and challenge the unlearned. For those who itch for new things will soon be sated and tired with it all, as they were heretofore in the Latin service. There was singing and reading in the churches every day, and yet the churches remained deserted and empty. Already they do the same in the German service. Therefore, it is best to plan the services in the interest of the young and such of the unlearned as may happen to come. With the others neither law nor order, neither scolding nor coaxing, will help. Allow them to leave those things in the service alone which they refuse to do willingly and gladly. God is not pleased with unwilling services; they are futile and vain.

18.  Christian Gerber, *Historie der Kirchen Ceremonien in Sachsen* (1732). Quoted in Günther Stiller, *Johann Sebastian Bach and Liturgical Life in Leipzig*, trans. Herbert J. A. Bouman, Daniel F. Poellot, and Hilton C. Oswald (St. Louis: Concordia Press, 1984), p. 55.

Happy is he who can live in a city where worship is conducted publicly every day. In this respect, the inhabitants of Dresden and Leipzig are fortunate, because in these two cities preaching and prayer services are held every day, so that they are enriched with all speech and knowledge and are not lacking in any spiritual gift.

19.  Francisco de Quiñones, *Preface, Breviarium Romanae Curiae* (1535 and 1536). Trans. from both 1535 and 1536 editions in the sequence used by Thomas Cranmer, texts in *Cranmer's Liturgical Projects*, ed. J. Wickham Legg (London: Henry Bradshaw Society, 1915), HBS, L, 168–182.

[1536] Nothing was ever worked out by human cleverness so completely from the beginning but that it was possible to be restored more perfectly after the judgments of many; this we have seen to have happened especially in the restoration of the church according to the primitive church. . . .

[1535] And truly if one may consider carefully what manner of praying was passed down formerly from most people, he discovers the reasonable character of all the hours to be clear.

[1536, 1536] But the fact is that I do not know how through what neglect of the stipulated practice of praying that little by little it departed from that most sacred practice put in place by the ancient fathers.

[1535] Now at first the books of holy scripture, which were appointed for reading through in the times of the year, scarcely began but they were passed over for prayers.

For example could be the book of Genesis, which is begun in Septuagesima, and the book of Isaiah, which in Advent, of which scarcely a single chapter is read through, and in the same means others of the Old Testament books we taste rather than we read.

[1535, 1536] The order became so complex, the calculation of the prayers so difficult, that sometimes it was little less work in finding what was laid down than after finding it, in reading it.

[1535, 1536] Which perception of things, happily having pondered, Pope Clement VII, when he considered it to be his duty . . . has encouraged me, and given authority, that with as much care and diligence as is possible, to distribute the prayers of the hours rationally, and to take away, as I have said, the difficulties and so dispose, that clergy in major orders may be more conveniently attracted to praying.

[1535] Antiphons, chapters, responses, and many hymns and other things of that sort which are a hindrance to the reading of sacred scripture are omitted; the breviary consists of psalms and sacred scripture of the Old and New Testaments, and histories of the saints which we have gathered from approved and serious greek and latin authors.

20. *The First and Second Prayer Books of Edward VI* (London: J. M. Dent & Sons, 1910; spelling, capitalization, and punctuation modernized).

a. *The Booke of the Common Prayer* (1549), "The Preface," pp. 3–5.
   There was never any thing by the wit of man so well devised, or so surely established, which (in continuance of time) hath not been corrupted: as (among other things) it may plainly appear by the common prayers in the Church, commonly called divine service:

the first original and ground whereof . . . was . . . that all the whole Bible (or the greatest part thereof) should be read over once in the year. . . . And further, that the people (by daily hearing of holy scripture read in the Church) should continually profit more and more in the knowledge of God, and be the more inflamed with the love of his true religion. But these many years passed this Godly and decent order of the ancient fathers, hath been so altered, broken, and neglected . . . that commonly when any book of the Bible was begun: before three or four chapters were read out, all the rest were unread. And in this sort the book of Isaiah was begun in Advent, and the book of Genesis in Septuagesima; but they were only begun, and never read through. . . . Many times, there was more business to find out what should be read, then to read it when it was found out.

These inconveniences therefore considered: here is set forth such an order, whereby the same shall be redressed. And for a readiness in this matter, here is drawn out a Calendar for that purpose, which is plain and easy to be understood, wherein (so much as may be) the reading of holy scripture is so set forth, that all things shall be in order, without breaking one piece thereof from another. For this cause be cut off anthems, responds, invitatories, and such like things, as did break the continual course of the reading of the scripture. . . .

Yet it is not meant, but when men say matins and evensong privately, they may say the same in any language that they themselves do understand.

b. "The Table and Kalender . . . ," p. 6.
The Psalter shall be read through once every month, and because that some months, be longer than some other be; it is thought good, to make them even by this means.

c. *The Booke of Common Prayer* (1552), "The Preface," p. 323.
And all priests and deacons shall be bound to say daily the morning and evening prayer, either privately or openly, except they be letted [prevented] by preaching, studying of divinity, or by some other urgent cause.

And the curate that ministers in every parish church or chapel, being at home, and not being otherwise reasonably letted, shall say the same in the parish church or chapel where he ministers, and shall toll a bell thereto, a convenient time before he begin, that such as be disposed may come to hear God's word, and to pray with him.

d. "The Order How the Rest of Holy Scripture (Beside the Psalter) Is Appointed to Be Read," p. 329.

The Old Testament is appointed for the first lessons, at morning and evening prayer, and shall be read through every year once, except certain books and chapters, which be least edifying, and might best be spared, and therefore be left unread.

The New Testament is appointed for the second lessons, at morning and evening prayer, and shall be read over orderly every year thrice, beside the epistles and gospels: except the Apocalypse, out of the which there be only certain lessons appointed, upon divers proper feasts.

## B. Family worship on a daily basis becomes an important part of Christian devotion.

21. Church of Scotland, *The Directory for Family-Worship*, I, II, IV (1647). *The Confession of Faith; . . . Directories for Public and Family Worship* (Philadelphia, 1829), pp. 595–596.

Besides the publick worship in congregations, mercifully established in this land in great purity, it is expedient and necessary that secret worship of each person alone, and private worship of families, be pressed and set up; that with national reformation, the profession and power of godliness, both personal and domestick, be advanced.

I. And first, for secret worship, it is most necessary . . . to perform this duty morning and evening, and at other occasions. . . .

II. The ordinary duties comprehended under the exercise of piety, which should be in families, when they are convened to this effect, are these: First, Prayer and praises performed with a special reference as well to the publick condition of the kirk of God in this kingdom, as to the present case of the family, and every member thereof. Next, Reading of the scriptures, with catechising in a plain way, that the understandings of the simpler may be the better enabled to profit under the publick ordinances, and they made more capable to understand the scriptures when they are read; together with godly conferences tending to the edification of all members in the most holy faith: as also, admonition and rebuke, upon just reasons, from those who have authority in the family. . . .

IV. The head of the family is to take care that none of the family withdraw himself from any part of family-worship.

## C. Wesley combines set forms and extempore daily prayer.
22. John Wesley.

*a.* Letter of September 10, 1784 bound with *Sunday Service* (1784). *John Wesley's Sunday Service* (Nashville: United Methodist Publishing House, 1984), n.p.

And I have prepared a liturgy little differing from that of the church of England (I think, the best constituted national church in the world) which I advise all the travelling-preachers to use, on the Lord's day, in all their congregations, reading the litany only on Wednesdays and Fridays, and praying extempore on all other days. I also advise the elders to administer the supper of the Lord on every Lord's day.

*b.* Letter of September 9, 1784 bound with *Sunday Service* (1784). Ibid.
Many Psalms left out, and many parts of the others, as being highly improper for the mouths of a Christian Congregation.

## D. The midweek prayer meeting recovers some of the characteristics of the early people's office (frequent use of familiar hymns and prayers) and leads to transformation of society (abolition of slavery, temperance movements, etc.).
23. Charles G. Finney, *Lectures on Revivals of Religion* (1835), ed. William G. McLoughlin (Cambridge, Mass.: Harvard University Press, 1960), p. 259.

*Female Prayer Meetings.* Within the last few years [1830s], female prayer meetings have been extensively opposed in this state [New York]. What dreadful things! A minister, now dead, said that when he first attempted to establish these meetings, he had all the clergy around opposed to him. "Set women to praying? Why, the next thing, I suppose, will be to set them preaching." And serious apprehensions were entertained for the safety of Zion, if women should be allowed to get together to pray. And even now, they are not tolerated in some churches.

### E. The liturgy of the hours is reformed by Roman Catholics in the 1970s.

24. *General Instruction on the Liturgy of the Hours*, XXIX, CXXVI, CXLIII. Trans. Peter Coughlin and Peter Purdue, *The Liturgy of the Hours* (London: Geoffrey Chapman, 1971), pp. 27, 45, 48.

They are to give due importance to the Hours which are the two hinges on which this Liturgy turns, that is, Lauds as morning prayer and Vespers; let them take care not to omit these hours, unless for a serious reason.

They are also to carry out faithfully the Office of Readings, which is above all the liturgical celebration of the word of God. . . .

That the day may be completely sanctified, they will desire to recite the middle Hour and Compline, thus commending themselves to God and completing the entire "Opus Dei" before going to bed. . . .

The psalms are distributed over a four-week cycle. In this cycle, a very small number of psalms are omitted, while the traditionally more important ones are repeated more frequently. Lauds, Vespers and Compline have psalms corresponding with their respective Hour. . . .

The reading of scripture in the Liturgy of the Hours is linked with and completes the reading at Mass; in this way the history of salvation is viewed as a whole.

### Select Bibliography on Daily Public Prayer

Bradshaw, Paul F. *Daily Prayer in the Early Church*. London: Alcuin Club/SPCK, 1981.
Guiver, George. *Company of Voices*. New York: Pueblo Publishing Co., 1988.

Jasper, R. C. D., ed. *The Daily Office*. London: SPCK and Epworth Press, 1968.

*Liturgy of the Hours: The General Instruction*, with commentary by A. M. Roguet, O.P. Translated by Peter Coughlan and Peter Purdue. London: Geoffrey Chapman, 1971.

Mateos, Juan. "The Origins of the Divine Office." *Worship* 41 (October 1967): 477–485.

———. "The Morning and Evening Office." *Worship* 42 (January 1968): 31–47).

Old, Hughes Oliphant. "Daily Prayer in the Reformed Church of Strasbourg." *Worship* 52 (1978): 121–138.

Salmon, Pierre. *The Breviary Through the Centuries*. Collegeville, Minn.: Liturgical Press, 1962.

Scotto, Dominic F. *The Liturgy of the Hours*. Petersham, Mass.: St. Bede's Publications, 1987.

Taft, Robert. *The Liturgy of the Hours in East and West*. Collegeville, Minn.: Liturgical Press, 1986.

# CHAPTER V

# The Service of the Word

## I. EARLY ACCOUNTS
### A. Continuity with synagogue worship is suggested.
1. Scripture.

*a.* Luke 4:16–21 (see also Matt. 7:28–29; Mark 1:21–28).
> When he came to Nazareth, where he had been brought up, he
> went to the synagogue on the sabbath day, as was his custom. He
> stood up to read, and the scroll of the prophet Isaiah was given to
> him. He unrolled the scroll and found the place where it was
> written:
>
> "The Spirit of the Lord is upon me,
>   because he has anointed me to bring good news to the poor.
> He has sent me to proclaim release to the captives
>   and recovery of sight to the blind,
>     to let the oppressed go free,
> to proclaim the year of the Lord's favor."
>
> And he rolled up the scroll, gave it back to the attendant, and sat
> down. The eyes of all in the synagogue were fixed on him. Then

he began to say to them, "Today this scripture has been fulfilled in your hearing."

*b.* Acts 13:14–16.

But they went on from Perga and came to Antioch in Pisidia. And on the sabbath day they went into the synagogue and sat down. After the reading of the law and the prophets, the officials of the synagogue sent them a message, saying, "Brothers, if you have any word of exhortation for the people, give it." So Paul stood up and with a gesture began to speak.

2. Justin Martyr, *First Apology*, LXVII (c. 155). Trans. Edward Rochie Hardy, LCC, I, 287.

And on the day called Sunday there is a meeting in one place of those who live in cities or the country, and the memoirs of the apostles or the writings of the prophets are read as long as time permits. When the reader has finished, the president in a discourse urges and invites [us] to the imitation of these noble things. Then we all stand up together and offer prayers.

## B. Ordines describe worship in Rome and become the model for high mass in medieval Europe.

3. *Ordo Romanus Primus*, VIII–XI (c. 700). Trans. E. G. Cuthbert F. Atchley (London: De La More Press, 1905), pp. 129–133 (altered).

The pope passes between them [bearers of candlesticks] to the upper part of the choir, and bows his head to the altar. He then rises up, and prays, and makes the sign of the cross on his forehead; after which he gives the kiss of peace to one of the hebdomadary bishops [on duty that week], and to the archpresbyter, and to all the deacons. Then, turning towards the precentor, he signals to him to sing *Gloria Patri* and the precentor bows to the pope, and begins it. Meanwhile the ruler of the choir precedes the pope in order to set his cushion before the altar, if it should be the season for it [Lent or penitential days]: and approaching it, the pope prays there until the repetition of the verse [entry anthem]. Now when "As it was in the beginning" is said, the deacons rise up in order to salute the sides of the altar, first two, and then the rest by twos, and return to the pope. And then, the latter rises, and kisses the book of the gospels and the altar, and, going to his throne, stands there facing eastwards.

Now, after the anthem is finished, the choir begins *Kyrie eleison.* But the precentor keeps his eye on the pope, so that the latter may signal him if he wishes to change the number of the Kyries, and bows to him. When they have finished, the pope turns himself round towards the people, and begins, *Gloria in excelsis Deo,* if it be the season for it [not Lent], and at once turns back again to the east until it is finished. Then, after turning again to the people, he says, *Pax vobis,* and once more turning to the east, says *Oremus,* and the collect follows. At the end of it, he sits, and the bishops and presbyters sit in like manner.

Meanwhile, the district-subdeacons go up to the altar, and place themselves at the right and left of the altar. Then the pope signals to the bishops and presbyters to sit. Now, as soon as the sub-deacon who is going to read perceives that the bishops and pres-byters are sitting down after the pope, he goes up into the ambo and reads the epistle. When he has finished reading, a chorister goes up into the same with the book of chants and sings the re-spond. And then *Alleluia* is sung by another singer, if it should be the season when *Alleluia* is said; if not, a tract [penitential verse]; if when neither one nor the other is appointed, only the respond is sung.

Then the deacon kisses the pope's feet, and the latter says to him in an undertone, *"Dominus sit in corde tuo et in labiis tuis."* Then the deacon comes before the altar, and after kissing the book of the gospels, takes it up in his hands; and there walk before him [to the ambo] two district-subdeacons, who have taken the censer from the hand of the subdeacon-attendant, diffusing incense. And in front of them they have two acolytes carrying two candlesticks. On coming to the ambo, the acolytes part before it, and the sub-deacons and the deacon with the gospel-book pass between them. The subdeacon who is not carrying the censer then turns towards the deacon, and offers him his left arm on which to rest the gospel-book, in order that the former may open it with his right hand at the place where the mark for reading was put: then, slip-ping his finger into the place where he has to begin, the deacon goes up to read, while the two subdeacons turn back to stand before the step coming down from the ambo. The gospel ended, the pope says *Pax tibi;* and then *Dominus vobiscum.* Answer is made, *Et cum spiritu tuo;* and he says, *Oremus.*

When the deacon is come down from the ambo, the subdeacon who first opened the gospel-book previously, takes it from him and hands it to the subdeacon-attendant, who stands in his rank. Then the latter, holding the book before his breast, outside his planet [chasuble], offers it to be kissed by all who stand [in the choir] in the order of their rank. And after this, an acolyte is ready on the step by the ambo with the case, in which the same subdeacon puts the gospel-book so that it may be sealed. But the acolyte of the same district as that to which the subdeacon belongs carries it back to the Lateran.

## II. REFORMATION CHANGES
### A. Luther's changes in the Service of the Word are conservative.
4. *Formula Missae* (1523). Trans. Paul Zeller Strodach and Ulrich S. Leupold, LW, LIII, 20–25.

We therefore first assert: It is not now nor ever has been our intention to abolish the liturgical service of God completely, but rather to purify the one that is now in use from the wretched accretions which corrupt it and to point out an evangelical use. We cannot deny that the mass, i.e., the communion of bread and wine is a rite divinely instituted by Christ himself and that it was observed first by Christ and then by the apostles, quite simply and evangelically without any additions. But in the course of time so many human inventions were added to it that nothing except the names of the mass and communion has come down to us.

Now the additions of the early fathers who, it is reported, softly prayed one or two Psalms before blessing the bread and wine are commendable. Athanasius and Cyprian are supposed to be some of these. Those who added the *Kyrie eleison* also did well. We read that under Basil the Great, the *Kyrie eleison* was in common use by all the people. The reading of the Epistles and Gospels is necessary, too. Only it is wrong to read them in a language the common people do not understand. Later, when chanting began, the Psalms were changed into the introit; the Angelic Hymn *Gloria in*

*Excelsis: et in terra pax,* the graduals, the alleluias, the Nicene Creed, the *Sanctus,* the *Agnus Dei,* and the *communio* were added. All of these are unobjectionable, especially the ones that are sung *de tempore* [temporal cycle] on Sundays. For these days by themselves testify to ancient purity, the canon excepted. . . .

We will set forth the rite according to which we think that it [the mass] should be used.

First, we approve and retain the introits for the Lord's days and the festivals of Christ, such as Easter, Pentecost, and the Nativity, although we prefer the Psalms from which they were taken as of old. But for the time being we permit the accepted use. And if any desire to approve the introits (inasmuch as they have been taken from Psalms or other passages of Scripture) for apostles' days, for feasts of the Virgin and of other saints, we do not condemn them. . . . [See chapter II, document 41].

Second, we accept the *Kyrie eleison* in the form in which it has been used until now, with the various melodies for different seasons, together with the Angelic Hymn, *Gloria in Excelsis,* which follows it. However the bishop [pastor] may decide to omit the latter as often as he wishes.

Third, the prayer or collect which follows, if it is evangelical (and those for Sunday usually are), should be retained in its accepted form; but there should be only one. After this the Epistle is read. Certainly the time has not yet come to attempt revision here, as nothing unevangelical is read, except that those parts from the Epistles of Paul in which faith is taught are read only rarely, while the exhortations to morality are most frequently read. The Epistles seems to have been chosen by a singularly unlearned and superstitious advocate of works. But for the service those sections in which faith in Christ is taught should have been given preference. The latter were certainly considered more often in the Gospels by whosoever it was who chose these lessons. In the meantime, the sermon in the vernacular will have to supply what is lacking. If in the future the vernacular be used in the mass (which Christ may grant), one must see to it that Epistles and Gospels chosen from the best and most weighty parts of these writings be read in the mass.

Fourth, the gradual of two verses shall be sung, either together with the Alleluia, or one of the two, as the bishop may decide. But the Quadragesima [Lenten] graduals and others like them that exceed two verses may be sung at home by whoever wants them. In church we do not want to quench the spirit of the faithful with tedium. Nor is it proper to distinguish Lent, Holy Week, or Good Friday from other days, lest we seem to mock and ridicule Christ with half of a mass and the one part of the sacrament. For the Alleluia is the perpetual voice of the church, just as the memorial of His passion and victory is perpetual.

Fifth, we allow no sequences or proses [verses] unless the bishop wishes to use the short one for the Nativity of Christ: *"Grates nunc omnes."* . . .

Sixth, the Gospel lesson follows, for which we neither prohibit nor prescribe candles or incense. Let these things be free.

Seventh, the custom of singing the Nicene Creed does not displease us; yet this matter should also be left in the hands of the bishop. Likewise, we do not think that it matters whether the sermon in the vernacular comes after the Creed or before the introit of the mass; although it might be argued that since the Gospel is the voice crying in the wilderness and calling unbelievers to faith, it seems particularly fitting to preach before mass. For properly speaking, the mass consists in using the Gospel and communing at the table of the Lord. Inasmuch as it belongs to believers, it should be observed apart [from unbelievers]. Yet since we are free, this argument does not bind us, especially since everything in the mass up to the Creed is ours, free and not prescribed by God; therefore it does not necessarily have anything to do with the mass.

## B. Calvin introduces sung congregational psalmody.
5. John Calvin, *Articles Concerning the Organization of the Church and of Worship at Geneva Proposed by the Ministers at the Council January 16, 1537.* Trans. J. K. S. Reid, LCC, XXII, 53–54.

There are psalms which we desire to be sung in the Church, as we have it exemplified in the ancient Church and in the evidence of Paul himself, who says it is good to sing in the congregation with mouth and heart. We are unable to compute the profit and edification which will arise from this, except after having experimented. Certainly as things are, the prayers of the faithful are so cold, that we ought to be ashamed and dismayed. The psalms can incite us to lift up our hearts to God and to move us to an ardor in invoking and exalting with praises the glory of his Name. Moreover, it will be thus appreciated of what benefit and consolation the pope and those that belong to him have deprived the Church; for he has reduced the psalms, which ought to be true spiritual songs, to a murmuring among themselves without any understanding.

This manner of proceeding seemed specially good to us, that children, who before hand have practiced some modest church song, sing in a loud distinct voice, the people listening with all attention and following heartily what is sung with the mouth, till all become accustomed to sing communally. But in order to avoid all confusion, you must not allow that anyone by his insolence, and to put the congregation to derision, should come to disturb the order you have adopted.

## C. In the Church of England, the Service of the Word becomes detached from the Eucharist when there are no communicants. Ceremonial is reduced but not eliminated.

6. *The Booke of the Common Prayer* (1549). *First and Second Prayer Books of Edward VI* (London: J. M. Dent & Sons, 1910; spelling modernized).

a. Rubric at end of eucharist, p. 229.
   Upon Wednesdays and Fridays the English Litany shall be said or sung in all places, after such form as is appointed by the king's majesty's injunctions: Or as is or shall be otherwise appointed by his highness. And though there be none to communicate with the priest, yet these days (after the Litany [is] ended) the priest shall put upon him a plain alb or surplice, with a cope, and say all things at the altar (appointed to be said at the celebration of the Lord's Supper), until the offertory. And then [he] shall add one or two of the collects aforewritten, as occasion shall serve by his discretion. And then turning him to the people shall let them depart with the accustomed blessing. And the same order shall be used all other days whensoever the people be customarily assembled to pray in his church, and none [be] disposed to communicate with the priest.

*b.* "Of Ceremonies, Why Some Be Abolished and Some Retained," pp. 287–288.

> Furthermore, the most weighty cause of the abolishment of certain ceremonies was, that they were so far abused, partly by the superstitious blindness of the rude and unlearned, and partly by the insatiable avarice of such as sought more their own lucre than the glory of God; that the abuses could not well be taken away, the thing remaining still.
>
> But now as concerning those persons, which peradventure will be offended for that some of the old ceremonies are retained still: If they consider, that without some ceremonies it is not possible to keep any order or quiet discipline in the church: they shall easily perceive just cause to reform their judgments. And if they think much that any of the old do remain, and would rather have all devised anew: then such men (granting some ceremonies convenient to be had), surely where the old may be well used: there they cannot reasonably reprove the old (only for their age) without betraying of their own folly. For in such a case they ought rather to have reverence unto them for their antiquity, if they will declare themselves to be more studious of unity and concord, than of innovations and newfangledness, which (as much as may be with the true setting forth of Christ's religion) is always to be eschewed.
>
> Furthermore, such shall have no just cause with the ceremonies reserved, to be offended: for as those be taken away which were most abused, and did burden men's consciences without any cause: So the other that remain are retained for a discipline and order, which (upon just causes) may be altered and changed, and therefore are not to be esteemed equal with God's law. And moreover they be neither dark nor dumb ceremonies, but are so set forth that every man may understand what they do mean, and to use what they do serve. . . . We think it convenient that every country should use such ceremonies, as they shall think best to the setting forth of God's honor, and glory.

**D. The Puritans object to many remaining ceremonies but finally succeed in shaping the Service of the Word according to their own consensus.**

7. *The Millenary Petition* (1603). *Documents Illustrative of English Church History,* ed. Henry Gee and William John Hardy (London: Macmillan & Co., 1910), pp. 509–510.

Our humble suit, then, unto your majesty is that these offenses following, some may be removed, some amended, some qualified:

In the Church service: that the cross in baptism, interrogatories ministered to infants, confirmation, as superfluous, may be taken away; baptism not to be ministered by women, and so explained; the cap and surplice not urged; that examination may go before the communion; that it be ministered with a sermon; that divers terms of priests, and absolution, and some other used, with the . ring in marriage, and other such like in the book, may be corrected; the longsomeness of service abridged, Church songs and music moderated to better edification; that the Lord's Day be not profaned; the rest upon holy days not so strictly urged; that there may be a uniformity of doctrine prescribed; no popish opinion to be any more taught or defended; no ministers charged to teach their people to bow at the name of Jesus; that the canonical Scriptures only be read in the Church.

Concerning Church ministers: that none hereafter be admitted into the ministry but able and sufficient men, and those to preach diligently and especially upon the Lord's day; that such as be already entered and cannot preach, may either be removed, and some charitable course taken with them for their relief.

8. *A Directory for the Publique Worship of God* [Westminster *Directory*] (London, 1644 [1645]). Copy in University Library, Cambridge, pp. 9–38.

*Of the Assembling of the Congregation and Their Behaviour in the Publique Worship of God.*
When the congregation is to meet for Publique Worship, the people (having before prepared their hearts thereunto) ought all to come, and joyne therein: not absenting themselves from the Publique Ordinances, through negligence, or upon pretence of Private meetings.

Let all enter the Assembly, not irreverently, but in a grave and seemly manner, taking their seats or places without Adoration, or Bowing themselves towards one place or other.

The Congregation being assembled: the Minister, after solemne calling on them to the worshiping of the great name of God, is to begin with prayer. . . .

### Of Publique Reading of the holy Scriptures.

Reading of the Word in the Congregation being part of the Publique Worship of God, (wherein we acknowledge our dependence upon him, and subjection to him) and one means sanctified by him for the edifying of his People, is to be performed by the Pastors and Teachers. . . .

How large a portion shall be read at once, is left to the wisdome of the Minister: but it is convenient, that ordinarily one Chapter of each Testament be read at every meeting: and sometimes more, where the chapters be short, or the coherence of matter requireth it.

It is requisite that all the Canonical Books be read over in order, that the people may be better acquainted with the whole Body of the Scriptures: And ordinarily, where the Reading in either testament endeth on one Lord's Day, it is to begin the next.

Wee commend also the more frequent reading of such Scriptures, as hee that readeth shall thinke best for edification of his Hearers: as the Book of Psalmes, and such like.

When the Minister, who readeth, shall judge it necessary to expound any part of what is read, let it not bee done until the whole Chapter, or Psalme be ended: and regard it alwayes to be had unto the time, that neither Preaching or other Ordinance be straitned, or rendred tedious. Which Rule is to be observed in all other publique performance. . . .

### Of Publike Prayer before the Sermon.

After reading of the Word (and singing of the Psalme) the Minister who is to Preach, is to endeavor to get his own, and his Hearers hearts to be rightly affected with their Sinnes, that they may all mourn in sense thereof before the Lord, and hunger and thirst after the grace of God in Jesus Christ, by proceeding to a more full Confession of sinne with shame and holy confusion of face, and to Call upon the Lord to this effect. . . .

### Of the Preaching of the Word.

Preaching of the Word, being the power of God unto Salvation, and one of the greatest and most excellent Works belonging to the ministry of the Gospell, should be so performed, that the Work-man need not be ashamed, but may save himself, and those that heare him. . . .

Ordinarily, the subject of his Sermon is to be some Text of Scrip-ture, holding forth some principle of head of Religion; or suitable to some speciall occasion emergent; or he may goe on in some Chapter, Psalme, or Booke of the holy Scripture as he shall see fit. . . .

But the servant of Christ, whatever his Method be, is to perform the whole ministery: painfully, . . . . plainly, . . . . faithfully, . . . . wisely, . . . . gravely, . . . . with loving affection, . . . . as taught of God, and perswaded in his own heart. . . .

### Of Prayer after the Sermon.

The sermon being ended, the minister is:

To give thanks . . . to pray for the continuance of the Gospell. . . . to turn the chief and most usefull heads of the Sermon into some few Petitions. . . . to pray for preparation for Death, and Judge-ment. . . .

And because the prayer which Christ taught his Disciples is not only a Pattern of Prayer, but it selfe a most comprehensive Prayer, we recommend it also to be used in the Prayers of the Church. . . .

Every Minister is herein to apply himselfe in his Prayer before, or after his Sermon to those occasions: [of sacraments, fasts, and thanksgiving], but for the manner, he is left to his liberty, as God shall direct and inable him, in piety and wisdom to discharge his duty.

The Prayer ended, let a Psalme be sung, if with conveniency it may be done. After which (unless some other Ordinance of Christ that concerneth the congregation at that time be to follow) let the Minister dismisse the Congregation with a solemne Blessing.

**E. The order of service in Leipzig, 1714, is noted by J. S. Bach (1685–1750).**

9. "Order of Divine Service in Leipzig," (December 2, 1714). Trans. Arthur Mendel, *The Bach Reader*, rev. ed., ed. by Hans T. David and Arthur Mendel (New York: W. W. Norton & Company, 1966), p. 70.

> *First Sunday in Advent: Morning*
> (1) Preluding
> (2) *Motetta*
> (3) Preluding on the Kyrie, which is performed throughout in concerted music
> (4) Intoning before the altar
> (5) Reading of the Epistle
> (6) Singing of the Litany
> (7) Preluding on [and singing of] the Chorale
> (8) Reading of the Gospel
> (9) Preluding on [and performance of] the principal composition [cantata]
> (10) Singing of the Creed
> (11) The Sermon
> (12) After the Sermon, as usual, singing of several verses of a hymn
> (13) Words of Institution [of the Sacrament]
> (14) Preluding on [and performance of] the composition [probably the second part of the cantata]. After the same, alternate preluding and singing of chorales until the end of the Communion, *et sic porro.*

10. B. W. Gorham, *Camp Meeting Manual: A Practical Book for the Camp Ground* (Boston: H. V. Degen, 1854), pp. 155–156.

> As to the order of exercises and of domestic arrangements, I have generally noticed that the following worked well:
>
> 1. Rise at five, or half-past five in the morning.
>
> 2. Family prayer and breakfast from half-past six to half-past seven.
>
> 3. General prayer meeting at the altar, led by several ministers appointed by the Presiding Elder, at half-past eight, A.M.

4. Preaching at half-past ten, followed by prayer meeting to twelve, M.

5. Dine at half-past twelve, P.M.

6. Preaching at two, or half-past two, P.M., followed by prayer at the altar till five.

7. Tea at six, P.M.

8. Preaching at half-past seven, followed by prayer meeting at the altar till nine or ten.

9. All strangers to leave the ground and the people to retire at ten, or immediately thereafter.

The prayer meetings at the altar, after preaching, should be strongly manned with a good number of preachers and official members, and under the control of the Presiding Elder, who should lead the exercises from the stand, or employ some other person to do so.

Special circumstances will occasionally dictate a departure from any prescribed routine, and yet it is good to have an established order, and to adhere to it with some tenacity.

On the last night of the meeting, the services are sometimes protracted through the night. Commonly this is of doubtful utility. A very appropriate method of closing the services is, after taking the names of such as have been converted, with the view to proper future attentions to them, to administer the sacrament of the Lord's supper.

## III. MODERN CHANGES
### A. The frontier camp meeting reshapes Protestant worship to focus on individual religious experience.
11. "Hymn 94" (early nineteenth century). *The Wesleyan Camp-Meeting Hymn-Book,* compiled by Joseph Meriam, 4th ed. (Wendell, Mass.: J. Metcalf, 1829), pp. 131–132.

What hath the world to equal this?
The solid peace, the heavenly bliss;
The joys immortal, love divine,
The love of Jesus ever mine:
Greater joys I'm born to know,
From terrestrial to celestial,
When I up to Jesus go.

When I shall leave this house of clay,
Glorious angels shall convey;
Upon their golden wings shall I
Be wafted far above the sky;
There behold him free from harm,
Beauties vernal, spring eternal,
In my lovely Jesus' arms.

There in sweet silent raptures wait,
Till the saints' number is complete,
Till the last trump of God shall sound,
Break up the graves and tear the ground.
There descending with the Lamb,
Ev'ry spirit shall inherit
Bodies of eternal frame.

O tiresome world, when will it end,
When shall I see my heavenly Friend,
When will my lovely Jesus come,
And take his weary pilgrims home!
When shall I meet him in the sky,
There adore him, fall before him,
And holy, holy, holy cry.

12. African American spiritual, "Steal Away" (nineteenth century).
*Songs of Zion* (Nashville: Abingdon Press, 1981), p. 134.

*Response:*

Steal away, steal away, steal away to Jesus!
Steal away, steal away home, I ain't got long to stay here.

*Leader:*

1. My Lord calls me, He calls me by the thunder;
2. Green trees are bending, Poor sinner stands a-trembling;
3. Tombstones are bursting, Poor sinner stands a-trembling;
4. My Lord calls me, He calls me by the lightning,
   The trumpet sounds with-in-a my soul,

*Response:*

I ain't got long to stay here.

**B. The Sunday service becomes oriented to producing converts. Charles G. Finney (1792–1875) leads the way in promoting a pragmatic approach to worship and argues that, since worship forms have changed over time, nothing biblical or historical is normative except that which works at the present.**
13. Charles G. Finney, "Measures to Promote Revivals" (1835). *Lectures on Revivals of Religion,* ed. William G. McLoughlin (Cambridge, Mass.: Harvard University Press, 1960), pp. 250, 256–257, 273, 276.

Our present forms of public worship, and every thing, so far as *measures* are concerned, have been arrived at *by degrees,* and by *a succession of New Measures.* . . .

*Choirs.* . . . O how many congregations were torn and rent in sunder, by the desire of ministers and some leading individuals to bring about an improvement in the cultivation of music, by forming choirs of singers. . . .

*Instrumental Music.* . . . And there are many churches now who would not tolerate an organ. They would not be half so much excited to be told that sinners are going to hell, as to be told that there is going to be an organ in the meeting house. . . .

*Extemporary Prayers.* How many people are there, who talk just as if the Prayer Book was of divine institution! And I suppose multitudes believe it is. And in some parts of the church a man would not be tolerated to pray without his book before him. . . .

*Kneeling in Prayer.* This has made a great disturbance in many parts of the country. The time has been in the Congregational churches in New England, when a man or woman would be ashamed to be seen kneeling at a prayer meeting, for fear of being taken for a Methodist. I have prayed in families where I was the only person that would kneel. The others all stood, lest they should imitate the Methodists, I suppose, and thus countenance innovations upon the established form. . . .

It is evident that we must have more exciting preaching, to meet the character and wants of the age. . . . The character of the age is changed, and these men [preachers] have not conformed to it, but retain the same stiff, dry, prosing styles of preaching that answered half a century ago.

Look at the Methodists. Many of their ministers are unlearned, in the common sense of the term, many of them taken right from the shop or farm, and yet they have gathered congregations, and pushed their way, and won souls every where. Wherever the Methodists have gone, their plain, pointed and simple but warm and animated mode of preaching has always gathered congregations. . . . We must have exciting, powerful preaching, or the devil will have the people, except what the Methodists can save. . . .

But it is just as absolutely fanatical for the Presbyterian church, or any other church, to be sticklish for her particular forms, and to act as if *they* were established by divine authority. The fact is, that God has established in no church, any particular *form*, or manner of worship, for promoting the interests of religion. The scriptures are entirely silent on these subjects, under the gospel dispensation, and the church is left to exercise her own discretion in relation to all such matters. . . .

The only thing insisted upon under the gospel dispensation, in regard to measures, is that there should be *decency and order*. . . . But I do not suppose that by "order" we are to understand any particular set mode, in which any church may have been accustomed to perform their service.

14. "Of Public Worship" (1844). *The Doctrines and Discipline of the Methodist Episcopal Church* (Cincinnati: L. Swormstedt & J. T. Mitchell, 1844), p. 78.

*Quest.* What directions shall be given for the establishment of uniformity in public worship among us, on the Lord's Day?

*Answ.* 1. Let the morning service consist of singing, prayer, the reading of a chapter out of the Old Testament, and another out of the New, and preaching.

2. Let the afternoon service consist of singing, prayer, the reading of one or two chapters out of the Bible, and preaching.

3. Let the evening service consist of singing, prayer, and preaching.

4. But on the days of administering the Lord's supper, the two chapters in the morning service may be omitted.

5. In administering the ordinances, and in the burial of the dead, let the form of Discipline invariably be used. Let the Lord's prayer also be used on all occasions of public worship in concluding the first prayer, and the apostolic benediction [2 Cor. 13:13] in dismissing the congregation.

6. Let the society be met, wherever it is practicable, on the sabbath day.

**C. Fanny J. Crosby (1820–1915) becomes the most popular American hymn writer and the preeminent popular saint of her time.**
15. "Blessed Assurance" (1873). *The Methodist Hymnal* (Nashville: Publishing House, Methodist Episcopal Church, South, 1905), p. 548.

1. Blessed assurance, Jesus is mine!
   O what a foretaste of glory divine!
   Heir of salvation, purchase of God,
   Born of his Spirit, washed in his blood.

2. Perfect submission, perfect delight,
   Visions of rapture now burst on my sight,
   Angels descending, bring from above,
   Echoes of mercy, whispers of love.

3. Perfect submission, all is at rest,
   I in my Saviour am happy and best,
   Watching and waiting, looking above,
   Filled with his goodness, lost in his love.


*Refrain:*


This is my story, this is my song,
Praising my Saviour all the day long;
This is my story, this is my song,
Praising my Saviour all the day long.


## D. Roman Catholics reform the Service of the Word after Vatican II (1962–1965).

16. *Constitution on the Sacred Liturgy,* LI–LIII (Collegeville, Minn.: Liturgical Press, 1963), pp. 31–32.


51. The treasures of the Bible are to be opened up more lavishly, so that richer fare may be provided for the faithful at the table of God's word. In this way a more representative portion of the holy scriptures will be read to the people in the course of a prescribed number of years.


52. By means of the homily the mysteries of the faith and the guiding principles of the Christian life are expounded from the sacred text, during the course of the liturgical year; the homily, therefore, is to be highly esteemed as part of the liturgy itself; in fact, at those Masses which are celebrated with the assistance of the people on Sundays and feasts of obligation, it should not be omitted except for a serious reason.


53. Especially on Sundays and feasts of obligation there is to be restored, after the Gospel and the homily, "the common prayer" or "the prayer of the faithful." By this prayer, in which the people are to take part, intercession will be made for holy Church, for the civil authorities, for those oppressed by various needs, for all mankind, and for the salvation of the entire world.

## Select Bibliography on the Service of the Word

Brightman, F. E. *The English Rite*. 2 vols. London: Rivingtons, 1921.

Cabié, Robert. *The Church at Prayer*, vol. 2: *The Eucharist*. Collegeville, Minn.: Liturgical Press, 1986.

Cuming, G. J. *A History of Anglican Liturgy*. 2nd ed. London, Macmillan & Co., 1982.

————. *The Godly Order*. London: Alcuin Club/ SPCK, 1983.

Davies, Horton. *The Worship of the English Puritans*. London: Dacre Press, 1948.

Jungmann, Joseph A. *The Mass of the Roman Rite*. 2 vols. New York: Benziger Brothers, 1951–1955.

————. *The Liturgy of the Word*. Collegeville, Minn.: Liturgical Press, 1966.

Old, Hughes Oliphant. *Worship That Is Reformed According to Scripture*. Atlanta: John Knox Press, 1984.

————. *The Patristic Roots of Reformed Worship*. Zurich: Theologischer Verlag, 1975.

Reed, Luther D. *The Lutheran Liturgy*. Philadelphia: Fortess Press, 1960.

Van Dijk, S. J. P., and J. H. Walker. *The Origins of the Modern Roman Liturgy*. London: Darton, Longman & Todd, 1960.

White, James F. *Protestant Worship: Traditions in Transition*. Louisville, Ky.: Westminster/John Knox Press, 1989.

# CHAPTER VI

# Sacraments in General

## I. DEFINITIONS OF A SACRAMENT, KEY CONCEPTS, AND THE NUMBER OF SACRAMENTS IN EARLY AND MEDIEVAL THEOLOGIANS

**A. Augustine articulates key concepts of later sacramental theology.**

1. Augustine.

*a. Treatise on the Gospel of John,* LXXX, 3 (c. 416). Trans. Paul F. Palmer, *Sacraments and Worship* (London: Darton, Longman & Todd, 1957), pp. 127–128.

> Why does He not say: you are clean because of the baptism with which you were washed, but says: "because of the word that I have spoken to you" [John 15:3], unless the reason is that even in water it is the word that cleanses? Take away the word and what is water but water? The word is joined to the element and the result

is a sacrament, itself becoming, in a sense, a visible word as well.
. . . Whence this power of water so exalted as to bathe the body
and cleanse the soul, if it is not through the action of the word; not
because it is spoken, but because it is believed?. . . . This word of
faith is of such efficacy in the Church of God that it washes clean
not only the one who believes in the word, the one who presents
[the child for baptism], the one who sprinkles [the child], but the
child itself, be it ever so tiny, even though it is as yet incapable of
believing unto justice with the heart or of making profession unto
salvation with the lips. All this takes place through the word, concerning which the Lord says: "You are already clean because of
the word that I have spoken to you."

b. *Against Faustus the Manichaean*, XIX, 11 (c. 398). Trans. Bernard
Leeming, *Principles of Sacramental Theology* (London: Longmans, 1960),
pp. 562–563.

In no religion, whether true or whether false, can men be held in
association, unless they are gathered together with a common
share in some visible signs or sacraments; and the power of these
sacraments is inexpressibly effective, and hence if contemned is
accounted to be a sacrilege.

c. *Questions on the Heptateuch*, III, 84 (c. 410). Trans. Bernard Leeming,
ibid., p. 563.

How, then, do both Moses and the Lord sanctify? . . . . Moses, by
the visible sacraments through his ministry; God by invisible grace
through the Holy Spirit, wherein is the whole fruit of the visible
sacraments; for without that sanctification of invisible grace, what
use are visible sacraments?

d. *Commentary on the Psalms*, LXXIII, 2 (c. 416). Trans. Paul F. Palmer,
*Sacraments and Worship* (London: Darton, Longman & Todd, 1957), pp.
128–129.

If we weigh well the two testaments, the old and the new, the
sacraments are not the same, nor are the promises made the same.
. . . The sacraments are not the same, since there is a difference
between sacraments that give salvation and those that promise a
Saviour. The sacraments of the New Law give salvation, the sacraments of the Old Law promised a Saviour.

*e. On Baptism against the Donatists,* IV, 11, 18 (c. 400). Trans. Palmer, ibid., p. 123.

> When baptism is given in the words of the gospel, no matter how great the perverseness of either minister or recipient, the sacrament is inherently holy on His account whose sacrament it is. And if any one receives baptism from a misguided man, he does not on that account receive the perversity of the minister, but only the holiness of the mystery, and if he is intimately united to the Church in good faith and hope and charity, he receives the remission of his sins. . . . But if the recipient himself is perverse, that which is given is of no profit while he remains in his perversity; and yet that which is received does remain holy within him, nor is the sacrament repeated when he has been corrected.

## B. Hugh of St. Victor attempts a precise definition of a sacrament yet enumerates more than a dozen including monastic vows, dedication of a church, and death and judgment.

2. Hugh of St. Victor, *On the Sacraments of the Christian Faith,* I, 9 (1140). Trans. Roy J. Deferrari, *Hugh of Saint Victor on the Sacraments of the Christian Faith* (Cambridge: Medieval Academy of America, 1951), p. 155.

> Now if any one wishes to define more fully and more perfectly what a sacrament is, he can say: "A sacrament is a corporeal or material element set before the senses without, representing by similitude and signifying by institution and containing by sanctification some invisible and spiritual grace." This definition is recognized as so fitting and perfect that it is found to befit every sacrament and a sacrament alone. For every thing that has these three is a sacrament, and every thing that lacks these three can not be properly called a sacrament.

> For every sacrament ought to have a kind of similitude to the thing itself of which it is the sacrament, according to which it is capable of representing the same thing; every sacrament ought to have also institution through which it is ordered to signify this thing and finally sanctification through which it contains that thing and is efficacious for conferring the same on those to be sanctified.

## C. Peter Lombard completes a synthesis of theology to his time and defines the number of sacraments.

3. Peter Lombard, *The Four Books of Sentences,* IV (c. 1152).

a. *Distinction I, 2–7.* Trans. Owen R. Ott, LCC, X, 338–341.

"A sacrament is a sign of a sacred thing" [Augustine]. However a sacrament is also called a sacred secret just as it is called a sacrament of the deity, so that a sacrament both signifies something sacred and is something sacred signified; but now it is a question of a sacrament as a sign.

Again, "A sacrament is the visible form of an invisible grace" [Augustine].

"A sign is something beyond the appearance, which it presses on the senses, for it makes something else enter thought" [Augustine].

"Some signs are natural, such as smoke signifying fire; others are given" [Augustine] and of those which are given, certain ones are sacraments, certain ones are not, for every sacrament is a sign, but not conversely.

A sacrament bears a likeness of that thing, whose sign it is. "For if sacraments did not have a likeness of the things whose sacraments they are, they would properly not be called sacraments" [Augustine]. For that is properly called a sacrament which is a sign of the grace of God and a form of invisible grace, so that it bears its image and exists as its cause. Sacraments were instituted, therefore, for the sake, not only of signifying, but also of sanctifying. . . .

"The sacraments were instituted for a threefold cause: as a means of increasing humility, as a means of instruction, and as a spur to activity" [Hugh of St. Victor]. . . .

"Moreover, there are two constituents of a sacrament, namely, words and things: words such as the invocation of the Trinity; things such as water, oil, and the like."

Now there remains to be seen the difference between the old sacraments and the new, so that we may call sacraments what in former times used to signify sacred things, such as sacrifices and oblations and the like.

Augustine, indeed, briefly indicated the difference between these, when he said, "While the former only promised and signified, the latter gave salvation."

Nevertheless there was among them a certain sacrament, namely circumcision, conferring the same remedy against sin which baptism now does. . . .

Through circumcision, from the time of its institution, the remission of original and actual sin for young and old was offered by God, just as now it is given in baptism.

b. *Distinction II, 1.* Ibid., 344–345.

Now let us approach the sacraments of the new law, which are: baptism, confirmation, the bread of blessing, that is the eucharist, penance, extreme unction, orders, marriage. Of these, some provide a remedy against sin and confer assisting grace, such as baptism; others are only a remedy, such as marriage; others strengthen us with grace and power, such as the eucharist and orders.

If it is asked why the sacraments were not instituted soon after the fall of man, since righteousness and salvation are in them, we say that the sacraments of grace were not to be given before the coming of Christ, who brought grace, for they receive power from his death and Passion. Christ did not wish to come before man was convinced that neither the natural nor the written law could support him.

"Marriage, however, was certainly not instituted before sin [the fall] as a remedy, but as a sacrament and a duty" [Hugh of St. Victor]; after sin, indeed, it was a remedy against the corrupting effect of carnal concupiscence, with which we shall deal in its place.

c. *Distinction IV, 1.* Trans. Elizabeth Frances Rogers, *Peter Lombard and the Sacramental System* (Merrick, N.Y.: Richwood Publishing Co., 1976), p. 95.

[Baptism]: Here we must say that some receive the sacrament and the thing [*res*], some the sacrament and not the thing, some the thing and not the sacrament.

*d. Distinction VIII, 6–7. Ibid., p. 122.*

[Eucharist]: Now let us see what is the sacrament and what the thing [*res*]: "The sacrament is the visible form of invisible grace" [Augustine]; the form therefore of the bread and wine which appears here is the sacrament, that is "the sign of a sacred thing, because it calls something to mind beyond the appearance which it presents to the senses." Therefore the appearances "keep the names of the things which they were before, namely, bread and wine."

"Moreover the thing [*res*] of this sacrament is two-fold: one, what is contained and signified, the other what is signified but not contained. The thing contained and signified is the flesh of Christ which he received from the Virgin and the blood which he shed for us. The thing signified and not contained is the unity of the Church in those who are predestined, called, justified, and glorified."

*e. Distinction XXIII, 3. Ibid., p. 221.*

[Extreme unction] This sacrament of the unction of the sick is said to have been instituted by the apostles. For James says: "Is any sick among you?" [James 5:14].

*f. Distinction XXIV, 1–3. Trans. Owen R. Ott, LCC, X, 349.*

[Ordination] Let us now enter upon the consideration of sacred orders.

There are seven degrees or orders of spiritual function, as is plainly handed down by the writings of the holy Fathers and is shown by the example of our head, namely, Jesus Christ. He exhibited the functions of all in himself and left to his body, which is the Church, the same orders to be observed.

Moreover there are seven on account of the sevenfold grace of the Holy Spirit, and those who are not partakers of the Spirit approach ecclesiastical orders unworthily. . . .

In the sacrament of the sevenfold Spirit there are seven ecclesiastical degrees, namely, doorkeeper, lector, exorcist, acolyte, subdeacon, deacon, priest; all, however, are called clerics, that is, those chosen by lot [Acts 1:26].

*g. Distinction XXIV,* Trans. Elizabeth Rogers, *Peter Lombard and the Sac-ramental System* (Merrick, N.Y.: Richwood Publishing Co., 1976), p. 231.
Wherefore also among men of old times bishops and presbyters were the same, because it is the name of a dignity, not of an age.

*h. Distinction XXIV, 12–16.* Trans. Owen R. Ott, LCC, X, 350–351.
Although all spiritual states are sacred, the canons well conclude that only two are so called, namely, the diaconate and the presbyt-erate; for "it is written that the primitive Church had these alone" [Gratian]. . . . The Church appointed subdeacons and acolytes for itself as time went on" [Gratian].

If it is asked what that which is called an order is, it can definitely be said that it is a certain sign, that is, a sacred something, by which spiritual power and office are handed to the ordinand. Therefore a spiritual character in which there is an increase of power is called an order or grade.

And these orders are called sacraments because in receiving them a sacred thing, grace, which the things that are there done figure, is conferred.

There are certain other names, not of orders, but of dignities and offices. "Bishop" is both the name of a dignity and of an office. . . .

"The bishop is the chief of priests, as it were the path of those who follow. He is also called the highest priest; for he makes priests and deacons, and distributes all ecclesiastical orders" [Isidore of Seville].

## D. Later Scholastic theologians refine these concepts.
4. Thomas Aquinas, *Summa Theologica,* Part III, 61–65 (c. 1271). Trans. Fathers of the English Dominican Province (New York: Benziger Broth-ers, [1947]), II. 2352–2379.

*Question 61: First Article: "Whether Sacraments Are Necessary for Man's Salvation?"* . . .
*I answer that,* Sacraments are necessary unto man's salvation for three reasons. The first is taken from the condition of human na-ture which is such that it has to be led by things corporeal and sensible to things spiritual and intelligible. . . . The second reason

is taken from the state of man who in sinning subjected himself by his affections to corporeal things. . . . The third reason is taken from the fact that man is prone to direct his activity chiefly toward material things. . . .

### Question 62: First Article: "Whether the Sacraments Are the Cause of Grace?" . . .

*I answer that*, We must needs say that in some way the sacraments of the New Law cause grace. For it is evident that through the sacraments of the New Law man is incorporated with Christ. . . .

### Fourth Article: "Whether There Be in the Sacraments a Power of Causing Grace?" . . .

*I answer that*, . . . . If we hold that a sacrament is an instrumental cause of grace, we must needs allow that there is in the sacraments a certain instrumental power of bringing about the sacramental effects. . . .

### Sixth Article: "Whether the Sacraments of the Old Law Caused Grace?" . . .

*I answer that*, It cannot be said that the sacraments of the Old Law conferred sanctifying grace of themselves, i.e., by their own power: since thus Christ's Passion would not have been necessary. . . .

### Question 63: First Article: "Whether a Sacrament Imprints a Character on the Soul?" . . .

*I answer that*, . . . . Since, therefore by the sacraments, men are deputed to a spiritual service pertaining to the worship of God, it follows that by their names the faithful receive a certain spiritual character. . . .

### Fifth Article: "Whether a Character Can Be Blotted out from the Soul?" . . .

*I answer that*, . . . . It is clear that the intellect being perpetual and incorruptible, a character cannot be blotted out from the soul. . . .

### Sixth Article: "Whether a Character Is Imprinted by Each Sacrament of the New Law?" . . .

*I answer that*, . . . . These three sacraments imprint a character, namely, Baptism, Confirmation, and Order. . . .

*Question 64: Second Article: "Whether the Sacraments Are Instituted by God Alone?" . . .*
*I answer that,* . . . . Since, therefore, the power of the sacrament is from God alone, it follows that God alone can institute the sacraments. . . .

*Fifth Article: "Whether the Sacraments Can be Conferred by Evil Ministers?" . . .*
*I answer that,* . . . . The ministers of the Church can confer the sacraments, though they be wicked. . . .

*Seventh Article: "Whether Angels Can Administer Sacraments?" . . .*
*I answer that,* . . . . It belongs to men, but not to angels, to dispense the sacraments and to take part in their administration. . . .

*Ninth Article: "Whether Faith Is Required of Necessity in the Minister of a Sacrament?" . . .*
*I answer that,* . . . . Wherefore, just as the validity of a sacrament does not require that the minister should have charity, and even sinners can confer sacraments, . . . so neither is it necessary that he should have faith, and even an unbeliever can confer a true sacrament, provided that the other essentials are there. . . .

*Question 65: First Article: "Whether There Should Be Seven Sacraments?" . . .*
*I answer that,* As stated above, . . . the sacraments of the Church were instituted for a twofold purpose: namely, in order to perfect man in things pertaining to the worship of God according to the religion of Christian life, and to be a remedy against the defects caused by sin. And in either way it is becoming that there should be seven sacraments. . . .

*Third Article: "Whether the Eucharist Is the Greatest of the Sacraments?" . . .*
*I answer that,* Absolutely speaking, the sacrament of the Eucharist is the greatest of all the sacraments: and this may be shown in three ways. First of all because it contains Christ Himself substantially. . . . Secondly, this is made clear by considering the relation of the sacraments to one another. For all the other sacraments seem to be ordained to this one as to their end. . . . Thirdly, this is

made clear by considering the rites of the sacraments. For nearly all the sacraments terminate in the Eucharist. . . .

*Fourth Article: "Whether All the Sacraments Are Necessary to Salvation?"* . . .
*I answer that,* . . . . In the first way, three sacraments are necessary for salvation. Two of them are necessary for the individual; Baptism, simply and absolutely; Penance, in the case of mortal sin committed after Baptism; while the sacrament of Order is necessary to the Church, since *where there is no governor the people shall fall* (Prov. 11:14).

But in the second way the other sacraments are necessary. For in a sense Confirmation perfects Baptism; Extreme Unction perfects Penance; while Matrimony, by multiplying them, preserves the numbers in the Church.

**E. The medieval sacramental system is summed up in the "Decree for the Armenians," which relies largely on Aquinas.**
5. "Decree for the Armenians" (1439). Trans. from *Enchiridion Symbolorum Definitionum et Declarationum*, ed. Henry Denzinger and Adolf Schönmetzer, 33rd ed. (Freiburg: Herder, 1965), pp. 332–333.

Fifthly, we have set down in briefest form the truth about the sacraments of the Church for the easier instruction of the Armenians at present or in the future. There are seven sacraments of the new law: namely, baptism, confirmation, eucharist, penance, extreme unction, ordination and marriage. These differ much from the sacraments of the old law. The latter did not cause grace but only served as a figure of the passion of Christ. Ours truly contain grace and confer it on those who worthily receive it.

Of these, five pertain to the spiritual perfecting of individuals, the other two are ordained to the governing and increase of the Church. Through baptism we are spiritually reborn; through confirmation we are made to grow in grace and are strengthened in faith. When we have been reborn and strengthened, we are sustained by the divine nourishment of the eucharist. But if through sin we incur sickness of the soul, through penance we are made healthy; we are healed, spiritually and physically according as the soul needs, through extreme unction. Through ordination the

Church is governed and increased spiritually, through marriage it grows physically.

All these sacraments are made complete by three things, namely things or matter, words or form, and the person of the minister performing the sacrament with the intention of doing what the Church does. If any of these is absent, the sacrament is not complete.

Among these sacraments there are three—baptism, confirmation, and ordination—which impose on the soul indelibly a character, a certain spiritual sign distinguished from all others. These are not repeated for the same person. The other four do not impose a character and allow repetition.

## II. REFORMATION CONFLICTS OVER THE NATURE AND NUMBER OF SACRAMENTS
### A. Martin Luther lays the foundation for Protestant sacramental theology, rejecting much of the medieval sacramental system. Zwingli follows suit.
6. Martin Luther.

*a. Babylonian Captivity of the Church* (1520). Trans. A. T. W. Steinhäuser, Frederick C. Ahrens, and Abdel Ross Wentz, LW, XXXVI, 18, 91–92, 106–107, 117–118, 123–125

> To begin with, I must deny that there are seven sacraments, and for the present maintain that there are but three: baptism, penance, and the bread. All three have been subjected to a miserable captivity by the Roman curia, and the church has been robbed of all her liberty. Yet, if I were to speak according to the usage of the Scriptures, I should have only one single sacrament [Christ, 1 Tim. 3:16], but with three sacramental signs, of which I shall treat more fully at the proper time. . . .

### Confirmation
It is amazing that it should have entered the minds of these men to make a sacrament of confirmation out of the laying on of hands. . . .

I do not say this because I condemn the seven sacraments, but because I deny that they can be proved from the Scriptures. Would that there were in the church such a laying on of hands as there was in apostolic times, whether we chose to call it confirmation or healing! But there is nothing left of it now but what we ourselves have invented to adorn the office of bishops, that they may not be entirely without work in the church. . . .

For to constitute a sacrament there must be above all things else a word of divine promise, by which faith may be exercised. . . .

These things cannot be called sacraments of faith, because they have no divine promise connected with them, neither do they save, but the sacraments do save those who believe the divine promise.

### Marriage

Not only is marriage regarded as a sacrament without the least warrant of Scripture, but the very ordinances which extol it as a sacrament have turned it into a farce. Let us look into this a little.

We have said that in every sacrament there is a word of divine promise, to be believed by whoever receives the sign, and that the sign alone cannot be a sacrament. . . .

### Ordination

Of this sacrament the church of Christ knows nothing; it is an invention of the church of the pope. Not only is there nowhere any promise of grace attached to it, but there is not a single word said about it in the whole New Testament. Now it is ridiculous to put forth as a sacrament of God something that cannot be proved to have been instituted by God. . . . We ought to see that every article of faith of which we boast is certain, pure, and based on clear passages of Scripture. But we are utterly unable to do that in the case of the sacrament under consideration. . . .

### The Sacrament of Extreme Unction

To this rite of anointing the sick the theologians of our day have made two additions which are worthy of them: first, they call it a sacrament, and second, they make it the last sacrament. . . .

I still would say, that no aspostle [James] has the right on his own authority to institute a sacrament, that is, to give a divine promise with a sign attached. For this belongs to Christ alone. . . .

*There are still a few other things which it might seem possible to regard as sacraments;* namely, all those things to which a divine promise has been given, such as prayer, the Word, and the cross. . . .

*Nevertheless, it has seemed proper to restrict the name of sacrament to those promises which have signs attached to them.* The remainder, not being bound to signs, are bare promises. *Hence there are, strictly speaking, but two sacraments in the church of God—baptism and the bread.* For only in these two do we find both the divinely instituted sign and the promise of forgiveness of sins. The sacrament of penance, which I added to these two, lacks the divinely instituted visible sign, and is, as I have said, nothing but a way and a return to baptism. Nor can the scholastics say that their definition fits penance, for they too ascribe to the true sacraments a visible sign, which is to impress upon the senses the form of that which it effects invisibly. But penance or absolution has no such sign. Therefore they are compelled by their own definition either to admit that penance is not a sacrament and thus to reduce their number, or else to bring forth another definition of a sacrament.

Baptism, however, which we have applied to the whole of life, will truly be a sufficient substitute for all the sacraments which we might need as long as we live. And the bread is truly the sacrament of the dying and departing; for in it we commemorate the passing of Christ out of this world, that we may imitate him. . . . Thus he clearly seems to have instituted the sacrament of the bread with a view to our entrance into the life to come. For then, when the purpose of both sacraments is fulfilled, baptism and bread will cease.

*b. The Large Catechism* (1529). Trans. Theodore G. Tappert, *The Book of Concord* (Philadelphia: Fortress Press, 1959), p. 436.

It remains for us to speak of our two sacraments, instituted by Christ. Every Christian ought to have at least some brief, elementary instruction in them because without these no one can be a Christian, although unfortunately in the past nothing was taught about them.

7. Ulrich Zwingli, *Commentary on True and False Religion* (1525). Trans. Samuel Macauley Jackson and Clarence Nevin Heller (Durham, N.C.: Labyrinth Press, 1981), p. 184.

> The sacraments are, then, signs or ceremonials—let me say it with the good permission of all both of the new school and the old—by which a man proves to the Church that he either aims to be, or is, a soldier of Christ, and which inform the whole Church rather than yourself of your faith. For if your faith is not so perfect as not to need a ceremonial sign to confirm it, it is not faith. For faith is that by which we rely on the mercy of God unwaveringly, firmly, and singleheartedly, as Paul shows us in many passages.

> So much for the meaning of the name. Christ left us two sacraments and no more, Baptism and The Lord's Supper. By these we are initiated, giving the name with the one, and showing by the other that we are mindful of Christ's victory and are members of His Church. In Baptism we receive a token that we are to fashion our lives according to the rule of Christ; by the Lord's Supper we give proof that we trust in the death of Christ, glad and thankful to be in that company which gives thanks to the Lord for the blessing of redemption which He freely gave us by dying for us. The other sacraments are rather ceremonials, for they have no initiatory function in the Church of God. Hence it is not improper to exclude them; for they were not instituted by God to help us initiate anything in the Church.

## B. John Calvin refines the concepts of Luther and Zwingli.

8. John Calvin, *Institutes of the Christian Religion*, IV, 14, 1–26 (1559). Trans. Ford Lewis Battles, LCC, XXI, 1277–1303.

> *Chapter XIV. The Sacraments.*
> 1. First, we must consider what a sacrament is. It seems to me that a simple and proper definition would be to say that it is an outward sign by which the Lord seals on our consciences the promises of his good will toward us in order to sustain the weakness of our faith; and we in turn attest our piety toward him in the presence of the Lord and of his angels and before men. Here is another briefer definition: one may call it a testimony of divine grace toward us, confirmed by an outward sign, with mutual attestation of our piety toward him. Whichever of these definitions you

may choose, it does not differ in meaning from that of Augustine, who teaches that a sacrament is a "visible sign of a sacred thing," or "a visible form of an invisible grace," but it better and more clearly explains the thing itself. . . .

3. But as our faith is slight and feeble unless it be propped on all sides and sustained by every means, it trembles, wavers, totters, and at last gives way. Here our merciful Lord, according to his infinite kindness, so tempers himself to our capacity that, since we are creatures who always creep on the ground, cleave to the flesh, and, do not think about or even conceive of anything spiritual, he condescends to lead us to himself even by these earthly elements, and to set before us in the flesh a mirror of spiritual blessings. For if we were incorporated (as Chrysostom says), he would give us these very things naked and incorporeal. Now, because we have souls engrafted in bodies, he imparts spiritual things under visible ones. . . .

7. It is therefore certain that the Lord offers us mercy and the pledge of his grace both in his Sacred Word and in his sacraments. But it is understood only by those who take Word and sacraments with sure faith, just as Christ is offered and held forth by the Father to all unto salvation, yet not all acknowledge and receive him. In one place Augustine, meaning to convey this, said that the efficacy of the Word is brought to light in the sacrament, not because it is spoken, but because it is believed. . . .

9. But the sacraments properly fulfill their office only when the Spirit, that inward teacher, comes to them, by whose power alone hearts are penetrated and affections moved and our souls opened for the sacraments to enter in. If the Spirit be lacking, the sacraments can accomplish nothing more in our minds than the splendor of the sun shining upon blind eyes, or a voice sounding in deaf ears. Therefore, I make such a division between Spirit and the sacraments that the power to act rests with the former, and the ministry alone is left to the latter—a ministry empty and trifling, apart from the action of the Spirit, but charged with great effect when the Spirit works within and manifests his power. . . .

17. Therefore, let it be regarded as a settled principle that the sacraments have the same office as the Word of God: to offer and set forth Christ to us, and in him the treasures of heavenly grace. . . .

They do not bestow any grace of themselves, but announce and tell us, and (as they are guarantees and tokens) ratify among us, those things given us by divine bounty. . . .

God therefore truly executes whatever he promises and represents in signs; nor do the signs lack their own effect in proving their Author truthful and faithful. . . .

20. These [circumcision, purifications, sacrifices, and other rites] were the sacraments of the Jews until the coming of Christ. When at his coming these were abrogated, two sacraments were instituted which the Christian church now uses, Baptism and the Lord's Supper [Matt. 28:19; 26:26–28]. I am speaking of those which were established for the use of the whole church. I would not go against calling the laying on of hands, by which ministers of the church are initiated into their office, a sacrament, but I do not include it among the ordinary sacraments. In what place the rest of what are commonly considered sacraments should be held, we shall soon see.

Yet those ancient sacraments looked to the same purpose to which ours now tend: to direct and almost lead men by the hand to Christ, or rather, as images, to represent him and show him forth to be known. . . . There is only one difference: the former foreshadowed Christ promised while he was as yet awaited: the latter attest him as already given and revealed.

21. When these things are individually explained, they will become much clearer.

For the Jews, circumcision was the symbol by which they were admonished that whatever comes forth from man's seed, that is, the whole nature of mankind, is corrupt and needs pruning. Moreover, circumcision was a token and reminder to confirm them in the promise given to Abraham of the blessed seed in which all nations of the earth were to be blessed [Gen. 22:18], from whom they were also to await their own blessing. Now that saving seed (as we are taught by Paul) was Christ [Gal. 3:16]. . . .

26. It is good that our readers be briefly apprised of this thing also: whatever the Sophists have dreamed up concerning the *opus ope-*

*ratum* is not only false but contradicts the nature of the sacraments, which God so instituted that believers, poor and deprived of all goods, should bring nothing to it but begging. From this it follows that in receiving the sacraments believers do nothing to deserve praise, and that even in this act (which on their part is merely passive) no work can be ascribed to them.

## C. The Council of Trent (1545–1563) reaffirms medieval Western teachings on the sacraments.

9. Council of Trent, *The Canons and Decrees of the Council of Trent* (1547). Trans. Philip Schaff, *The Creeds of Christendom* (Grand Rapids: Baker Book House, n.d.), II, 119–122.

*Seventh Session, held March 3, 1547*

**Canon I.**—If any one saith, that the sacraments of the New Law were not all instituted by Jesus Christ, our Lord; or, that they are more, or less, than seven, to wit, Baptism, Confirmation, the Eucharist, Penance, Extreme Unction, Order, and Matrimony; or even that any one of these seven is not truly and properly a sacrament: let him be anathema.

**Canon II.**—If any one saith, that these said sacraments of the New Law do not differ from the sacraments of the Old Law, save that the ceremonies are different, and different the outward rites: let him be anathema.

**Canon III.**—If any one saith, that these seven sacraments are in such wise equal to each other, as that one is not in any way more worthy than another: let him be anathema.

**Canon IV.**—If any one saith, that the sacraments of the New Law are not necessary unto salvation, but superfluous; and that without them, or without the desire thereof, men obtain of God, through faith alone, the grace of justification;—though all [the sacraments] are not indeed necessary for every individual: let him be anathema.

**Canon V.**—If any one saith, that these sacraments were instituted for the sake of nourishing faith alone: let him be anathema.

**Canon VI.**—If any one saith, that the sacraments of the New Law do not contain the grace which they signify; or, that they do not confer that grace on those who do not place an obstacle thereunto; as though they were merely outward signs of grace or justice received through faith, and certain marks of the Christian profession, whereby believers are distinguished amongst men from unbelievers: let him be anathema.

**Canon VII.**—If any one saith, that grace, as far as God's part is concerned, is not given through the said sacraments, always, and to all men, even though they receive them rightly but [only] sometimes, and to some persons: let him be anathema.

**Canon VIII.**—If any one saith, that by the said sacraments of the New Law grace is not conferred through the act performed, but that faith alone in the divine promise suffices for the obtaining of grace: let him be anathema.

**Canon IX.**—If any one saith, that, in the three sacraments, to wit, Baptism, Confirmation, and Order, there is not imprinted in the soul a character, that is, a certain spiritual and indelible sign, on account of which they can not be repeated: let him be anathema.

**Canon X.**—If any one saith, that all Christians have power to administer the word, and all the sacraments: let him be anathema.

**Canon XI.**—If any one saith, that, in ministers, when they effect, and confer the sacraments, there is not required the intention at least of doing what the Church does: let him be anathema.

**Canon XII.**—If any one saith, that a minister, being in moral sin,—if so be that he observe all the essentials which belong to the effecting, or conferring of, the sacrament,—neither effects, nor confers the sacrament: let him be anathema.

**Canon XIII.**—If any one saith, that the received and approved rites of the Catholic Church, wont to be used in the solemn administration of the sacraments, may be contemned, or without sin be omitted at pleasure by the ministers, or be changed, by every pastor of the churches, into other new ones: let him be anathema.

**D. The various British churches make their own statements.**
10. Church of Scotland, *The Scotch Confession of Faith* (1560). *The Creeds of Christendom*, ed. Philip Schaff (Grand Rapids: Baker Book House, 1969), III, 467–468 (spelling, capitalization, and punctuation modernized).

### Article XXI. Of the Sacraments
As the fathers under the law, besides the verity of the sacrifices, had two chief sacraments, to wit, circumcision and the Passover, the despisers and contemners whereof were not reputed for God's people; so do we acknowledge and confess that we now in the time of the Evangel have two chief sacraments, only instituted by the Lord *Jesus* and commanded to be used of all they that will be reputed members of his body, to wit Baptism and the Supper or Table of the Lord *Jesus*, called the Communion of his Body and his Blood. And these sacraments, as well of Old as of New Testament, now instituted of God, not only to make any visible difference betwixt his people and they that were without his league: But also to exercise the faith of his children, and, by participation of the same sacraments, to seal in their hearts the assurance of his promise, and of that most blessed conjunction, union, and society, which the elect have with their head *Christ Jesus*. And thus we utterly damn the vanity of they that affirm sacraments to be nothing else but naked and bare signs.

11. Church of England, *Articles of Religion* (1563). *Book of Common Prayer* (Oxford, 1784). Bracketed items omitted or modernized by John Wesley (1784). *John Wesley's Sunday Service* (Nashville: United Methodist Publishing House, 1984), pp. 311–312.

### Article XXV [XVI]. Of the Sacraments.
Sacraments ordained of Christ, [be] not only badges or tokens of Christian men's profession; but rather they [be] certain [sure witnesses, and effectual] signs of grace, and God's good will towards us, by the which he doth work invisibly in us, and doth not only quicken, but also strengthen and confirm our Faith in him.

There are two Sacraments ordained of Christ our Lord in the Gospel; that is to say, Baptism, and the Supper of the Lord.

Those five commonly called Sacraments, that is to say, Confirmation, Penance, Orders, Matrimony, and Extreme Unction, are not to be counted for Sacraments of the Gospel, being such as have grown partly of the corrupt following of the Apostles, partly are states of life allowed in the Scriptures: but yet have not like nature of [Sacraments with] Baptism, and the Lord's Supper, [for that] they have not any visible sign or ceremony ordained by God.

The Sacraments were not ordained [of] Christ to be gazed upon, or to be carried about; but that we should duly use them. And in such only as worthily receive the same, they have a wholesome effect or operation: but they that receive them unworthily, purchase to themselves [damnation], as Saint *Paul* saith.

12. The Puritans, *Westminster Confession of Faith* (1647). *The Creeds of Christendom*, ed. Philip Schaff (Grand Rapids: Baker Book House, 1969), III, 660–661.

### Chapter XXVII. Of the Sacraments.
I. Sacraments are holy signs and seals of the covenant of grace, immediately instituted by God, to represent Christ and his benefits, and to confirm our interest in him: as also to put a visible difference between those that belong unto the Church and the rest of the world; and solemnly to engage them to the service of God in Christ, according to his Word.

II. There is in every sacrament a spiritual relation or sacramental union, between the sign and the thing signified; whence it comes to pass that the names and the effects of the one are attributed to the other.

III. The grace which is exhibited in or by the sacraments, rightly used, is not conferred by any power in them; neither doth the efficacy of a sacrament depend upon the piety or intention of him that doth administer it, but upon the work of the Spirit, and the word of institution, which contains, together with a precept authorizing the use thereof, a promise of benefit to worthy receivers.

IV. There be only two sacraments ordained by Christ our Lord in the gospel, that is to say, Baptism and the Supper of the Lord:

neither of which may be dispensed by any but by a minister of the Word lawfully ordained.

V. The sacraments of the Old Testament, in regard to the spiritual things thereby signified and exhibited, were, for substance, the same with those of the New.

13. Society of Friends, Robert Barclay, *An Apology for the True Christian Divinity* (English trans. from Latin, 1678; Manchester: William Irwin, 1869), pp. 215, 222, 240, 257, 280.

### *Proposition Eleventh. Concerning Worship.*

All true and acceptable *worship* to God is offered in the inward and immediate moving and drawing of his own Spirit, which is neither limited to places, times, nor persons. . . .

And there being many joined together in the same work, there is an inward travail and wrestling; and also, as the measure of grace is abode in, an overcoming of the power and spirit of darkness; and thus we are often greatly strengthened and renewed in the spirits of our minds without a word, and we enjoy and possess the *holy fellowship*, and *communion of the body and blood of Christ*, by which our inward man is nourished and fed; which makes us not to dote upon outward *water*, and *bread* and *wine*, in our spiritual things. . . .

He [God] causeth the inward life (which is also many times not conveyed by the outward senses,) the more to abound, when his children assemble themselves diligently together to wait upon him; so that *as iron sharpeneth iron* [Prov. 27:17], the seeing of the faces one of another, when both are inwardly gathered unto the life, giveth occasion for the life secretly to arise, and pass from vessel to vessel. And as many candles lighted, and put in one place, do greatly augment the light, and make it more to shine forth, so when many are gathered together into the same life, there is more of the glory of God, and his power appears to the refreshment of each individual; for that he partakes not only of the light and life raised in himself but in all the rest. And therefore Christ hath particularly promised a blessing to such as assemble together in his *name*, seeing he will be *in the midst of them*, Matt. 18:20. . . .

*Proposition Twelfth. Concerning Baptism.*
And this baptism is a pure and spiritual thing, to wit, the baptism
of the Spirit and fire, by which we are buried with him, that being
washed and purged from our sins, we may *walk in newness of life;*
of which the baptism of John was a figure, which was commanded
for a time, and not to continue for ever. As to the baptism of *in-*
*fants,* it is a mere human tradition, for which neither *precept* nor
*practice* is to be found in all the scripture. . . .

*Proposition Thirteenth. Concerning the Communion, or*
*Participation of the Body and Blood of Christ.*
The *communion* of the body and blood of Christ is *inward* and
*spiritual,* which is the participation of his flesh and blood, by
which the *inward man* is daily nourished in the hearts of those in
whom Christ dwells; of which things the *breaking of bread* by
Christ with his disciples was a *figure,* which even they who had
received the substance used in the church for a time, for the sake
of the weak; even as *abstaining from things strangled, and from*
*blood;* the *washing one another's feet,* and the *anointing of the sick*
*with oil;* all which are commanded with no less authority and solemnity than the former; yet seeing they are but *shadows* of better
things, they cease in such as have obtained the *substance.*

## E. The Enlightenment values the sacraments chiefly as moral exhortations.

14. Immanuel Kant, *Religion within the Limits of Reason Alone* (1793).
Trans. Theodore M. Greene and Hoyt H. Hudson (New York: Harper &
Row, 1960), pp. 182–189.

There can, indeed, be three kinds of *illusory faith* that involve the
possibility of our overstepping the bounds of our reason in the
direction of the supernatural (which is not, according to the laws
of reason, an object either of theoretical or practical use). *First,* . . .
(the faith in *miracles*). *Second,* . . . (the faith in *mysteries*). *Third,*
the illusion of being able to bring about, through the use of merely
natural means, an effect which is, for us, a mystery, namely the
influence of God upon our morality (the faith in *means of grace*).
. . . It still remains, therefore, for us to treat of the means of grace,
(which are further distinguished from *works of grace, i.e.* supernatural moral influences in relation to which we are merely passive;

but the imagined experience of these is a fanatical illusion pertaining entirely to the emotions).

1. *Praying*, thought of as an *inner formal* service of God and hence as a means of grace, is a superstitious illusion. . . .

2. *Church-going*, thought of as the ceremonial *public service of God* in a church, *in general*, . . . [only as] a *means of grace*, . . . is an illusion.

3. The ceremonial *initiation*, taking place but once, into the church. . . . community, that is, one's first acceptance *as a member of a church* (in the Christian Church through *baptism*) is a highly significant ceremony which lays a grave obligation either upon the initiate, if he is in a position himself to confess his faith, or upon the witnesses who pledge themselves to take care of his education in this faith. This aims at something holy (the development of a man into a citizen in a divine state) but this act performed by others is not in itself holy or productive of holiness and receptivity for the divine grace in this individual; hence it is no *means of grace*, however exaggerated the esteem in which it was held in the early Greek church, where it was believed capable, in an instant, of washing away all sins—and here this illusion publicly revealed its affinity to an almost more than heathenism superstition.

4. The oft-repeated ceremony (*communion*) of a *renewal, continuation, and propagation of this churchly community* under laws of *equality*, a ceremony which indeed can be performed, after the example of the Founder of such a church (and, at the same time, in memory of him), through the formality of a common partaking at the same table, contains within itself something great, expanding the narrow selfish, and unsociable cast of mind among men, especially in matters of religion, towards the idea of a cosmopolitan *moral community*; and it is a good means of enlivening a community to the moral disposition of brotherly love which it represents. But to assert that God has attached special favors to the celebration of this solemnity, and to incorporate among the articles of faith the proposition that this ceremony, which is after all but a churchly act, is, in addition, a *means of grace*—this is a religious illusion which can do naught but work counter to the spirit of religion. *Clericalism* in general would therefore be the dominion of

the clergy over men's hearts, usurped by the dint of arrogating to themselves the prestige attached to exclusive possession of means of grace.

All such artificial self-deceptions in religious matters have a common basis. Among the three divine attributes, holiness, mercy, and justice, man habitually turns directly to the second in order thus to avoid the forbidding condition of conforming to the requirements of the first. . . .

To this end man busies himself with every conceivable formality, designed to indicate how greatly he *respects* the divine commands, in order that it may not be necessary for him to *obey* them; and, that his idle wishes may serve also good to make good the disobedience of these commands, he cries: "Lord, Lord," so as not to have to "do the will of his heavenly Father" (Mt. 7:21). . . . He busies himself with *piety* (a passive respect for the law of God) rather than with *virtue*. . . .

When the illusion of this supposed favorite of heaven mounts to the point where he fanatically imagines that he feels special works of grace within himself (or even where he actually presumes to be confident of a fancied occult *intercourse* with God), virtue comes at last actually to arouse his loathing and becomes for him an object of contempt.

## III. A NEW ERA IN SACRAMENTAL THEOLOGY
### A. Edward Schillebeeckx (1914-) points in new directions.
15. Edward Schillebeeckx, *Christ the Sacrament of the Encounter with God* (1960). Trans. Paul Barrett et al. (New York: Sheed & Ward, 1963), pp. 15-17, 44-45.

The man Jesus, as the personal visible realization of the divine grace of redemption, is *the* sacrament, the primordial sacrament, because this man, the Son of God himself, is intended by the Father to be in his humanity the only way to the actuality of redemption. "For there is one God, and one mediator of God and men, the man Christ Jesus" [1 Tim. 2:5]. Personally to be approached by the man Jesus was, for his contemporaries, an invitation to a personal encounter with the life-giving God, because personally that man was the Son of God. Human encounter with Jesus is therefore the sacrament of the encounter with God, or of the religious life as a theologal [sic] attitude of existence towards God. Jesus' human redeeming acts are therefore a "sign and cause of grace." "Sign" and "cause" of salvation are not brought together here as two elements fortuitously conjoined. Human bodiliness is human interiority itself in visible form.

Now because the inward power of Jesus' will to redeem and of his human love is God's own saving power realized in human form, the human saving acts of Jesus are the divine bestowal of grace itself realized in visible form; that is to say they cause what they signify; they are sacraments. . . .

From this account of the sacraments as the earthly prolongation of Christ's glorified bodiliness, it follows immediately that the Church's sacraments are not things but encounters of men on earth with the glorified man Jesus by way of a visible form. On the plane of history they are the visible and tangible embodiment of the heavenly saving action of Christ. They are this saving action itself in its availability to us; a personal act of the Lord in earthly visibility and open availability.

Here the first and most fundamental definition of sacramentality is made evident. In an earthly embodiment which we can see and touch, the heavenly Christ sacramentalizes both his continual intercession for us and his active gift of grace. Therefore the sacraments are the visible realization on earth of Christ's mystery of saving worship. "What was visible in Christ has now passed over into the sacraments of the Church" [Ascension Day sermon of Leo I].

The fact which we must now begin to analyze in detail is therefore this: Through the sacraments we are placed in living contact with the mystery of Christ the High Priest's saving worship. In them we encounter Christ in his mystery of Passover and Pentecost. The sacraments *are* this saving mystery in earthly guise. This visible manifestation is the visible Church.

## Select Bibliography on Sacraments in General

Baillie, Donald. *Theology of the Sacraments,* New York: Charles Scribner's Sons, 1957.

Cooke, Bernard J. *Sacraments and Sacramentality.* Mystic, Conn.: Twenty-Third Publications, 1983.

Hellwig, Monika. *The Meaning of the Sacraments.* Dayton, Ohio: Pflaum/Standard, 1972.

Jenson, Robert. *Visible Words.* Philadelphia: Fortress Press, 1978.

Leeming, Bernard. *Principles of Sacramental Theology.* London: Longmans, 1960.

Martos, Joseph. *Doors to the Sacred.* New York: Doubleday & Co., 1981.

Osborne, Kenan B. *Sacramental Theology: A General Introduction.* New York: Paulist Press, 1989.

Palmer, Paul F. *Sacraments and Worship.* London: Darton, Longman & Todd, 1957.

Powers, Joseph. *Spirit and Sacrament.* New York: Seabury Press, 1973.

Rahner, Karl. *The Church and the Sacraments.* London: Burns & Oates, 1963.

Schillebeeckx, Edward. *Christ the Sacrament of the Encounter with God.* New York: Sheed & Ward, 1963.

Schmemann, Alexander. *For the Life of the World.* Crestwood, N.Y.: St. Vladimir's Seminary Press, 1973.

Segundo, Juan Luis. *The Sacraments Today.* Maryknoll, N.Y.: Orbis Books, 1974.

White, James F. *Sacraments as God's Self Giving.* Nashville: Abingdon Press, 1983.

# CHAPTER VII

# Christian Initiation

## I. FOUR CENTURIES OF IMAGES OF CHRISTIAN INITIATION
### A. The Bible uses a variety of metaphors to describe what the Christian experiences in baptism.
1. Scripture.

*a.* The baptism of Jesus: Mark 1:9–11 (see also Matt. 3:13–17; Luke 3:21–22; John 1:29–34).

> In those days Jesus came from Nazareth of Galilee and was baptized by John in the Jordan. And just as he was coming up out of the water, he saw the heavens torn apart and the Spirit descending like a dove on him. And a voice came from heaven, "You are my Son, the Beloved; with you I am well pleased."

*b.* Romans 6:3–5.

> Do you not know that all of us who have been baptized into Christ Jesus were baptized into his death? Therefore we have been buried with him by baptism into death, so that, just as Christ was raised from the dead by the glory of the Father, so we too might

walk in newness of life. For if we have been united with him in a death like his, we will certainly be united with him in a resurrection like his.

c. 1 Corinthians 12:13 (see also Gal. 3:27–28).
> For in the one Spirit we were all baptized into one body—Jews or Greeks, slaves or free—and we were all made to drink of one Spirit.

d. Acts 2:38 (see also Acts 22:16).
> Peter said to them [at Pentecost], "Repent, and be baptized every one of you in the name of Jesus Christ so that your sins may be forgiven; and you will receive the gift of the Holy Spirit."

e. John 3:5 (see also Titus 3:5).
> Jesus answered, "Very truly, I tell you, no one can enter the kingdom of God without being born of water and Spirit."

f. Acts 8:36–38.
> As they were going along the road, they came to some water; and the eunuch said, "Look, here is water! What is to prevent me from being baptized? [And Philip said, "If you believe with all your heart, you may." And he replied, "I believe that Jesus Christ is the Son of God."] He commanded the chariot to stop, and both of them, Philip and the eunuch, went down into the water, and Philip baptized him.

g. Acts 8:15–17 (but see also Acts 10:47 and 19:2–6).
> The two went down [to Samaria] and prayed for them that they might receive the Holy Spirit (for as yet the Spirit had not come upon any of them; they had only been baptized in the name of the Lord Jesus). Then Peter and John laid their hands on them, and they received the Holy Spirit.

h. Acts 10:48 (see also Acts 2:38; 8:12, 16; 19:5; and 22:16).
> So he ordered them to be baptized in the name of Jesus Christ.

i. Matthew 28:19.
> Go therefore and make disciples of all nations, baptizing them in the name of the Father and of the Son and of the Holy Spirit.

**B. Second century documents add to our knowledge of initiation practices.**
2. *The Didache*, VII (late first or early second century). Trans. Cyril C. Richardson, LCC, I, 174.

> Now about baptism: this is how to baptize. Give public instruction on all these points, and then "baptize" in running water, "in the name of the Father and of the Son and of the Holy Spirit." If you do not have running water, baptize in some other. If you cannot in cold, then in warm. If you have neither, then pour water on the head three times "in the name of the Father, Son, and Holy Spirit." Before the baptism, moreover, the one who baptizes and the one being baptized must fast, and any others who can. And you must tell the one being baptized to fast for one or two days beforehand.

3. Justin Martyr, *First Apology*, LXI, LXV (c. 155). Trans. Edward Rochie Hardy, LCC, I, 282–283, 285–286.

> 61. How we dedicated ourselves to God when we were made new through Christ I will explain, since it might seem to be unfair if I left this out from my exposition. Those who are persuaded and believe that the things we teach and say are true, and promise that they can live accordingly, are instructed to pray and beseech God with fasting for the remission of their past sins, while we pray and fast along with them. Then they are brought by us where there is water, and are reborn by the same manner of rebirth by which we ourselves were reborn; for they are then washed in the water in the name of God the Father and Master of all, and of our Saviour Jesus Christ, and of the Holy Spirit. . . . There is named at the water, over him who has chosen to be born again and has repented of his sinful acts, the name of God the Father and Master of all. Those who lead to the washing the one who is to be washed call on [God by] this term only. For no one may give a proper name to the ineffable God, and if anyone should dare to say that there is one, he is hopelessly insane. This washing is called illumination, since those who learn these things are illumined within. The illuminand is also washed in the name of Jesus Christ, who was crucified under Pontius Pilate, and in the name of the Holy Spirit, who through the prophets foretold everything about Jesus. . . .

65. We, however, after thus washing the one who has been convinced and signified his assent, lead him to those who are called brethren, where they are assembled. They then earnestly offer common prayers for themselves and the one who has been illuminated and all others everywhere, that we may be made worthy, having learned the truth, to be found in deed good citizens and keepers of what is commanded, so that we may be saved with eternal salvation. On finishing the prayers we greet each other with a kiss.

4. Irenaeus of Lyons, *Against the Heresies*, III, xvii, 2 (c. 190). Trans. Henry Bettenson, *The Early Christian Fathers* (London: Oxford University Press, 1963), p. 129.

As dry flour cannot be united into a lump of dough, or a loaf, but needs moisture; so we who are many cannot be made one in Christ Jesus without the water which comes down from heaven. And as dry earth does not produce fruit unless it receives moisture; so we who are at first "a dry tree," would never have yielded the fruit of life without the "willing rain" from above. For our bodies have received the unity which brings us to immortality, by means of the washing [*of Baptism*]; our souls receive it by means of [*the gift of*] the Spirit. Thus both of these are needed, for together they advance man's progress towards the life of God.

5. Clement of Alexandria, *The Teacher*, I, vi, 26 (c. 200). Ibid., p. 247.

Being baptized, we are enlightened: being enlightened, we are adopted as sons; being adopted, we are made perfect; being made complete, we are made immortal. The Scripture says, "I said, You are gods, and are all sons of the Highest" [John 10:34]. This work has many names; gift of grace, enlightenment, perfection, washing. Washing, by which we are cleansed from the filth of our sins; gift of grace, by which the penalties of our sins are cancelled; enlightenment, through which that holy light which saves us is perceived, that is, by which our eyes are made keen to see the divine; perfection means the lack of nothing, for what is still lacking to him who has the knowledge of God?

**C. The early third century provides details of an elaborate process for the making of a Christian.**
6. Tertullian.

*a. On Baptism* (c. 200). Trans. Ernest Evans, *Tertullian's Homily on Baptism* (London: SPCK, 1964), pp. 11, 17, 31, 35, 39, 41.

4. Therefore, in consequence of that ancient original privilege, all waters, when God is invoked, acquire the sacred significance of conveying sanctity: for at once the Spirit comes down from heaven and stays upon the waters, sanctifying them from within himself, and when thus sanctified they absorb the power of sanctifying. . . . Thus when the waters have in some sense acquired healing power by an angel's intervention, the spirit is in those waters corporally washed, while the flesh is in those same waters spiritually cleansed. . . .

7. After that we come up from the washing and are anointed with the blessed unction, following that ancient practice by which, ever since Aaron was anointed by Moses, there was a custom of anointing them for priesthood with oil out of a horn. That is why [the high priest] is called a christ, from "chrism" which is [the Greek for] "anointing": and from this also our Lord obtained his title, though it had become a spiritual anointing, in that he was anointed with the Spirit of God the Father. . . .

8. Next follows the imposition of the hand in benediction, inviting and welcoming the Holy Spirit. . . .

13. For there has been imposed a law of baptizing, and its form prescribed: *"Go,"* he says, *"teach the nations, baptizing them in the Name of the Father and the Son and the Holy Ghost"* [Matt. 28:19]. . . .

17. It remains for me to advise you of the rules to be observed in giving and receiving baptism. The supreme right of giving it belongs to the high priest, which is the bishop: after him, to the presbyters and deacons, yet not without commission from the bishop, on account of the Church's dignity: for when this is safe, peace is safe. Except for that, even laymen have the right: for that which is received on equal terms can be given on equal terms." . . .

18. It follows that deferment of baptism is more profitable, in accordance with each person's character and attitude, and even age: and especially so as regards children. For what need is there, if

there really is no need, for even their sponsors to be brought into peril, seeing they may possibly themselves fail of their promises by death, or be deceived by the subsequent development of an evil disposition? It is true our Lord says, *"Forbid them not to come to me"* [Matt. 19:14]. So let them come when they are growing up, when they are learning, when they are being taught what they are coming to: let them be made Christians when they have become competent to know Christ. Why should innocent infancy come with haste to the remission of sins? Shall we take less cautious action in this than we take in worldly matters? Shall one who is not trusted with earthly property be entrusted with heavenly? Let them first learn how to ask for salvation, so that you may be seen to have given to one that asketh. With no less reason ought the unmarried also to be delayed until they either marry or are firmly established in continence. . . .

19. The Passover provides the day of most solemnity for baptism, for then was accomplished our Lord's passion, and into it we are baptized. . . . After that, Pentecost is a most auspicious period for arranging baptisms, for during it our Lord's resurrection was several times made known among the disciples, and the grace of the Holy Spirit first given. . . . For all that, every day is a Lord's day: any hour, any season, is suitable for baptism. If there is a difference of solemnity, it makes no difference to the grace. . . .

20. Those who are at the point of entering upon baptism ought to pray, with frequent prayers, fastings, bendings of the knee, and all-night vigils, along with the confession of all their sins, so as to make a copy of the baptism of John.

b. *Of the Crown* (c. 211). Ibid., p. xxiii.
    In short, to begin with baptism, when on the point of coming to the water we then and there, as also somewhat earlier in church under the bishop's control, affirm that we renounce the devil and his pomp and his angels. After this we are thrice immersed, while we answer interrogations rather more extensive than our Lord has prescribed in the gospel. Made welcome then [into the assembly] we partake of a compound of milk and honey, and from that day for a whole week we abstain from our daily bath.

7.  Hippolytus, *The Apostolic Tradition,* XV–XXI (c. 217). Trans. Geoffrey J. Cuming, *Hippolytus: A Text for Students* (Bramcote, Notts.: Grove Books, 1976), pp. 15–21.

### Of Newcomers to the Faith
15. Those who come forward for the first time to hear the word shall first be brought to the teachers before all the people arrive, and shall be questioned about their reason for coming to the faith. And those who have brought them shall bear witness about them, whether they are capable of hearing the word. They shall be questioned about their state of life: Has he a wife? Is he the slave of a believer? Does his master allow him? Let him hear the word. If his master does not bear witness about him that he is a good man, he shall be rejected. If his master is a heathen, teach him to please his master, that there be no scandal. If any man has a wife or a woman a husband, they shall be taught to be contented, the man with his wife and the women with her husband. But if any man is not living with a wife, he shall be instructed not to fornicate, but to take a wife lawfully or remain as he is. If anyone is possessed by a demon, he shall not hear the word of teaching until he is pure.

### Of Crafts and Professions
16. Inquiry shall be made about the crafts and professions of those who are brought for instruction. If a man is a brothel-keeper, let him cease or be rejected. If anyone is a sculptor or a painter, let them be instructed not to make idols; let them cease or be rejected. If anyone is an actor or gives theatrical performances, let him cease or be rejected. He who teaches children had best cease; but if he has no craft, let him have permission.

Similarly, a charioteer who competes in the games, or goes to them, let him cease or be rejected. One who is a gladiator or teaches gladiators to fight, or one who fights with beasts in the games, or a public official employed on gladiatorial business, let him cease or be rejected.

If anyone is a priest, or keeper, of idols, let him cease or be rejected.

A soldier under authority shall not kill a man. If he is ordered to, he shall not carry out the order; nor shall he take the oath. If he is unwilling, let him be rejected. He who has the power of the sword, or is a magistrate of a city who wears the purple, let him cease or be rejected. A catechumen or believer who want to become soldiers should be rejected, because they have despised God.

A prostitute, a profligate, a eunuch, or anyone else who does things of which it is a shame to speak, let them be rejected, for they are impure. Neither shall a magician be brought for examination. A charmer, an astrologer, a diviner, an interpreter of dreams, a mountebank, a cutter of fringes of clothes, or a maker of phylacteries, let them be rejected.

A man's concubine, if she is his slave and has reared her children and remained faithful to him alone, may be a hearer; otherwise, let her be rejected. Let any man who has a concubine cease, and take a wife lawfully; but if he is unwilling, let him be rejected.

If we have left anything out, the facts themselves will teach you; for we all have the Spirit of God.

### Of the Time of Hearing the Word after (Examination of) Crafts and Professions
17. Catechumens shall continue to hear the word for three years. But if a man is keen, and perseveres well in the matter, the time shall not be judged, but only his conduct.

### Of the Prayer of Those Who Hear the Word
18. When the teacher has finished giving instruction, let the catechumens pray by themselves, separated from the faithful; and let the women, whether faithful or catechumens, stand by themselves in some place in the church when they pray. And when they have finished praying, they shall not give the Peace, for their kiss is not yet holy. But let only the faithful greet one another, men with men and women with women; but the men shall not greet the women. And let all the women cover their heads with a hood, but (not) just with a piece of linen, for that is no veil.

### Of Laying Hands on the Catechumens
19. After their prayer, when the teacher has laid hands on the catechumens, he shall pray and dismiss them. Whether the teacher is a cleric or a layman, let him act thus.

If a catechumen is arrested for the name of the Lord, let him not be in two minds about his witness. For if he suffers violence and is killed (before he has received baptism) for the forgiveness of his sins, he will be justified, for he has received baptism in his blood.

### Of Those Who Will Receive Baptism
20. And when those who are to receive baptism are chosen, let their life be examined: have they lived good lives when they were catechumens? Have they honoured the widows? Have they visited the sick? Have they done every kind of good work? And when those who brought them bear witness to each: "He has," let them hear the gospel.

From the time they were set apart, let hands be laid on them daily while they are exorcized. And when the day of their baptism approaches, the bishop shall exorcize each one of them, in order that he may know whether he is pure. And if anyone is not good or not pure, let him be put aside, because he has not heard the word with faith, for it is impossible that the Alien should hide himself for ever.

Those who are to be baptized should be instructed to bathe and wash themselves on the Thursday. And if a woman is in her period, let her be put aside, and receive baptism another day. Those who are to receive baptism shall fast on the Friday. On the Saturday those who are to receive baptism shall be gathered in one place at the bishop's decision. They shall all be told to pray and kneel. And he shall lay his hand on them and exorcize all alien spirits, that they may flee out of them and never return into them. And when he has finished exorcizing them, he shall breathe on their faces; and when he has signed their foreheads, ears, and noses, he shall raise them up.

And they shall spend the whole night in vigil; they shall be read to and instructed. Those who are to be baptized shall not bring with them any other thing, except what each brings for the eucharist. For it is suitable that he who has been made worthy should offer an offering then.

### Of the Conferring of Holy Baptism
21. At the time when the cock crows. First let prayer be made over the water. Let the water be flowing in the font or poured over it.

Let it be thus unless there is some necessity; if the necessity is permanent and urgent, use what water you can find. They shall take off their clothes. Baptize the little ones [*parvulos*] first. All those who can speak for themselves shall do so. As for those who cannot speak for themselves, their parents or someone from their family shall speak for them. Then baptize the men, and lastly the women, who shall have loosened all their hair, and laid down the gold and silver ornaments which they have on them. Let no-one take any alien object down into the water.

And at the time fixed for baptizing, the bishop shall give thanks over the oil, which he puts in a vessel: one calls it "oil of thanksgiving." And he shall also take other oil and exorcize it: one calls it "oil of exorcism." And a deacon takes the oil of exorcism and stands on the priest's left; and another deacon takes the oil of thanksgiving and stands on the priest's right. And when the priest takes each one of those who are to receive baptism, he shall bid him renounce, saying:

> I renounce you, Satan, and all your service and all your works.

And when each one has renounced all this, he shall anoint him with the oil of exorcism, saying to him:

> Let every spirit depart far from you.

And in this way, he shall hand him over naked to the bishop or the priest who stands by the water to baptize. In the same way a deacon shall descend with him into the water and say, helping him to say:

> I believe in one God, the Father almighty . . .

And he who receives shall say according to all this:

> I believe in this way.

And the giver, having his hand placed on his head, shall baptize him once. And then he shall say:

Do you believe in Christ Jesus, the Son of God, who was born from the holy Spirit from the Virgin Mary, and was crucified under Pontius Pilate, and died, and rose again on the third day alive from the dead, and ascended into heaven, and sits at the right hand of the Father, and will come to judge the living and the dead?

And when he has said, "I believe," he shall be baptized again. And he shall say again:

Do you believe in the holy Spirit and the holy Church and the resurrection of the flesh?

Then he who is being baptized shall say, "I believe," and thus he shall be baptized a third time.

And then, when he has come up, he shall be anointed from the oil of thanksgiving by the presbyter, who says:

I anoint you with holy oil in the name of Jesus Christ.

And so each of them shall wipe themselves and put on their clothes, and then they shall enter into the church.

And the bishop shall lay his hands on them and invoke, saying:

Lord God, you have made them worthy to receive remission of sins through the laver of regeneration of the holy Spirit: send upon them your grace, that they may serve you according to your will; for to you is glory, to Father and Son with the holy Spirit in the holy Church, both now and to the ages of ages. Amen.

Then, pouring the oil of thanksgiving from his hand and placing it on his head, he shall say:

I anoint you with holy oil in God the Father almighty and Christ Jesus and the holy Spirit.

And having signed him on the forehead, he shall give him a kiss and say:

The Lord be with you.

And he who has been signed shall say:

And with your spirit.

So let him do with each one. And then they shall pray together with all the people: they do not pray with the faithful until they have carried out all these things. And when they have prayed, they shall give the kiss of peace.

8. *Didascalia Apostolorum*, XVI (c. 250). Trans. R. Hugh Connolly (Oxford: Clarendon Press, 1969), pp. 146–147.

In many other matters the office of a woman deacon is required. In the first place, when women go down into the water, those who go down into the water ought to be anointed by a deaconess with the oil of anointing; and where there is no woman at hand, and especially no deaconess, he who baptizes must of necessity anoint her who is being baptized. But where there is a woman, and especially a deaconess, it is not fitting that women should be seen by men: but with the imposition of hands do thou anoint the head only. . . . Let a woman deacon, as we have already said, anoint the women. But let a man pronounce over them the invocation of the divine Names in the water.

And when she who is being baptized has come up from the water, let the deaconess receive her, and teach and instruct her how the seal of baptism ought to be (kept) unbroken in purity and holiness. For this cause we say that the ministry of a woman deacon is especially needful and important. For our Lord and Saviour also was ministered unto by women.

**D. Fourth century documents show theological reflection on the meanings of Christian initiation.**
9. Cyril of Jerusalem.

*a. Catechetical Lectures (c. 350).* Trans. William Telfer, LCC, IV, 64–65, 68, 71, 80.

**Procatechesis 1.** Already the savour of bliss is upon you, who have come to be enlightened [those to be baptized at the end of Lent]; you have begun to pluck spiritual flowers with which to weave heavenly crowns. Already are you redolent of the fragrance of the Holy Spirit. You have reached the royal vestibule. O may the King himself conduct you within.

Lo, now the trees are in blossom; and grant the fruit be duly gathered.

So far, your names have been enrolled, and you have been called up for service. . . .

4. You have a long period of grace, forty days for repentance. . . .

## Verbal and Conceptual Progression of Baptism

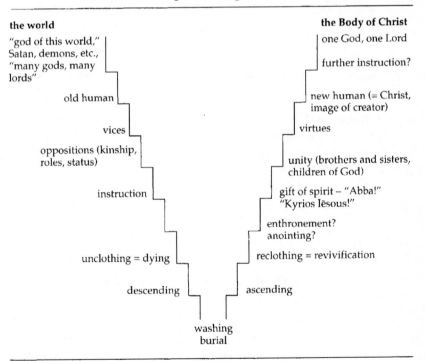

**Table 10.** From Wayne A. Meeks, *The First Urban Christians* (New Haven: Yale University Press, 1983), p. 156.

11. Let this be your solemn charge; learn the things that are told you, and keep them for ever. . . .

**Lecture I.** 4. You were a catechumen till now but now you are to be called believer. Henceforth you are transplanted among the olives of that paradise: or are being grafted on a good olive tree being taken from a wild olive.

*b. Mystagogical Catechesis* (c. 348). Trans. R. W. Church, *St. Cyril of Jerusalem's Lectures on the Christian Sacraments,* ed. Frank Leslie Cross (London: SPCK, 1960), pp. 53, 55, 60, 61, 64.

**Catechesis I.** 1. Let us now teach you exactly about these things that ye may know the deep meaning to you-ward of what was done on that evening of your baptism.

2. First, ye entered into the outer hall of the Baptistery, and there facing towards the West, ye heard the command to stretch forth your hand, and as in the presence of Satan ye renounced him. . . .

4. What then did each of you standing up say? "I renounce thee, Satan, thou wicked and most cruel tyrant!" meaning, "I fear thy might no longer; for Christ hath overthrown it."

**Catechesis II:** 4. After these things, ye were led to the holy pool of Divine Baptism, as Christ was carried from the Cross to the Sepulchre which is before our eyes [in Jerusalem]. And each of you was asked, whether he believed in the name of the Father, and of the Son, and of the Holy Ghost, and ye made that saving confession, and descended three times into the water, and ascended again, here also covertly pointing by a figure at the three-days of burial of Christ. . . .

5. O strange and inconceivable thing! we did not really die, we were not really buried, we were not really crucified and raised again, but our imitation was but in a figure [*mimēsis*], while our salvation is in reality.

**Catechesis III.** 1. In the same manner to you also, after you had come up from the pool of the sacred streams, was given the Unction, the emblem [*antitypon*] of that wherewith Christ was anointed; and this is the Holy Ghost.

10. Ambrose of Milan, *On the Sacraments*, Book III, 1, 5, 8 (c. 390). Trans. T. Thompson, *St. Ambrose "on the Mysteries" and the Treatise "on the Sacraments"* (London: SPCK, 1919), pp. 96, 98–99, 100.

> 1. Yesterday we discoursed on the font, whose appearance is somewhat like that of a tomb in shape; into which, believing in the Father and the Son and the Holy Ghost, we are received, and plunged, and emerge, that is, we are raised up. Moreover thou receivest *myron*, that is *ointment upon the head.* . . .

> 5. We are not ignorant that the Roman Church has not this custom [footwashing]. Her type and form we follow in all things; however, she has not this custom of washing the feet. See then, perhaps she has declined it on account of the numbers. There are, however, some who say and try to urge that this ought to be done, not as a sacrament, not at baptism, not at the regeneration; but only as we should wash the feet of a guest. The latter is an act of humility, the former a work of sanctification. Accordingly, learn how it is a sacrament and a means of sanctification. *"Unless I wash thy feet, thou wilt have no part with me"* [John 13:8]. This I say, not to find fault with others, but to recommend my own usage. In all things I desire to follow the Roman Church. Yet we too are not without discernment; and what other places have done well to retain, we too, do well to maintain. . . .

> 8. There follows the spiritual seal, which you have heard mentioned in the lesson to-day. For after the font, it remains for the "perfecting" to take place, when, at the invocation of the priest, the Holy Spirit is bestowed, *"the spirit of wisdom and understanding, the spirit of counsel and strength, the spirit of knowledge and godliness, the spirit of holy fear"* [Isa. 11:2–3], as it were the seven virtues of the Spirit.

11. John Chrysostom, *Baptismal Instructions* II (c. 390). Trans. Paul W. Harkins, *St. John Chrysostom: Baptismal Instructions* (Westminster, Md.: Newman Press, 1963), pp. 51, 52–53.

> 21. Did you see what the terms of the agreement are? After the renunciation of the wicked one and of all things which are important to him, the priest again has you say: "And I enter into thy service, O Christ." Did you see his boundless goodness? Receiving

only these words from you, he entrusts to you such a store of treasures! He has forgotten all your former ingratitude, he reminds you of none of your past deeds, but he is content with these few words. . . .

25. After this anointing, the priest makes you go down into the sacred waters, burying the old man and at the same time raising up the new, who is renewed in the image of his Creator. It is at this moment that, through the words and the hand of the priest, the Holy Spirit descends upon you. Instead of the man who descended into the water, a different man comes forth, one who has wiped away all the filth of his sins, who has put off the old garment of sin and has put on the royal robe.

26. That you may also learn from this that the substance of the Father, Son, and Holy Spirit is one, baptism is conferred in the following manner. When the priest says: "So-and-so is baptized in the name of the Father, and of the Son, and of the Holy Spirit," he puts your head down into the water three times and three times he lifts it up again, preparing you by this mystic rite to receive the descent of the Spirit. For it is not only the priest who touches the head, but also the right hand of Christ, and this is shown by the very words of the one baptizing. He does not say: "I baptize so-and-so," but: "So-and-so is baptized," showing that he is only the minister of grace and merely offers his hand because he has been ordained to this end by the Spirit. The one fulfilling all things is the Father, and the Son and the Holy Spirit, the undivided Trinity.

12. Theodore of Mopsuestia, *Instructions to Candidates for Baptism* (c. 390). Trans. A. Mingana, *Woodbrooke Studies* (Cambridge: Cambridge University Press, 1933), VI, 31, 54–55, 68.

**Part 2, Sermon 2.** Because you are unable by yourselves to plead against Satan and to fight against him, the services of the persons called exorcists have been found indispensable, as they act as your surety for divine help. They ask in a loud and prolonged voice that your enemy should be punished and by a verdict from the judge be ordered to retire and stand far. . . . You stand, therefore, with outstretched arms in the posture of one who prays, and look downwards and remain in that state in order to move the judge to mercy.

**Sermon 4.** After you have taken off your garments, you are rightly anointed all over your body with the holy Chrism: a mark and a sign that you will be receiving the covering of immortality, which through baptism you are about to put on. . . .

It is necessary that the priest should have beforehand made use of clear words, according to the rite of the priestly service, and asked God that the grace of the Holy Spirit might come on the water and impart to it the power both of conceiving that awe-inspiring child and becoming a womb to the sacramental birth. . . .

When you go out (of the water) you wear a garment that is wholly radiant. . . .

After you have received the grace of baptism and worn a white garment that shines, the priest draws nigh unto you and signs you on the forehead and says: "So-and-so is signed in the Name of the Father and of the Son and of the Holy Spirit." When Jesus came out of the water he received the grace of the Holy Spirit who descended like a dove and lighted on him, and this is the reason why he is said to have been anointed: "The Spirit of the Lord is upon me, because of which the Lord hath anointed me" [Luke 4:18].

## The Ceremonies of the Baptismal Initiation

| Cyril | Chrysostom | Theodore | Ambrose |
|---|---|---|---|
| | | | Anointing |
| Renunciation-Commitment | Renunciation-Commitment Anointing | Renunciation-Commitment Anointing | Renunciation |
| Stripping | Stripping | Stripping | |
| Anointing | Anointing | ˙Anointing | |
| BAPTISM | BAPTISM | BAPTISM | BAPTISM |
| Anointing | | White Garment | Anointing |
| | (Kiss) | | (Foot-Washing) |
| White Garment | White Garment | Anointing | White Garment |
| | (Lamp?) | | Consignation |

**Table 11.** From Hugh M. Riley, *Christian Initiation* (Washington, D.C.: Catholic University of America Press, 1974), p. 21.

13. Egeria (c. 384). Trans. John Wilkinson, *Egeria's Travels* (London: SPCK, 1971), pp. 143–146.

45.1 I feel I should add something about the way they instruct those who are to be baptized at Easter. Names must be given in before the first day of Lent, which means that a presbyter takes down all the names before the start of the eight weeks for which Lent lasts here, as I have told you. Once the priest has all the names, on the second day of Lent at the start of the eight weeks, the bishop's chair is placed in the middle of the Great Church, the Martyrium, the presbyters sit in chairs on either side of him, and all the clergy stand. Then one by one those seeking baptism are brought up, men coming with their fathers and women with their mothers. As they come in one by one, the bishop asks their neighbours questions about them: "Is this person leading a good life?" . . . And if his inquiries show him that someone has not committed any of these misdeeds, he himself puts down his name. . . .

They have here the custom that those who are preparing for baptism during the season of the Lenten fast go to be exorcized by the clergy first thing in the morning. . . . All those to be baptized, the men and the women, sit round him [bishop] in a circle. . . . though not catechumens, who do not come in while the bishop is teaching.

His subject is God's Law; during the forty days he goes through the whole Bible, beginning with Genesis, and first relating the literal meaning of each passage, then interpreting its spiritual meaning. He also teaches them at this time all about the resurrection and the faith. And this is called *catechesis*. After five weeks' teaching they receive the Creed, whose content he explains article by article in the same way as he explained the Scriptures, first literally and then spiritually. . . . all through Lent, three hours' catechesis a day. . . .

[During Holy Week] the candidates go up to the bishop, men with their fathers and women with their mothers, and repeat the Creed to him. When they have done so, the bishop speaks to them all as follows: "During these seven weeks you have received instruction in the whole biblical Law. You have heard about the faith, and the resurrection of the body. You have also learned all you can as catechumens of the content of the Creed. But the teaching about baptism itself is a deeper mystery, and you have not the right to hear it while you remain catechumens. Do not think it will never be explained; you will hear it all during the eight days of Easter after you have been baptized. But so long as you are catechumens you cannot be told God's deep mysteries." . . .

[After Easter, the bishop] interprets all that takes place in Baptism. . . . Indeed the way he expounds the mysteries and interprets them cannot fail to move his hearers.

14. *Apostolic Constitutions*, VII (c. 375). Trans. James Donaldson, ANF, VII, 477.

22. Now concerning baptism, O bishop, or presbyter, we have already given direction, and we now say, that thou shalt so baptize as the Lord commanded us, saying: "Go ye, and teach all nations, baptizing them in the name of the Father, and of the Son, and of the Holy Ghost (teaching them to observe all things whatsoever I have commanded you" [Matt. 28:19]: of the Father who sent, of Christ who came, of the Comforter who testified. But thou shalt beforehand anoint the person with holy oil, and afterward baptize him with water, and in the conclusion shalt seal him with the ointment; that the anointing with oil may be a participation of the Holy Spirit, and the water, a symbol of the death *of Christ*, and the ointment the seal of the covenants. But if there be neither oil nor ointment, water is sufficient both for the anointing, and for the seal, and for the confession of him that is dead, or indeed is dying together *with Christ*. But before baptism, let him that is to be baptized fast. . . .

43. Him [the Father], therefore, let the priest even now call upon in baptism, and let him say: Look down from heaven and sanctify this water, and give it grace and power, that so he that is to be baptized, according to the command of Thy Christ, may be crucified with Him, and may die with Him, and may be buried with Him, and may rise with Him to the adoption which is in Him, that he may be dead to sin, and live to righteousness.

15. Augustine of Hippo, *Enchiridion*, XIII (421). Trans. Albert C. Outler, LCC, VII, 365–367.

42. This is the meaning of the great sacrament of baptism, which is celebrated among us. All who attain to this grace die thereby to sin—as he himself is said to have died to sin because he died in the flesh, that is, "in the likeness of sin"—and they are thereby alive by being reborn in the baptismal font, just as he rose again from the sepulcher. This is the case no matter what the age of the body.

43. For whether it be a newborn infant or a decrepit old man—since no one should be barred from baptism—just so, there is no one who does not die to sin in baptism. Infants die to original sin only; adults, to all those sins which they have added, through their evil living, to the burden they brought with them at birth. . . .

45. Still, even in that one sin—which "entered into the world by one man and so spread to all men" [Rom. 5:12], and on account of which infants are baptized—one can recognize a plurality of sins, if that single sin is divided, so to say, into its separate elements. . . .

46. It is also said—and not without support—that infants are involved in the sins of their parents, not only of the first pair, but even of their own, of whom they were born. . . .

This is why each one of them must be born again, so that he may thereby be absolved of whatever sin was in him at the time of birth. For the sins committed by evil-doing after birth can be healed by repentance—as, indeed, we see it happen even after baptism. For the new birth [*regeneratio*] would not have been instituted except for the fact that the first birth [*generatio*] was tainted.

## II. THE MEDIEVAL LEGACY
### A. Two sacraments of initiation are described in the "Decree for the Armenians," 1439.
16. "The Decree for the Armenians" (1439). Trans. from *Enchiridion Symbolorum Definitionum et Declarationum*, ed. Henry Denzinger and Adolf Schönmetzer, 33rd ed. (Freiburg: Herder, 1965), pp. 333–334.

Holy baptism holds the first place of all the sacraments, which is the doorway to the life of the spirit, and through it we are made members of Christ and his body, the Church. And since with the first man death entered the world, unless we are reborn of water and the Spirit, we are not able, as Truth says, to enter the kingdom of heaven. The matter of this sacrament is water, pure and natural: it does not matter if it be cold or warm.

The form is: "I baptize you in the name of the Father and of the Son and of the Holy Spirit." We do not deny, however, that at the words, "So and so, the servant of Christ, is baptized in the name of the Father and of the Son and of the Holy Spirit," or "So and so is baptized by my hands in the name of the Father and of the Son and of the Holy Spirit," baptism is truly conferred, seeing that the sacrament is conferred if the chief cause from which baptism receives its power, the holy Trinity, [is invoked] by the minister or the instrument who passes on the external sacrament, that is, if the power is expressed through which he works, namely, by the invocation of the holy Trinity.

The minister of this sacrament is a priest, who from his office is competent to baptize. In the case of necessity, however, not only a priest but a deacon, or even a lay man or woman, or indeed even a pagan or heretic, is able to baptize, as long as he uses the form of the Church, and intends to do what the Church does.

The effect of this sacrament is the remission of all sin, original and actual, and all punishment which is due for this guilt. On account of this, no satisfaction for previous sin is imposed on those being baptized; but if they die before they commit another sin, they attain immediately the kingdom of heaven and the vision of God.

The second sacrament is confirmation. The matter is chrism, made from oil whose glow suggests conscience and balsam whose odor signifies a good reputation. The chrism is blessed by the bishop. The form is: "I sign you in the sign of the cross, and confirm you with the chrism of salvation, in the name of the Father and of the Son and of the Holy Spirit."

The ordinary minister is the bishop. And although for other anointings a simple priest suffices; this ought not be conferred except by a bishop: because of the Apostles alone (whose place the bishops hold) is it written, that they gave the Holy Spirit by the imposition of hands, in which manner the Acts of the Apostles manifests: When the Apostles who were in Jerusalem had heard that Samaria had received the word of God, they sent Peter and John to them. They, when they had come, prayed for them, that they might receive the Holy Spirit: for it had not yet come on them, but they had been baptized in the name of the Lord Jesus. Then they laid hands on them and they received the Holy Spirit [Acts 8:14–17]. The place of this imposition of hands is given to confirmation in the Church. It is also appointed that on occasion, through the Apostolic See, for reasonable and urgent needs, a dispensation is given to simple priests to administer the sacrament of confirmation with chrism blessed by a bishop.

The effect of this sacrament is that through it the Holy Spirit is given to strengthen those to whom it is given, as it was given to the Apostles in the day of Pentecost, namely that the Christian might boldly confess the name of Christ. Thus the confirmand is anointed, on the forehead, where the seat of shame is, that he may never blush to confess the name of Christ especially his cross, which is a scandal to the Jews and folly to the Gentiles according to the Apostle; on account of which he is signed with the sign of the cross.

### III. REFORMATION PERSPECTIVES ON CHRISTIAN INITIATION
**A. Luther seeks few changes in baptismal practice but a new baptismal spirituality.**
17. Martin Luther.

a. *The Holy and Blessed Sacrament of Baptism* (1519). Trans. Charles M. Jacobs and E. Theodore Bachmann, LW, XXXV, 29, 30, 34, 36, 42.
1. Although in many places it is no longer customary to thrust and dip infants into the font, but only with the hand to pour the baptismal water upon them out of the font, nevertheless the former is what should be done. . . .

3. The significance of baptism is a blessed dying unto sin and a resurrection in the grace of God, so that the old man, conceived and born in sin, is there drowned, and a new man, born in grace, comes forth and rises. . . .

11. There is no greater comfort on earth than baptism. . . .

12. For this reason we must boldly and without fear hold fast to our baptism, and set it high against all sins and terrors of conscience. We must humbly admit, "I know full well that I cannot do a single thing that is pure. But I am baptized, and through my baptism God, who cannot lie, has bound himself in a covenant with me. He will not count my sin against me, but will slay it and blot it out." . . .

19. If, then, the holy sacrament of baptism is a matter so great, gracious, and full of comfort, we should diligently see to it that we ceaselessly, joyfully, and from the heart thank, praise, and honor God for it.

*b. Babylonian Captivity* (1520). Trans. A. T. W. Steinhäuser, Frederick C. Ahrens, and Abdel Ross Wentz, LW, XXXVI, 59.

This message should have been impressed upon the people untiringly, and this promise should have been dinned into their ears without ceasing. Their baptism should have been called to their minds again and again, and their faith constantly awakened and nourished. For just as the truth of this divine promise, once pronounced over us, continues until death, so our faith in it ought never to cease, but to be nourished and strengthened until death by the continual remembrance of this promise made to us in baptism.

*c.* "Flood Prayer," *The Order of Baptism Newly Revised* (1526). Trans. Paul Zeller Strodach and Ulrich S. Leupold, LW, LIII, 107–108.

Almightly eternal God, who according to thy righteous judgment didst condemn the unbelieving world through the flood and in thy great mercy didst preserve believing Noah and his family, and who didst drown hardhearted Pharaoh with all his host in the Red Sea and didst lead thy people Israel through the same on dry ground, thereby prefiguring this bath of thy baptism, and who through the baptism of thy dear Child, our Lord Jesus Christ, hast consecrated and set apart the Jordan and all water as a salutary flood and a rich and full washing away of sins: We pray through the same thy groundless mercy that thou wilt graciously behold this N. and bless him with true faith in the spirit so that by means of this saving flood all that has been born in him from Adam and which he himself has added thereto may be drowned in him and engulfed, and that he may be sundered from the number of the unbelieving, preserved dry and secure in the holy ark of Christendom, serve thy name at all times fervent in spirit and joyful in hope, so that with all believers he may be made worthy to attain eternal life according to thy promise; through Jesus Christ our Lord. Amen.

d. *Large Catechism* (1529). Trans. Theodore G. Tappert, *The Book of Concord* (Philadelphia: Fortress Press, 1959), p. 444.

We do the same in infant Baptism. We bring the child with the purpose and hope that he may believe, and we pray God to grant him faith. But we do not baptize him on that account, but solely on the command of God. Why? Because we know that God does not lie. My neighbor and I—in short, all men—may err and deceive, but God's Word cannot err.

## B. The Anabaptists protest that baptism is for believers only.

18. *The Schleitheim Confession* (1527). Trans. Walter Klaassen, *Anabaptism in Outline* (Scottdale, Pa.: Herald Press, 1981), p. 168.

1. Notice concerning baptism. Baptism shall be given to all those who have been taught repentance and the amendment of life and [who] believe truly that their sins are taken away through Christ and to all those who desire to walk in the resurrection of Jesus Christ and be buried with him in death, so that they might rise with him; to all those who with such an understanding themselves desire and request it from us; hereby is excluded all infant baptism, the greatest and first abomination of the Pope. For this you have the reasons and the testimony of the writings and the practice of the apostles. We wish simply yet resolutely and with assurance to hold to the same.

19. Menno Simons, *Foundation of Christian Doctrine* (1539). Trans. Leonard Verduin, *The Complete Writings of Menno Simons* (Scottdale, Pa.: Herald Press, 1956), pp. 120, 126–127.

Christ, after His resurrection, commanded His apostles saying, Go ye therefore, and teach all nations, baptizing them in the name of the Father, and of the Son, and the Holy Ghost; teaching them to observe all things whatsoever I have commanded you; and, lo, I am with you always, even unto the end of the world. Amen [Matt. 28:19].

Here we have the Lord's commandment concerning baptism, as to when according to the ordinance of God it shall be administered and received; namely, that the Gospel must first be preached, and then those baptized who believe it, as Christ says: Go ye into all the world, and preach the gospel to every creature; he that believeth and is baptized shall be saved, but he that believeth not, shall be damned [Mark 16:16]. Thus has the Lord commanded and ordained; therefore, no other baptism may be taught or practiced forever. The Word of God abideth forever.

Young children are without understanding and unteachable; therefore baptism cannot be administered to them without perverting the ordinance of the Lord, misusing His exalted name, and doing violence to His holy Word. In the New Testament no ceremonies for infants are enjoined, for it treats both in doctrines and sacraments with those who have ears to hear and hearts to understand. Even as Christ commanded, so the holy apostles also taught and practiced, as may be plainly perceived in many parts of the New Testament. Peter said, Repent and be baptized everyone of you in the name of Jesus Christ for the remission of sins, and ye shall receive the gift of the Holy Ghost [Acts 2:38]. And Philip said to the eunuch, If thou believest with all thine heart, thou mayest [Acts 8:37]. Faith does not follow from baptism, but baptism follows from faith. . . .

Luther writes that children should be baptized in view of their own faith and adds, If children had no faith, then their baptism would be blaspheming the sacrament. It appears to me to be a great error in this learned man, through whose writings at the outset the Lord effected no little good, that he holds that children without knowledge and understanding have faith, whereas the Scriptures teach so plainly that they know neither good nor evil, that they cannot discern right from wrong. Luther says that faith is dormant and lies hidden in children, even as in a believing person who is asleep, until they come to years of understanding. If Luther writes this as his sincere opinion, then he proves that he has written in vain a great deal concerning faith and its power. But if he writes this to please men, may God have mercy on him, for I know of a truth that it is only human reason and invention of men. It shall not make the Word and ordinance of the Lord to fall. We do not read in Scripture that the apostles baptized a single believer while he was asleep. They baptized those who were awake, and not sleeping ones. Why then do they baptize their children before their sleeping faith awakes and is confessed by them?

Bucer does not follow this explanation, but he defends infant baptism in a different way, namely, not that children have faith, but that they by baptism are incorporated in the church of the Lord so that they may be instructed in His Word. He admits that infant baptism is not expressly commanded by the Lord; nevertheless he maintains that it is proper. . . .

Since we have not a single command in the Scriptures that infants are to be baptized, or that the apostles practiced it, therefore we confess with good sense that infant baptism is nothing but human invention and notion, a perversion of the ordinances of Christ, a manifold abomination standing in the holy place where it ought not to stand.

### C. Zwingli responds to the Anabaptist challenge to infant baptism.
20. Ulrich Zwingli, *Of Baptism* (1525). Trans. G. W. Bromiley, LCC, XXIV, 138, 145–146, 156.

And in Genesis 17 God himself makes it quite clear that circumcision is not a sign for the confirmation of faith but a covenant sign: "This is my covenant, which ye shall keep, between me and you and thy seed after thee; every man child among you shall be circumcised." Note that God calls it a contract or covenant. Similarly, the feast of the paschal lamb was a covenant, as we read in Exodus 12: "And ye shall observe this thing for an ordinance to thee and to thy sons for ever." Note that the paschal lamb was a covenant sign. . . . Similarly, baptism in the New Testament is a covenant sign. It does not justify the one who is baptized, nor does it confirm his faith, for it is not possible for an external thing to confirm faith. For faith does not proceed from external things. . . .

Hence the meaning of the words "baptizing them" is this: with this external sign you are to dedicate and pledge them to the name of the Father, the Son and the Holy Ghost, and to teach them to observe all the things that I have committed to you. . . .

All that I am now claiming is this: I have proved that baptism is an initiatory sign, and that those who receive it are dedicated and pledged to the Lord God. I am not basing the baptism of infants upon this fact. I am simply following up my main argument or thesis, which is to prove from the words of Christ himself and of all the disciples that baptism is simply a mark or pledge by which those who receive it are dedicated to God. And in the dispute concerning Christ's words in Matthew 28 I claim only that we cannot use those words to disallow infant baptism. . . .

But it is clear that the external baptism of water cannot effect spiritual cleansing. Hence water-baptism is nothing but an external ceremony, that is, an outward sign that we are incorporated and engrafted into the Lord Jesus Christ and pledged to live to him and to follow him. And as in Jesus Christ neither circumcision nor uncircumcision avails anything, but a new creature, the living of a new life (Gal. 6), so it is not baptism which saves us, but a new life. Therefore one of the good results of the controversy has been to teach us that baptism cannot save or purify. Yet I cannot but think that in other respects the Anabaptists themselves set too great store by the baptism of water, and for that reason they err just as much on the one side as the papists do on the other. For though the whole world were arrayed against it, it is clear and indisputable that no external element or action can purify the soul.

## D. Calvin has a higher esteem for baptism.
21. John Calvin.

*a. Institutes of the Christian Religion,* IV (1559). Trans. Ford Lewis Battles, LCC, XXI, 1303–1304, 1323, 1325.

XV.1. Baptism is the sign of the initiation by which we are received into the society of the church, in order that, engrafted in Christ, we may be reckoned among God's children. Now baptism was given to us by God for these ends (which I have taught to be common to all sacraments): first, to serve our faith before him; secondly, to serve our confession before men. We shall treat in order the reasons for each aspect of its institution. Baptism brings three things to our faith which we must deal with individually.

The first thing that the Lord sets out for us is that baptism should be a token and proof of our cleansing; or (the better to explain what I mean) it is like a sealed document to confirm to us that all our sins are so abolished, remitted, and effaced that they can never come to his sight, be recalled, or charged against us. For he wills that all who believe be baptized for the remission of sins [Matt. 28:19; Acts 2:38].

Accordingly, they who regarded baptism as nothing but a token and mark by which we confess our religion before men, as soldiers bear the insignia of their commander as a mark of their profession, have not weighed what was the chief point of baptism. It is to receive baptism with this promise: "He who believes and is baptized will be saved" [Mark 16:16]. . . .

22. But this principle will easily and immediately settle the controversy: infants are not barred from the Kingdom of Heaven just because they happen to depart the present life before they have been immersed in water. Yet we have already seen that serious injustice is done to God's covenant if we do not assent to it, as if it were weak of itself, since its effect depends neither upon baptism nor upon any additions. Afterward, a sort of seal is added to the sacrament, not to confer efficacy upon God's promise as if it were invalid of itself, but only to confirm it to us. From this it follows that the children of believers are baptized not in order that they who were previously strangers to the church may then for the first time become children of God, but rather that, because by the blessing of the promise they already belonged to the body of Christ, they are received into the church with this solemn sign.

Accordingly, if, when the sign is omitted, this is neither from sloth nor contempt nor negligence, we are safe from all danger. It is, therefore, much more holy to revere God's ordinance, namely, that we should seek the sacraments from those only to whom the Lord has committed them. When we cannot receive them from the church, the grace of God is not so bound to them but that we may obtain it by faith from the Word of the Lord. . . .

XVI.2. It therefore now remains for us, from the promises given in baptism, to inquire what its force and nature are. Scripture declares that baptism first points to the cleansing of our sins, which we obtain from Christ's blood; then to the mortification of our flesh, which rests upon participation in his death and through which believers are reborn into newness of life and into the fellowship of Christ. All that is taught in the Scriptures concerning baptism can be referred to this summary, except that baptism is also a symbol for bearing witness to our religion before men.

*b. Draft Ecclesiastical Ordinances* (1541). Trans. J. K. S. Reid, LCC, XXII, 66.

Baptism is to take place at the time of Sermon, and should be administered only by ministers or coadjutors. The names of children with those of their parents are to be registered, that, if any be found a bastard, the magistrate may be informed.

The stone or baptismal font is to be near the pulpit, in order that there be better hearing for the recitation of this mystery and practice of baptism.

Only such strangers as are men of faith and of our communion are to be accepted as godparents, since others are not capable of making the promise to the Church of instructing the children as is proper.

### E. The Church of England retains traditional baptism but ties confirmation and first communion to catechizing.

22. Prayers over the font (1549; disappears in 1552). *First and Second Prayer Books of Edward VI* (London: J. M. Dent & Sons, 1910), p. 245 (spelling modernized).

*The water in the font shall be changed every month once at the least, and afore any child be Baptized in the water so changed, the priest shall say at the font these prayers following.*

O most merciful God our Saviour Jesus Christ, who hast ordained the element of water for the regeneration of thy faithful people, upon whom, being baptized in the river of Jordan, the Holy Ghost came down in the likeness of a dove: Send down we beseech thee the same thy Holy Spirit to assist us, and to be present at this our invocation of thy holy name: Sanctify this fountain of baptism, thou that art the sanctifier of all things, that by the power of thy word, all those that shall be baptized therein, may be spiritually regenerated, and made the children of everlasting adoption. Amen.

23. Martin Bucer, *Censura* (1551). Trans. E. C. Whitaker, *Martin Bucer and the Book of Common Prayer* (London: Alcuin Club, 1974), ACC, LV, 112, 114.

> Such an occasion [bishop's visitation], when the churches are thus visited and renewed in the religion of Christ would be particularly suitable for the solemn administration of confirmation to those who had reached that stage in the catechizing of our faith. Such care on the part of the bishops would go a long way to arouse the people to make progress in all true and effective knowledge of Christ. The men of old time, true bishops, gave care of this kind to their churches with the greatest zeal, and in Germany the superintendents, who commonly perform the function of bishops in our church, have carefully followed their example.
>
> The last of this series of instruction is a warning that no-one is to be admitted to Holy Communion unless he has been confirmed. This instruction will be very wholesome if only those are confirmed who have confirmed the confession of their mouth with a manner of life consistent with it and from whose conduct it can be discerned that they make profession of their own faith and not another's.

24. Church of England, *Articles of Religion* (1563). BCP (Oxford, 1784), n.p.

> ### XXVII. Of Baptism
> Baptism is not only a sign of profession, and mark of difference, whereby Christian men are discerned from others that be not christened, but it is also a sign of Regeneration or New-Birth, whereby, as by an instrument, they that receive Baptism rightly are grafted into the Church; the promises of the forgiveness of sin, and of our adoption to be the sons of God by the Holy Ghost, are visibly signed and sealed; Faith is confirmed, and Grace increased by virtue of prayer unto God.
>
> The Baptism of young Children is in any wise to be retained in the Church, as most agreeable with the institution of Christ.

25. Puritans, *A Directory for the Publique Worship of God* [Westminster *Directory*] (London: 1644 [1645]). Copy in University Library, Cambridge, pp. 39–40.

> Baptisme, as it is not unnecessarily to be delayed, so is it not to be administered in any case by any private person, but only by a Minister of Christ, called to be the Stewart of the Mysteries of God.
>
> Nor is it to be administered in private places, or privately, but in the place of Publique Worship, and in the face of the Congregation, where the people may most conveniently see and heare; and not in the places where Fonts in the time of Popery were unfitly and superstitiously placed.

**F. Wesley wrestles with the problems of the relation of baptism to conversion.**
26. John Wesley.

*a. Articles of Religion* (1784); Article XXVII revised in *John Wesley's Sunday Service* (United Methodist Publishing House, 1984), p. 312.

> *XVII. Of Baptism*
> Baptism is not only a sign of profession, and mark of difference, whereby Christians are distinguished from others that are not baptized; but it is also a sign of regeneration, or the new birth. The baptism of young children is to be retained in the church.

*b.* "The New Birth" (1760). *Sermons on Several Occasions* (London: Epworth Press, 1956), pp. 519–520, 523.

> II, 5. From hence it manifestly appears, what is the nature of the new birth. It is that great change which God works in the soul when He brings it into life; when He raises it from the death of sin to the life of righteousness. . . .
>
> IV, 2. From the preceding reflections we may, secondly, observe, that as the new birth is not the same thing with baptism, so it does not always accompany baptism: they do not constantly go together. A man may possibly be "born of water," and yet not be "born of the Spirit." There may sometimes be the outward sign, where there is not the inward grace. I do not now speak with

regard to infants: it is certain our Church [of England] supposes that all who are baptized in their infancy are at the same time born again; and it is allowed that the whole Office for the Baptism of Infants proceeds upon this supposition. Nor is it an objection of any weight against this, that we cannot comprehend how this work can be wrought in infants. For neither can we comprehend how it is wrought in a person of riper years. But whatever be the case with infants, it is sure all of riper years who are baptized are not at the same time born again. "The tree is known by its fruits." And hereby it appears too plain to be denied, that divers of those who were children of the devil before they were baptized continue the same after baptism: "for the works of their father they do": they continue servants of sin, without any pretence either to inward or outward holiness.

### G. Karl Barth makes a classic statement of the case against infant baptism.
27. Karl Barth, *The Teaching of the Church Regarding Baptism* (1943). Trans. Ernest A. Payne (London: SCM Press, 1948), pp. 9, 14, 27, 29, 33, 40–41, 49.

Christian baptism is in essence the representation (*Abbild*) of a man's renewal through his participation by means of the power of the Holy Spirit in the death and resurrection of Jesus Christ, and therewith the representation of man's association with Christ, with the covenant of grace which is concluded and realised in Him, and with the fellowship of His Church. . . .

Baptism testifies to a man that this event is not his fancy but is objective reality which no power on earth can alter and which God has pledged Himself to maintain in all circumstances. . . . Baptism then is a picture in which, man, it is true, is not the most important figure but is certainly the second most important. . . .

In baptism we have to do not with the *causa* but with the *cognitio salutis*. If one confounds *causa* and *cognitio*, at once and inevitably one overlooks and mistakes the peculiarity of the purpose which baptism serves (and also that of faith!). . . .

The sacramental happening in which a real gift comes to man from Jesus Christ Himself is not in fact any less genuine a happening, because Christ's word and work on this occasion in this dimension and form, and Christ's power on this occasion, have not a causative or generative, but a cognitive aim. . . .

The experience to which a man is subjected in baptism consists in being made sure with divine certainty and being placed under obligation by divine authority. . . .

Baptism without the willingness and readiness of the baptized is true, effectual and effective baptism, but it is not correct; it is not done in obedience, it is not administered according to proper order, and therefore it is necessarily clouded baptism. It must and ought not to be repeated. It is, however, a wound in the body of the Church and a weakness for the baptized, which can certainly be cured but which are so dangerous that another question presents itself to the Church: how long is she prepared to be guilty of the occasioning of this wounding and weakening through a baptismal practice which is, from this standpoint, arbitrary and despotic?

We have in mind here the custom of the baptism of children. . . .

From the standpoint of a doctrine of baptism, infant-baptism can hardly be preserved without exegetical and practical artifices and sophisms—the proof to the contrary has yet to be supplied! One wants to preserve it only if one is resolved to do so on grounds which lie outside the biblical passages on baptism and outside the thing itself. The determination to defend it on extraneous grounds has certainly found expression from century to century.

## H. Post-Vatican II Roman Catholicism reintroduces the process of adult initiation of the early church.

28. *Rite of Christian Initiation of Adults* (1972). *The Rites of the Catholic Church* (New York: Pueblo Publishing Company, 1988), IA, 36–37.

4. The initiation of catechumens is a gradual process that takes place within the community of the faithful. By joining the catechumens in reflecting on the value of the paschal mystery and by renewing their own conversion, the faithful provide an example that will help the catechumens to obey the Holy Spirit more generously.

5. The rite of initiation is suited to a spiritual journey of adults that varies according to the many forms of God's grace, the free cooperation of the individuals, the action of the Church, and the circumstances of time and place.

6. This journey includes not only the periods for making inquiry and for maturing, . . . but also the steps marking the catechumens' progress, as they pass, so to speak, through another doorway or ascend to the next level.

> 1. The first step: reaching the point of initial conversion and wishing to become Christians, they are accepted as catechumens, by the church.
> 2. The second step: having progressed in faith and nearly completed the catechumenate, they are accepted into a more intense preparation for the sacraments of initiation.
> 3. The third step: having completed their spiritual preparation, they receive the sacraments of Christian initiation.

These three steps are to be regarded as the major, more intense moments of initiation and are marked by three liturgical rites: the first by the rite of acceptance into the order of catechumens; . . . the second by the rite of election or enrollment of names; . . . and the third by the celebration of the sacraments of Christian initiation.

## Select Bibliography on Christian Initiation

Austin, Gerard. *The Rite of Confirmation: Anointing with the Spirit.* New York: Pueblo Publishing Co., 1985.

Beasley-Murray, G. R. *Baptism in the New Testament.* London: Macmillan & Co., 1962.

Burnish, Raymond. *The Meaning of Baptism.* London: Alcuin Club/SPCK, 1985.

Duffy, Regis. *On Becoming a Catholic.* San Francisco: Harper & Row, 1984.

Fisher, J. D. C. *Christian Initiation: The Reformation Period.* London: Alcuin Club, 1970.

———. *Christian Initiation: Baptism in the Medieval West.* London: SPCK, 1963.

Jagger, Peter J. *Christian Initiation: 1552–1969.* London: Alcuin Club, 1970.

Kavanagh, Aidan. *The Shape of Baptism.* New York: Pueblo Publishing Co., 1978.

Marsh, Thomas A. *Gift of Community: Baptism and Confirmation.* Wilmington, Del.: Michael Glazier, 1984.

Mitchell, Leonell. *Baptismal Anointing.* London: SPCK, 1966.

Neunheuser, Burkhard. *Baptism and Confirmation.* New York: Herder & Herder, 1964.

Riley, Hugh. *Christian Initiation.* Washington, D.C.: Catholic University of American Press, 1974.

Searle, Mark. *Christening: The Making of Christians.* Collegeville, Minn.: Liturgical Press, 1980.

Stevick, Daniel B. *Baptismal Movements: Baptismal Meanings.* New York: Church Hymnal Corporation, 1987.

Stookey, Laurence H. *Baptism: Christ's Act in the Church.* Nashville: Abingdon Press, 1982.

Whitaker, E. C. *Documents of the Baptismal Liturgy.* 2nd ed. London: SPCK, 1970.

Yarnold, Edward J. *The Awe-Inspiring Rites of Initiation.* Slough, Middlesex: St. Paul Publications, 1972.

# CHAPTER VIII

# The Eucharist

## I. EARLY EXPERIENCES OF THE EUCHARIST
**A. Multiple images of the eucharist appear in the New Testament.**
1. Scripture.

*a.* Exodus 12:6–8; 24–27.

"You shall keep it [the lamb] until the fourteenth day of this month; then the whole assembled congregation of Israel shall slaughter it at twilight. They shall take some of the blood and put it on the two doorposts and the lintel of the houses in which they eat it. They shall eat the lamb that same night; they shall eat it roasted over the fire with unleavened bread and bitter herbs. . . .

"You shall observe this rite as a perpetual ordinance for you and your children. When you come to the land that the LORD will give you, as he has promised, you shall keep this observance. And

when your children ask you, 'What do you mean by this observance?' you shall say, 'It is the passover sacrifice to the LORD, for
he passed over the houses of the Israelites in Egypt, when he
struck down the Egyptians but spared our houses.' " And the people bowed down and worshiped.

*b.* Mark 14:22–26 (see also Matt. 26:26–30; Luke 22:14–22 and 1 Cor.
11:23–26).
> While they were eating, he took a loaf of bread, and after blessing
it he broke it, gave it to them, and said, "Take; this is my body."
Then he took a cup, and after giving thanks he gave it to them,
and all of them drank from it. He said to them, "This is my blood
of the [new] covenant, which is poured out for many. Truly I tell
you, I will never again drink of the fruit of the vine until that day
when I drink it new in the kingdom of God." When they had sung
the hymn, they went out to the Mount of Olives.

*c.* 1 Corinthians 10:16–17; 21.
> The cup of blessing that we bless, is it not a sharing in the blood of
Christ? The bread that we break, is it not a sharing in the body of
Christ? Because there is one bread, we who are many are one
body, for we all partake of the one bread. . . . You cannot drink
the cup of the Lord and the cup of demons. You cannot partake of
the table of the Lord and the table of demons.

*d.* 1 Corinthians 11:27–29.
> Whoever, therefore, eats the bread or drinks the cup of the Lord in
an unworthy manner will be answerable for the body and blood
of the Lord. Examine yourselves, and only then eat of the bread
and drink of the cup. For all who eat and drink [in an unworthy
manner] without discerning the [Lord's] body, eat and drink judgment against themselves.

*e.* Acts 2:42, 46.
> They devoted themselves to the apostles' teaching and fellowship,
to the breaking of bread and the prayers. . . .

> Day by day, as they spent much time together in the temple, they
broke bread at home and ate their food with glad and generous
hearts.

## B. The second century gives us more information about the rite itself.

2. *Didache*, IX–X, XIV (late first or early second century). Trans. Cyril C. Richardson, LCC, I, 175–176, 178.

9. Now about the Eucharist: This is how to give thanks: First in connection with the cup:

"We thank you, our Father, for the holy vine of David, your child, which you have revealed through Jesus, your child. To you be glory forever."

Then in connection with the piece [broken off the loaf]:

"We thank you, our Father, for the life and knowledge which you have revealed through Jesus, your child. To you be glory forever.

"As this piece [of bread] was scattered over the hills and then was brought together and made one, so let your Church be brought together from the ends of the earth into your Kingdom. For yours is the glory and the power through Jesus Christ forever."

You must not let anyone eat or drink of your Eucharist except those baptized in the Lord's name. For in reference to this the Lord said, "Do not give what is sacred to dogs."

10. After you have finished your meal, say grace in this way:

"We thank you, holy Father, for your sacred name which you have lodged in our hearts, and for the knowledge and faith and immortality which you have revealed through Jesus, your child. To you be glory forever.

"Almighty Master, 'you have created everything' for the sake of your name, and have given men food and drink to enjoy that they may thank you. But to us you have given spiritual food and drink and eternal life through Jesus, your child.

"Above all, we thank you that you are mighty. To you be glory forever.

"Remember, Lord, your Church, to save it from all evil and to make it perfect by your love. Make it holy, 'and gather' it 'together from the four winds' into your Kingdom which you have made ready for it. For yours is the power and the glory forever."

"Let Grace come and let this world pass away."

"Hosanna to the God of David!"

"If anyone is holy, let him come. If not, let him repent."

"Our Lord, come!"

"Amen."

In the case of prophets, however, you should let them give thanks in their own way. . . .

14. On every Lord's Day—his special day—come together and break bread and give thanks, first confessing your sins so that your sacrifice may be pure. Anyone at variance with his neighbor must not join you, until they are reconciled, lest your sacrifice be defiled. For it was of this sacrifice that the Lord said, "Always and everywhere offer me a pure sacrifice; for I am a great King, says the Lord, and my name is marveled at by the nations."

3. Letter of Pliny to the Emperor Trajan (c. 112). Trans. Henry Bettenson, *Documents of the Christian Church* (New York: Oxford University Press, 1947), pp. 6–7.

But they declared that the sum of their guilt or error had amounted only to this, that on the appointed day they had been accustomed to meet before daybreak, and to recite a hymn [*carmen*] antiphonally to Christ, as to a god, and to bind themselves by an oath [*sacramentum*], not for the commission of any crime but to abstain from theft, robbery, adultery, and breach of faith, and not to deny a deposit when it was claimed. After the conclusion of this ceremony it was their custom to depart and meet again to take food; but it was ordinary and harmless food; and they had ceased this practice after my edict in which, in accordance with your orders, I had forbidden secret societies. I thought it the more necessary, therefore, to find out what truth there was in this by applying torture to two maidservants, who were called deaconesses [*ministrae*]. But I found nothing but a depraved and extravagant superstition, and I therefore postponed my examination and had recourse to you for consultation.

4. Ignatius of Antioch, *Letters* (c. 115). Trans. Cyril C. Richardson, LCC, I, 93, 114–115.

### To the Ephesians
20. At these meetings you should heed the bishop and presbytery attentively, and break one loaf, which is the medicine of immortality [*pharmakon athanasias*], and the antidote which wards off death but yields continuous life in union with Jesus Christ.

### To the Smyrnaeans
6. They [Docetists] hold aloof from the Eucharist and from services of prayer, because they refuse to admit that the Eucharist is the flesh of our Saviour Jesus Christ, which suffered for our sins and which, in his goodness, the Father raised [from the dead]. Consequently those who wrangle and dispute God's gift face death. . . .

8. You should regard that Eucharist as valid which is celebrated either by the bishop or by someone he authorizes. Where the bishop is present, there let the congregation gather, just as where Jesus Christ is, there is the Catholic Church. Without the bishop's supervision, no baptisms or love feasts are permitted.

5. Justin Martyr, *First Apology* (c. 155). Trans. Edward Rochie Hardy, LCC, I, 285–287.

65. We, however, after thus washing the one who has been convinced and signified his ascent, lead him to those who are called brethren, where they are assembled. They then earnestly offer common prayers for themselves and the one who has been illuminated and all others everywhere, that we may be made worthy, having learned the truth, to be found in deed good citizens and keepers of what is commanded, so that we may be saved with eternal salvation. On finishing the prayers we greet each other with a kiss. Then bread and a cup of water and mixed wine are brought to the president of the brethren and he, taking them,

sends up praise and glory to the Father of the universe through the name of the Son and of the Holy Spirit, and offers thanksgiving at some length that we have been deemed worthy to receive these things from him. When he has finished the prayers and the thanksgiving, the whole congregation present assents, saying, "Amen." "Amen" in the Hebrew language means, "So be it." When the president has given thanks and the whole congregation has assented, those whom we call deacons give to each of those present a portion of the consecrated bread and wine and water, and they take it to the absent.

66. This food we call Eucharist, of which no one is allowed to partake except one who believes that the things we teach are true, and has received the washing for forgiveness of sins and for rebirth, and who lives as Christ handed down to us. For we do not receive these things as common bread or common drink; but as Jesus Christ our Saviour being incarnate by God's word took flesh and blood for our salvation, so also we have been taught that the food consecrated by the word of prayer which comes from him, from which our flesh and blood are nourished by transformation, is the flesh and blood of that incarnate Jesus. For the apostles in the memoirs composed by them, which are called Gospels, thus handed down what was commanded them: that Jesus, taking bread and having given thanks, said, "Do this for my memorial, this is my body"; and likewise taking the cup and giving thanks he said, "This is my blood"; and gave it to them alone. This also the wicked demons in imitation handed down as something to be done in the mysteries of Mithra; for bread and a cup of water are brought out in their secret rites of initiation, with certain invocations which you either know or can learn.

67. After these [services] we constantly remind each other of these things. Those who have more come to the aid of those who lack, and we are constantly together. Over all that we receive we bless the Maker of all things through his Son Jesus Christ and through the Holy Spirit. And on the day called Sunday there is a meeting in one place of those who live in cities or the country, and the memoirs of the apostles or the writings of the prophets are read as long as time permits. When the reader has finished, the president in a discourse urges and invites [us] to the imitation of these noble things. Then we all stand up together and offer prayers. And, as

said before, when we have finished the prayer, bread is brought, and wine and water, and the president similarly sends up prayers and thanksgivings to the best of his ability, and the congregation assents, saying the Amen; the distribution, and reception of the consecrated [elements] by each one, takes place and they are sent to the absent by the deacons. Those who prosper, and who so wish, contribute, each one as much as he chooses to. What is collected is deposited with the president, and he takes care of orphans and widows, and those who are in want on account of sickness or any other cause, and those who are in bonds, and the strangers who are sojourners among [us], and, briefly, he is the protector of all those in need. We all hold this common gathering on Sunday. . . . (cf. chapter II, document 8, p. 19 above).

## C. Hippolytus provides our first detailed texts of the eucharist.
6. *The Apostolic Tradition*, IV, XXI (c. 217). Trans. Geoffrey J. Cuming, *Hippolytus: A Text for Students* (Bramcote, Notts.: Grove Books, 1976), pp. 10–11, 21–22.

### The Ordination of a Bishop
4. And when he has been made bishop, all shall offer the kiss of peace, greeting him because he has been made worthy. Then the deacons shall present the offering to him; and he, laying his hands on it with all the presbytery, shall give thanks, saying:

The Lord be with you;

and all shall say:

And with your spirit.

Up with your hearts.

We have them with the Lord.

Let us give thanks to the Lord.

It is fitting and right.

And then he shall continue thus:

We render thanks to you, O God, through your beloved child Jesus Christ, whom in the last times you sent to us a saviour and redeemer and angel of your will; who is your inseparable Word, through whom you made all things, and in whom you were well pleased. You sent him from heaven into the Virgin's womb; and, conceived in the womb, he was made flesh and was manifested as your Son, being born of the holy Spirit and the Virgin. Fulfilling your will and gaining for you a holy people, he stretched out his hands when he should suffer, that he might release from suffering those who have believed in you.

And when he was betrayed to voluntary suffering that he might destroy death, and break the bonds of the devil, and tread down hell, and shine upon the righteous, and fix a term, and manifest the resurrection, he took bread and gave thanks to you, saying, "Take, eat; this is my body, which shall be broken for you." Likewise also the cup, saying, "This is my blood, which is shed for you; when you do this, you make my remembrance."

Remembering therefore his death and resurrection, we offer to you the bread and the cup, giving you thanks because you have held us worthy to stand before you and minister to you. And we ask that you would send your holy Spirit upon the offering of your holy Church; that, gathering (it) into one, you would grant to all who partake of the holy things (to partake) for the fullness of the holy Spirit for the strengthening of faith in truth, that we may praise and glorify you through your child Jesus Christ, through whom be glory and honour to you with the holy Spirit, in your holy Church, both now and to the ages of ages. Amen.

*The Conferring of Holy Baptism* (follows immediately after chapter VII, document 7, p. 156 above)
21. And then the offering shall be presented by the deacons to the bishop; and he shall give thanks over the bread for the representation, which the Greeks call "antitype" [*antitypum*], of the body of Christ; and over the cup mixed with wine for the antitype, which the Greeks call "likeness" [*similitudinem*], of the blood which was shed for all who have believed in him; and over milk and honey mixed together in fulfillment of the promise which was made to the fathers, in which he said, "a land flowing with milk and honey," in which also Christ gave his flesh, through which those who believe are nourished like little children, making the bitterness of the heart sweet by the gentleness of his word; and over water, as an offering to signify the washing, that the inner man

also, which is the soul, may receive the same things as the body. And the bishop shall give a reason for all these things to those who receive.

And when he breaks the bread, in distributing fragments to each, he shall say:

The bread of heaven in Christ Jesus.

And he who receives shall answer:

Amen.

And if there are not enough presbyters, the deacons also shall hold the cups, and stand by in good order and reverence: first, he who holds the water; second, the milk; third, the wine. And they who receive shall taste of each thrice, he who gives it saying:

In God the Father almighty.

And he who receives shall say:

Amen.

And in the Lord Jesus Christ.

(Amen).

And in the holy Spirit and the holy Church.

And he shall say:

Amen.

So shall it be done with each one.

When these things have been done, each one shall hasten to do good works and to please God and to conduct himself rightly, being zealous for the Church, doing what he has learnt and advancing in piety.

7. Cyprian, *Letter 62, to Caecilius* (253). Trans. Ernest Wallis, ANF, V, 362.

13. For because Christ bore us all, in that He also bore our sins, we see that in the water is understood the people, but in the wine is showed the blood of Christ. But when the water is mingled in the

cup with wine, the people is made one with Christ, and the assembly of believers is associated and conjoined with Him on whom it believes; which association and conjunction of water and wine is so mingled in the Lord's cup, that the mixture cannot any more be separated. Whence, moreover, nothing can separate the Church—that is, the people established in the Church, faithfully and firmly persevering in that which they have believed—from Christ, in such a way as to prevent their undivided love from always abiding and adhering.

Thus, therefore, in consecrating the cup of the Lord, water alone cannot be offered, even as wine alone cannot be offered. For if any one offer wine only, the blood of Christ is dissociated from us, but if the water be alone, the people are dissociated from Christ; but when both are mingled, and are joined with one another by a close union, there is completed a spiritual and heavenly sacrament. Thus the cup of the Lord is not indeed water alone, nor wine alone, unless each be mingled with the other, just as, on the other hand, the body of the Lord cannot be flour alone or water alone, unless both should be united and joined together and compacted in the mass of one bread; in which very sacrament our people are shown to be made one, so that in like manner as many grains, collected, and ground, and mixed together into one mass, make one bread; so in Christ, who is the heavenly bread, we may know that there is one body, with which our number is joined and united.

## D. In the fourth century, reflections on the meaning of the eucharist are common but controversies few.

8. Ambrose of Milan, *On the Sacraments*, IV, 14–20 (c. 390). Trans. Darwell Stone, *A History of the Doctrine of the Holy Eucharist* (London: Longmans, Green & Co., 1909), I, 81–82.

14. This bread is bread before the sacramental words; when the consecration has taken place, from being bread it becomes the flesh of Christ. Let us then declare this. How can that which is bread be the body of Christ? By consecration. But by what words is the consecration effected, and who is He that spoke them? For everything else which is said before is spoken by the priest, prayer is offered to God, prayer is made for the people, for kings, for all others; but when the time comes for the making of the venerable

Sacrament, the priest no longer uses his own words, but he uses the words of Christ. Therefore the word of Christ makes this Sacrament.

15. What is the word of Christ? Assuredly that by which all things were made. The Lord commanded and the heaven was made; the Lord commanded and the earth was made; the Lord commanded and the seas were made. The Lord commanded and every creature was created. You see how powerful the word of Christ is. If then there is so great force in the word of the Lord Jesus that those things which were not should begin to be, how much more does it bring to pass that those things which were shall be and shall also be changed into something else. The heaven was not, the sea was not, the earth was not; but hear the words of David, "He spake and they were made; He commanded and they were created" [Ps. 33:9].

16. Therefore that I may give you an answer, before consecration it was not the body of Christ; but after consecration I tell you that it is now the body of Christ. He spake and it was made; He commanded and it was created. You were yourself, but you were an old creature; after you were consecrated you began to be a new creature. Do you wish to know how a new creature? "Every one," says Scripture, "in Christ is a new creature" [2 Cor. 5:17]. . . .

19. You have learnt that from bread the body of Christ comes to be, and that wine and water are placed in the cup but become blood by the consecration of the heavenly Word.

20. But perhaps you say, I do not see the nature of blood. Yet it has likeness; for as you have received the likeness of the death, so also you drink the likeness of the most precious blood, so that there may be no horror at gore and that none the less the price of redemption may accomplish its work. You have learnt then that what you receive is the body of Christ.

9. Cyril of Jerusalem, *Mystagogical Catecheses* (c. 350). Trans. R. W. Church, *St. Cyril of Jerusalem's Lectures on the Christian Sacraments*, ed. Frank Leslie Cross (London: SPCK, 1951), pp. 68, 74, 78–79.

IV. 3. Therefore with fullest assurance let us partake as of the Body and Blood of Christ: for in the figure [*typō*] of Bread is given to thee

His Body, and in the figure [*typō*] of Wine His Blood; that thou by partaking of the Body and Blood of Christ, mightest be made of the same body and the same blood with Him. For thus we come to bear Christ in us, because His Body and Blood are diffused through our members; thus it is that, according to the blessed Peter, "we become partakers of the divine nature" [2 Pet. 1:4]. . . .

V. 7. Then having sanctified ourselves by these spiritual Hymns, we call upon the merciful God to send forth His Holy Spirit upon the gifts lying before Him; that He may make the Bread the Body of Christ, and the Wine the Blood of Christ; for whatsoever the Holy Ghost has touched is sanctified and changed [*metabeblētai*]. . . .

20. After this ye hear the chanter, with a sacred melody inviting you to the communion of the Holy Mysteries, and saying, "O taste and see that the Lord is good" [Ps. 34:8]. Trust not the decision to thy bodily palate; no, but to faith unfaltering; for when we taste we are bidden to taste, not bread and wine, but the sign [*antitypon*] of the Body and Blood of Christ.

21. Approaching, therefore, come not with thy wrists extended, or thy fingers open; but make thy left hand as if a throne for thy right, which is on the eve of receiving the King. And having hollowed thy palm, receive the Body of Christ, saying after it, Amen.

10.  Augustine of Hippo.

*a. Treatise on the Gospel of St. John,* XXVI (c. 416). Trans. Darwell Stone, *A History of the Doctrine of the Holy Eucharist* (London: Longmans, Green and Co., 1909), I, 93–94.

He explains how it is that what He speaks of happens, and the meaning of eating His Body and drinking His blood. "He that eateth My flesh and drinketh My blood abideth in Me, and I in Him" [John 6:56]. This then is to eat that food and to drink that drink, to abide in Christ, and to have Him abiding in oneself. And in this way he who does not abide in Christ, and in whom Christ does not abide, without doubt neither eats His flesh nor drinks His blood, but rather to His own judgement eats and drinks the Sacrament of so great a thing.

b. *Sermon 272* (c. 415). Trans. Darwell Stone, ibid., I, 95–96.

If you wish to understand the body of Christ, hear the Apostle speaking to the faithful, "Now ye are the body and members of Christ" [1 Cor. 12:27]. If you then are the body and members of Christ, your mystery is laid on the Table of the Lord, your mystery you receive. To that which you are you answer Amen, and in answering you assent. For you hear the words, The body of Christ; and you answer Amen. Be a member of the body of Christ, that the Amen may be true. Wherefore then in the bread? Let us assert nothing of our own here; let us listen to the reiterated teaching of the Apostle, who when he spoke of this Sacrament said, "We who are many are one bread, one body" [1 Cor. 10:17]; understand and rejoice; unity, truth, goodness, love. "One bread." What is that one bread? "Many are one body." Remember that the bread is not made from one grain but from many. When ye were exorcised, ye were so to speak ground. When ye were baptized, ye were so to speak sprinkled. When ye received the fire of the Holy Ghost, ye were so to speak cooked. Be what you see, and receive what you are. . . . Many grapes hang on the cluster, but the juice of the grapes is gathered together in unity. So also the Lord Christ signified us, wished us to belong to Him, consecrated on His Table the mystery of our peace and unity.

c. *City of God*, Book X (c. 420). Trans. Darwell Stone, ibid., I, 123–124.

6. The whole redeemed City itself, that is the congregation and society of the saints, is offered as a universal sacrifice to God by the High Priest, who offered even Himself in suffering for us in the form of a servant, that we might be the body of so great a Head. For this form of a servant did He offer, in this was He offered: for in this is He mediator and priest and sacrifice. And so when the Apostle exhorted us that we should present our bodies a living sacrifice, holy, pleasing to God, our reasonable service [Rom. 12:1] and that we be not conformed to this world but reformed in the newness of our mind, to prove what is the will of God, that which is good and well-pleasing and complete, which whole sacrifice we ourselves are. . . .

This is the sacrifice of Christians: "the many one body in Christ." Which also the Church celebrates in the Sacrament of the altar, familiar to the faithful, where it is shown to her that in this thing which she offers she herself is offered. . . .

Thus is He priest, Himself offering, Himself also that which is offered. Of this thing He willed the sacrifice of the Church to be the daily Sacrament; and the Church, since she is the body of the Head Himself, learns to offer herself through Him.

## II. MEDIEVAL DEFINITIONS
### A. The limits of acceptable eucharistic doctrine begin to be tested in the ninth century.
11. Paschasius Radbertus of Corbie, *The Lord's Body and Blood*, I (c. 844). Trans. George E. McCracken and Allen Cabaniss, LCC, IX, 94.

> 2. It is . . . clear that nothing is possible outside the will of God or contrary to it, but all things wholly yield to him. Therefore, let no man be moved from this body and blood of Christ which in a mystery are true flesh and true blood since the Creator so willed it: "For all things whatsoever he willed he did in heaven and on earth" [Ps. 115:3], and because he willed, he may remain in the figure of bread and wine. Yet these must be believed to be fully, after the consecration, nothing but Christ's flesh and blood. As the Truth himself said to his disciples: "This is my flesh for the life of the world" [John 6:51], and, to put it in more miraculous terms, nothing different, of course, from what was born of Mary, suffered on the cross, and rose again from the tomb. . . . If our words seem unbelievable to anyone, let him note all the miracles of the Old and New Testaments which, through firm faith, were accomplished by God contrary to natural order, and he will see clearer than day that for God nothing is impossible, since all things that God wills to be, and whatsoever he wills, actually take place.

12. Ratramnus of Corbie, *Christ's Body and Blood*, X (c. 845). Trans. George E. McCracken and Allen Cabaniss, LCC, IX, 120–121.

> The wine also, which through priestly consecration becomes the sacrament of Christ's blood, shows, so far as the surface goes, one thing; inwardly it contains something else. What else is to be seen on the surface than the substance of wine? Taste it, and it has the flavor of wine; smell it, and it has the aroma of wine; look at it, and the wine color is visible. But if you think of it inwardly, it is now to the minds of believers not the liquid of Christ's blood, and when tasted, it has flavor; when looked at, it has appearance; and

when smelled, it is proved to be such. Since no one can deny that this is so, it is clear that that bread and wine are Christ's body and blood in a figurative sense. For as to outward appearance, the aspect of flesh is not recognized in that bread, nor in that wine is liquid blood shown, when, however, they are, after the mystical consecration, no longer called bread or wine but Christ's body and blood.

13. Berengarius, *Recantation* (1059). Trans. Darwell Stone, *A History of the Doctrine of the Holy Eucharist* (London: Longmans, Green & Co., 1909), I, 247.

I, Berengar, an unworthy deacon of the Church of St. Maurice of Angers, acknowledging the true Catholic and Apostolic faith, anathematize every heresy, especially that concerning which I have hitherto been in ill repute, which attempts to affirm that the bread and wine which are placed on the altar are after consecration only a Sacrament and not the real body and blood of our Lord Jesus Christ, and that these cannot be held or broken by the hands of the priests or crushed by the teeth of the faithful with the senses but only by way of sacrament. And I assent to the Holy Roman and Apostolic See, and with mouth and heart I profess that concerning the Sacrament of the Lord's Table I hold the faith which the Lord and venerable Pope Nicholas [II] and this holy synod have by evangelical and apostolic authority delivered to be held and have confirmed to me, namely that the bread and wine which are placed on the altar are after consecration not only a Sacrament but also the real body and blood of our Lord Jesus Christ, and that with the senses [*sensualiter*] not only by way of Sacrament but in reality [*non solum sacramento sed in veritate*] these are held and broken by the hands of the priests and are crushed by the teeth of the faithful.

## B. The Western church finally finds the key word to express the presence of Christ it had always experienced in the eucharist.

14. Fourth Lateran Council (1215). Trans. from *Enchiridion Symbolorum Definitionum et Declarationum*, ed. Henry Denzinger and Adolf Schönmetzer, 33rd ed. (Freiburg: Herder, 1965), p. 260.

There is truly one universal Church of the faithful, beyond which no one at all is saved. In it Jesus himself is both priest and sacrifice, whose body and blood are truly contained in the sacrament of the altar under the species of bread and wine by the transubstantiation [*transsubstantiatis*] of bread into body and wine into blood through divine power: that through the perfecting of the mystery of unity we receive of him from himself, that which he received from us. And certainly no one is able to accomplish this sacrament, except a priest, who has been properly ordained, according to the keys of the Church, which Jesus Christ himself gave to the Apostles and their successors. The sacrament of baptism (which is consecrated in water by the invocation of God and the individual members of the Trinity, namely, Father, Son, and Holy Spirit) assists to salvation both infants, as well as adults, when rightly performed in the form of the Church. And, if after the reception of baptism anybody has lapsed into sin, truly he is always able to be restored through penance. Not only virgins and continent ones, but also married persons, through right faith and working good are pleasing to God, and deserve to come to eternal blessedness.

15. Thomas Aquinas, *Summa Theologica*, Part III (c. 1271). Trans. Fathers of the English Dominican Province (New York: Benziger Brothers, 1947), II, 2447–2451.

### Question 75: Art. 2: Whether in This Sacrament the Substance of the Bread and Wine Remains after the Consecration? . . .

*I answer that*, Some have held that the substance of bread and wine remains in this sacrament after consecration. But this opinion cannot stand; first of all, because by such an opinion the truth of this sacrament is destroyed, to which it belongs that Christ's true body exists in this sacrament; which indeed was not there before consecration. . . .

### Art. 4: Whether Bread Can Be Converted into the Body of Christ? . . .

*I answer that*, As stated above (A.2), since Christ's true body is in this sacrament, and since it does not begin to be there by local motion, nor is it contained therein as in a place, as is evident from what was stated above (A.1, ad 2), it must be said then that it begins to be there by conversion of the substance of bread into itself.

Yet the change is not like natural changes, but is entirely supernatural, and effected by God's power alone. . . .

And this is done by Divine power in this sacrament; for the whole substance of the bread is changed into the whole substance of Christ's body, and the whole substance of the wine into the whole substance of Christ's blood. Hence this is not a formal, but a substantial conversion; nor is it a kind of natural movement: but, with a name of its own, it can be called *transubstantiation*. . . .

### Art. 5: Whether the Accidents of the Bread and Wine Remain in This Sacrament after the Change? . . .

*I answer that*, It is evident to sense that all the accidents of the bread and wine remain after the consecration. And this is reasonably done by Divine providence. First of all, because it is not customary, but horrible, for men to eat human flesh, and to drink blood. And therefore Christ's flesh and blood are set before us to be partaken of under the species of those things which are the more commonly used by men, namely, bread and wine.

16. "Decree for the Armenians" (1439). Trans. from *Enchiridion Symbolorum Definitionum et Declarationum*, ed. Henry Denzinger and Adolf Schönmetzer, 33rd ed. (Freiburg: Herder, 1965), pp. 334–335.

The third is the sacrament of the Eucharist. The matter is wheaten bread and wine of the grape, which before consecration ought to be mixed with a little water. The water is mixed, according to the true testimonies of the holy fathers and doctors of the Church set forth in former times in disputations. It is believed that the Lord himself instituted this sacrament with wine mixed with water. This conforms to the stories of the passion of the Lord. The blessed Pope Alexander [I] fifth [successor] to the blessed Peter, said: "In the offerings of sacred things offered to God in the solemnity of masses, bread and wine mixed with water are offered in sacrifice. For in the chalice of the Lord not only ought wine alone to be offered nor water, but both mixed, that is, blood and water, which it is said both flowed from the side of Christ [John 19:34]."

It agrees with signifying the effect of this sacrament, which is the union of the Christian people to Christ. The water signifies the people, according to the Apocalypse "many waters, many people" [Rev. 17:15]. And Pope Julius [I], second [successor] after the blessed Sylvester said: "The chalice of the Lord, according to canonical teaching, ought to be offered with wine and water mixed, which we see by the water to mean the people, and the wine shows forth the blood of Christ." Therefore when wine and water are mixed in the chalice, the people are united to Christ, and the company of the faithful is joined to him in whom it believes.

Therefore, since the holy Roman Church, taught by the most blessed apostles Peter and Paul, with all the other churches of the Latins and Greeks, in which the light of all holiness and doctrine have shined, from the beginnings of the Church, have observed this custom and observe it now. Still, it does not seem appropriate that any region depart from this universal and reasonable practice. We decree, therefore, that the Armenians conform themselves with the entire Christian world, and that their priests mix in the chalice of oblation a little water with the wine, accordingly.

## III. REFORMATION CONTROVERSIES
### A. Luther condemns various abuses while stressing the real presence of Christ in the eucharist.
17. Martin Luther.

a. *The Babylonian Captivity of the Church* (1520). Trans. A. T. W. Steinhäuser, Frederick C. Ahrens, and Abdel Ross Wentz, LW, XXXVI, 27, 28, 31–33, 35, 51–52.

*The first captivity of this sacrament,* therefore concerns its substance or completeness, which the tyranny of Rome has wrestled from us. . . . But they are the sinners, who forbid the giving of both kinds [bread and wine] to those who wish to exercise this choice. The fault lies not with the laity, but with the priests. The sacrament does not belong to the priests but to all men. The priests are not lords, but servants in duty bound to administer both kinds to those who desire them, as often as they desire them. . . .

*The second captivity of this sacrament* [transubstantiation] is less grievous as far as the conscience is concerned, yet the gravest of dangers threatens the man who would attack it, to say nothing of condemning it. . . .

We have to think of real bread and real wine, just as we do of a real cup (for even they do not say that the cup was transubstantiated). Since it is not necessary, therefore, to assume a transubstantiation effected by divine power, it must be regarded as a figment of the human mind, for it rests neither on the Scriptures nor on reason, as we shall see. . . .

And why could not Christ include his body in the substance of the bread just as well as in the accidents? In red-hot iron, for instance, the two substances, fire and iron, are so mingled that every part is both iron and fire. Why is it not even more possible that the body of Christ be contained in every part of the substance of the bread? . . .

What shall we say when Aristotle and the doctrines of men are made to be the arbiters of such lofty and divine matters? Why do we not put aside such curiosity and cling simply to the words of Christ, willing to remain in ignorance of what takes place here and content that the real body of Christ is present by virtue of the words? Or is it necessary to comprehend the manner of the divine working in every detail? . . .

Both natures are simply there in their entirety, and it is truly said: "This man is God; this God is man." Even though philosophy cannot grasp this, faith grasps it nonetheless. And the authority of God's Word is greater than the capacity of our intellect to grasp it. In like manner, it is not necessary in the sacrament that the bread and wine be transubstantiated and that Christ be contained under their accidents in order that the real body and real blood may be present. But both remain there at the same time. . . .

*The third captivity of this sacrament* is far the most wicked abuse of all. . . . The holy sacrament has been turned into mere merchandise, a market, and a profit-making business. . . .

It is certain, therefore, that the mass is not a work which may be communicated to others, but the object of faith (as has been said), for the strengthening and nourishing of each one's own faith.

Now there is yet a second stumbling block that must be removed, and this is much greater and the most dangerous of all. It is the common belief that the mass is a sacrifice, which is offered to God. Even the words of the canon seem to imply this, when they speak of "these gifts, these presents, these holy sacrifices," and further on "this offering." Prayer is also made, in so many words, "that the sacrifice may be accepted even as the sacrifice of Abel," etc. Hence Christ is termed "the sacrifice of the altar." Added to these are the sayings of the holy fathers, the great number of examples, and the widespread practice uniformly observed throughout the world.

Over against all these things, firmly entrenched as they are, we must resolutely set the words and example of Christ. For unless we firmly hold that the mass is the promise or testament of Christ, as the words clearly say, we shall lose the whole gospel and all its comfort. Let us permit nothing to prevail against these words— even though an angel from heaven should teach otherwise [Gal. 1:8]—for they contain nothing about a work or a sacrifice. Moreover, we also have the example of Christ on our side. When he instituted this sacrament and established this testament at the Last Supper, Christ did not offer himself to God the Father, nor did he perform a good work on behalf of others, but, sitting at the table, he set this same testament before each one and proffered to him the sign. Now, the more closely our mass resembles that first mass of all, which Christ performed at the Last Supper, the more Christian it will be. But Christ's mass was most simple, without any display of vestments, gestures, chants, or other ceremonies, so that if it had been necessary to offer the mass as a sacrifice, then Christ's institution of it was not complete.

*b. The Large Catechism* (1529). Trans. Theodore G. Tappert, *The Book of Concord* (Philadelphia: Fortress Press, 1959), p. 447.

Now, what is the Sacrament of the Altar? Answer: It is the true body and blood of the Lord Christ in and under the bread and wine which we Christians are commanded by Christ's word to eat and drink. As we said of Baptism that it is not mere water, so we say here that the sacrament is bread and wine, but not mere bread or wine such as is served at the table. It is bread and wine comprehended in God's Word and connected with it.

## B. Zwingli takes the debate in a much more radical direction.
18. Ulrich Zwingli, *On the Lord's Supper* (1526). Trans. G. W. Bromiley, LCC, XXIV, 195, 213, 234–235.

## Principal Eucharistic Rites, 1521–1571

| | Germany | Switzerland | Strasbourg | Scandinavia | Great Britain |
|---|---|---|---|---|---|
| 1520s | Andreas Karlstadt, *Christmas Mass*, 1521<br>Kaspar Kantz, *Evangelical Mass*, 1522<br>Luther, *Formula Missae*, 1523<br>Thomas Müntzer, *German Evangelical Mass*, 1524<br>Worms: *German Mass*, 1524<br>Döber, *Hospital Mass*, 1525<br>Luther, *German Mass*, 1525<br>Bugenhagen, Brunswick Order, 1528 | Zwingli, *De Canone Missae Epicheiresis*, 1523<br>Oecolampadius, *Testament of Jesus Christ*, 1523<br>Zwingli, *Action*, 1525<br>Oecolampadius, *Form and Manner*, 1525<br>Nicolsburg (Moravia): B. Hübmaier, 1527<br>Bern: *Use*, 1529 | D. Schwarz, *German Mass*, 1524<br>*Psalms, Prayers*, 1526 | | |
| 1530s | Brandenburg-Nuremberg Order, 1533 | G. Farel, *Manner*, 1533 | Martin Bucer, *Psalter*, 1539 | Sweden: Olavus Petri, 1531<br>Denmark/Norway: Bugenhagen, 1537 | |
| 1540s | Cologne: Hermann of Wied, *Simplex ac Pia Deliberatio*, 1545 | Geneva: Calvin, *Form*, 1542 | Calvin, *Form*, 1545 | Finland: M. Agricola, 1549 | *Order of Communion* 1548<br>BCP, 1549 |
| 1550s | | John Knox, *Forme*, 1556 | | | BCP, 1552<br>BCP, 1559 |
| 1560s | | | | | *Book of Common Order*, 1564 |
| 1570s | *Roman Missal*, imposed universally, 1570 | | | Sweden: L. Petri, 1571 | |

**Table 12**

For it is clear that if they insist upon a literal interpretation of the word "is" in the saying of Christ: "This is my body," they must inevitably maintain that Christ is literally there, and therefore they must also maintain that he is broken, and pressed with the teeth. Even if all the senses dispute it, that is what they must inevitably maintain if the word "is" is taken literally, as we have already shown. Hence they themselves recognize that the word "is" is not to be taken literally. . . .

This [human] nature was a guest in heaven, for no flesh had ever previously ascended up into it. Therefore when we read in Mark 16 that Christ was received up into heaven and sat on the right hand of God we have to refer this to his human nature, for according to his divine nature he is eternally omnipresent, etc. . . . The proper character of each nature must be left intact, and we ought to refer to it only those things which are proper to it. . . . The Ascension can be ascribed properly only to his humanity. . . .

And this he signified by the words: "This is (that is, represents) my body," just as a wife may say: "This is my late husband," when she shows her husband's ring. And when we poor creatures observe this act of thanksgiving amongst ourselves, we all confess that we are of those who believe in the Lord Jesus Christ, and seeing this confession is demanded of us all, all who keep the remembrance or thanksgiving are one body with all other Christians. Therefore if we are the members of his body, it is most necessary that we should live together as Christians, otherwise we are guilty of the body and blood of Christ, as Paul says.

19. Michael Sattler, *The Trial and Martyrdom of Michael Sattler* (1527). Trans. George Huntston Williams, LCC, XXV, 140.

The real body of Christ the Lord is not present in the sacrament, we admit. For the Scripture says: Christ ascended into heaven and sitteth on the right hand of his Heavenly Father, whence he shall come to judge the quick and the dead, from which it follows that, if he is in heaven and not in the bread, he may not be eaten bodily.

20. Balthasar Hübmaier, *Summa of the Entire Christian Life* (1525). Trans. H. Wayne Pipkin and John Howard Yoder, *Balthasar Hübmaier: Theologian of Anabaptism* (Scottdale, Pa.: Herald Press, 1989), p. 88.

From this it follows and is seen clearly that the Supper is nothing other than a memorial of the suffering of Christ who offered his body for our sake and shed his crimson blood on the cross to wash away our sins. But up to the present we have turned this Supper into a bear's mass, with mumbling and growling. We have sold the mass for huge amounts of possessions and money and, be it lamented to God, would gladly henceforth continue with it.

21. *Marburg Colloquy.*

*a.* Luther's comment to Bucer (1529). Trans. Martin E. Lehmann, LW, XXXVIII, 70–71.

"Our spirit is different from yours; it is clear that we do not possess the same spirit."

*b. The Marburg Articles* (1529). Trans. Martin E. Lehmann, LW, XXXVIII, 88–89.

### Concerning the Sacrament of the Body and Blood of Christ.

Fifteenth, we all believe and hold concerning the Supper of our dear Lord Jesus Christ that both kinds should be used according to the institution by Christ; [also that the mass is not a work with which one can secure grace for someone else, whether he is dead or alive;] also that the Sacrament of the Altar is a sacrament of the true body and blood of Jesus Christ and that the spiritual partaking of the same body and blood is especially necessary for every Christian. Similarly, that the use of the sacrament, like the word, has been given and ordained by God Almighty in order that weak consciences may thereby be excited to faith by the Holy Spirit. And although at this time, we have not reached an agreement as to whether the true body and blood of Christ are bodily present in the bread and wine, nevertheless, each side should show Christian love to the other side insofar as conscience will permit, and both sides should diligently pray to Almighty God that through his Spirit he might confirm us in the right understanding. Amen.

## C. Calvin refines the issues in a systematic attempt to balance Luther's and Zwingli's insights.

22. John Calvin.

*a. Short Treatise on the Holy Supper of Our Lord and Only Saviour Jesus Christ* (1541). Trans. J. K. S. Reid, LCC, XXII, 143–144.

We have already seen how Jesus Christ is the only provision by which our souls are nourished. But because it is distributed by the

Word of the Lord, which he has appointed as instrument to this end, it is also called bread and water. Now what is said of the Word fitly belongs also to the sacrament of the Supper, by means of which our Lord leads us to communion with Jesus Christ. For seeing we are so foolish, that we cannot receive him with true confidence of heart, when he is presented by simple teaching and preaching, the Father, of his mercy, not at all disdaining to condescend in this matter to our infirmity, has desired to attach to his Word a visible sign, by which he represents the substance of his promises, to confirm and fortify us, and to deliver us from all doubt and uncertainty. Since then it is a mystery so high and incomprehensible, when we say that we have communion with the body and blood of Jesus Christ, and since we on our side are so rude and gross that we cannot understand the smallest things concerning God, it was of consequence that he give us to understand, according as our capacity can bear it.

For this reason, the Lord instituted for us his Supper, in order to sign and seal in our consciences the promises contained in his gospel concerning our being made partakers of his body and blood; and to give us certainty and assurance that in this consists our true spiritual nourishment; so that, having such an earnest, we might entertain a right assurance about salvation. Second, for the purpose of inciting us to recognize his great goodness towards us, so that we praise and magnify it more fully. Third, to exhort us to all sanctity and innocence, seeing that we are members of Jesus Christ, and particularly to unity and brotherly charity, as is specially recommended to us. When we have noted well these three reasons, which our Lord imposed in ordaining his Supper for us, we shall be in a position to understand both what benefits accrue to us from it, and what is our duty in its right use.

b. *Institutes of the Christian Religion*, IV, 17 (1559). Trans. Ford Lewis Battles, LCC, XXI, 1364–1404.

5. Now here we ought to guard against two faults. First, we should not, by too little regard for the signs, divorce them from their mysteries, to which they are so to speak attached. Secondly, we should not, by extolling them immoderately, seem to obscure somewhat the mysteries themselves. . . .

7. Moreover, I am not satisfied with those persons who, recognizing that we have some communion with Christ, when they would show what it is, make us partakers of the Spirit only, omitting mention of flesh and blood. As though all these things were said in vain: that his flesh is truly food, that his blood is truly drink [John 6:55]; that none have life except those who eat his flesh and drink his blood [John 6:53]; and other passages pertaining to the same thing! Therefore, if it is certain that an integral communion of Christ reaches beyond their too narrow description of it, I shall proceed to deal with it briefly, in so far as it is clear and manifest, before I discuss the contrary fault of excess.

For I shall have a longer disputation with the extravagant doctors, who, while in the grossness of their minds they devise an absurd fashion of eating and drinking, also transfigure Christ, stripped of his own flesh, into a phantasm—if one may reduce to words so great a mystery, which I see that I do not even sufficiently comprehend with my mind. I therefore freely admit that no man should measure its sublimity by the little measure of my childishness. Rather, I urge my readers not to confine their mental interest within these too narrow limits, but to strive to rise much higher than I can lead them. For, whenever this matter is discussed, when I have tried to say all, I feel that I have as yet said little in proportion to its worth. And although my mind can think beyond what my tongue can utter, yet even my mind is conquered and overwhelmed by the greatness of the thing. Therefore, nothing remains but to break forth in wonder at this mystery, which plainly neither the mind is able to conceive nor the tongue to express. . . .

10. Even though it seems unbelievable that Christ's flesh, separated from us by such great distance, penetrates to us, so that it becomes our food, let us remember how far the secret power of the Holy Spirit towers above all our senses, and how foolish it is to wish to measure his immeasurableness by our measure. What, then, our mind does not comprehend, let faith conceive: that the Spirit truly unites things separated in space. . . .

19. But when these absurdities have been set aside, I freely accept whatever can be made to express the true and substantial partaking of the body and blood of the Lord, which is shown to believers

under the sacred symbols of the Supper—and so to express it that they may be understood not to receive it solely by imagination or understanding of mind, but to enjoy the thing itself as nourishment of eternal life. . . .

26. Not Aristotle, but the Holy Spirit teaches that the body of Christ from the time of his resurrection was finite, and is contained in heaven even to the Last Day [cf. Acts 3:21]. . . .

30. Unless the body of Christ can be everywhere at once, without limitation of place, it will not be credible that he lies hidden under the bread in the Supper. To meet this necessity, they [Luther] have introduced the monstrous notion of ubiquity. . . .

32. Now, if anyone should ask me how this takes place, I shall not be ashamed to confess that it is a secret too lofty for either my mind to comprehend or my words to declare. And, to speak more plainly, I rather experience than understand it. Therefore, I here embrace without controversy the truth of God in which I may safely rest. He declares his flesh the food of my soul, his blood its drink [John 6:53–56]. I offer my soul to him to be fed with such food. In his Sacred Supper he bids me take, eat, and drink his body and blood under the symbols of bread and wine. I do not doubt that he himself truly presents them, and that I receive them.

**D. The Council of Trent reaffirms the Western medieval concepts and terminology.**
23. *The Canons and Decrees of the Council of Trent* (1551, 1562). Trans. Philip Schaff, *The Creeds of Christendom* (Grand Rapids: Baker Book House, n.d.), II, 136–186.

*a. Thirteenth Session, held October 11, 1551.*

**Canon I.**—If any one denieth, that in the sacrament of the most Holy Eucharist, are contained truly, really, and substantially, the body and blood together with the soul and divinity of our Lord Jesus Christ, and consequently the whole Christ; but saith that he is only there as in a sign, or in figure, or virtue: let him be anathema.

**Canon II.**—If any one saith, that in the sacred and holy sacrament of the Eucharist, the substance of the bread and wine remains conjointly with the body and blood of our Lord Jesus Christ, and denieth that wonderful and singular conversion of the whole substance of bread into the body, and of the whole substance of the wine into the blood—the species only of the bread and wine remaining—which conversion indeed the Catholic Church most aptly [*aptissime*] calls Transubstantiation: let him be anathema.

**Canon III.**—If any one denieth, that, in the venerable sacrament of the Eucharist, the whole Christ is contained under each species, and under every part of each species, when separated: let him be anathema.

*b. Twenty-first Session, held July 16, 1562.*

**Canon I.**—If any one saith, that, by the precept of God, or by necessity of salvation, all and each of the faithful of Christ ought to receive both species of the most holy sacrament of the Eucharist: let him be anathema.

**Canon II.**—If any one saith, that the holy Catholic Church, was not induced by just causes and reasons, to communicate, under the species of bread only, laymen, and also clerics when not consecrating: let him be anathema.

*c. Twenty-second Session, held September 17, 1562.*

**Canon I.**—If any one saith, that in the mass a true and proper sacrifice is not offered to God; or, that to be offered is nothing else but that Christ is given us to eat: let him be anathema. . . .

**Canon III.**—If any one saith, that the sacrifice of the mass is only a sacrifice of praise and of thanksgiving; or, that it is a bare commemoration of the sacrifice consummated on the cross, but not a propriatory sacrifice; or, that it profits him only who receives; and that it ought not to be offered for the living and the dead for sins, pains, satisfactions, and other necessities: let him be anathema. . . .

**Canon VI.**—If any one saith, that the canon of the mass contains errors, and is therefore to be abrogated: let him be anathema.

**Canon VII.**—If any one saith, that the ceremonies, vestments, and outward signs, which the Catholic Church makes use of in the celebration of masses, are incentives to impiety, rather than offices of piety: let him be anathema.

**Canon VIII.**—If any one saith, that masses, wherein the priest alone communicates sacramentally, are unlawful, and are, therefore, to be abrogated: let him be anathema.

**Canon IX.**—If any one saith, that the rite of the Roman Church, according to which a part of the canon and the words of consecration are pronounced in a low tone, is to be condemned; or, that the mass ought to be celebrated in the vulgar tongue only; or, that water ought not to be mixed with the wine that is to be offered in the chalice, for that it is contrary to the institution of Christ: let him be anathema.

**E. The Church of England defines its eucharistic doctrine largely in opposition to Trent. Wesley retains the same statements for Methodists.**
24. Church of England, *Articles of Religion* (1563); *Book of Common Prayer* (London, 1784). From *John Wesley's Sunday Service* (1784) (Nashville: United Methodist Publishing House, 1984), pp. 312–313.

### XXVIII. *Of the Lord's Supper.* [Methodist XVIII.]
The Supper of the Lord is not only a sign of love that Christians ought to have among themselves one to another; but rather it is a Sacrament of our Redemption by Christ's death: insomuch that to such as rightly, worthily, and with faith, receive the same, the Bread which we break is a partaking of the Body of Christ; and likewise the Cup of Blessing is a partaking of the Blood of Christ.

Transubstantiation, (or the change of the substance of Bread and Wine) in the Supper of the Lord, cannot be proved by Holy Writ; but is repugnant to the plain words of Scripture, overthroweth the nature of a Sacrament, and hath given occasion to many superstitions.

The Body of Christ is given, taken, and eaten, in the Supper, only after an heavenly and spiritual manner. And the mean whereby the Body of Christ is received and eaten in the Supper, is faith.

The Sacrament of the Lord's Supper was not by Christ's ordinance reserved, carried about, lifted up, or worshipped.

### XXX. *Of both Kinds.* [Methodist XIX.]
The Cup of the Lord is not to be denied to the Lay-people: for both the parts of the Lord's Sacrament [Methodist: Supper], by Christ's ordinance and commandment, ought to be ministered to all Christian men alike.

### XXXI. *Of the one Oblation of Christ finished upon the Cross.* [Methodist XX.]
The Offering of Christ once made is that perfect redemption, propitiation, and satisfaction, for all the sins of the whole world, both original and actual; and there is none other satisfaction for sin, but that alone. Wherefore the sacrifices of Masses, in the which it was commonly said, that the Priest did offer Christ for the quick and the dead, to have remission of pain or guilt, were blasphemous fables, and dangerous deceits.

## F. The Enlightenment goes much further from traditional doctrine.
25. Benjamin Hoadly, *A Plain Account of the Nature and End of the Sacrament of the Lord's Supper* (London, 1735), pp. 23–24.

VIII. It appears from these *Passages* that the End for which our Lord instituted this Duty, was the *Remembrance* of Himself; that the *Bread*, to be taken and eaten, was appointed to be the *Memorial* of his *Body* broken; and the *Wine* to be drunk, was ordained to be the *Memorial* of his *Bloud* shed: Or, (according to the express Words of St. *Paul*) That the One was to be eaten, and the Other to be drunk in Remembrance of *Christ*; and this to be continued, until He, who was once *present* with his Disciples, and is now *absent*, shall *come again*.

## G. The Wesleys recapture many early Christian concepts in their eucharistic hymns.
26. John Wesley and Charles Wesley, *Hymns on the Lord's Supper* (1745). *The Eucharistic Hymns of John and Charles Wesley,* ed. J. Ernest Rattenbury (Cleveland: O.S.L. Publications, 1990), pp. H-19, H-23, H-30, H-37.

## No. 57

1. O the depth of love Divine,
     Th' unfathomable grace!
   Who shall say how bread and wine
     God into man conveys!
   *How* the bread His flesh imparts,
     *How* the wine transmits His blood,
   Fills His faithful people's hearts
     with all the life of God!

2. Let the wisest mortal show
     How we the grace receive,
   Feeble elements bestow
     A power not theirs to give.
   Who explains the wondrous way
     How through these the virtue came?
   These the virtue did convey,
     Yet still remain the same.

3. How can heavenly spirits rise,
     By earthly matter fed,
   Drink herewith Divine supplies,
     And eat immortal bread?
   Ask the Father's Wisdom *how*;
     Him that did the means ordain!
   Angels round our altars bow
     To search it out in vain.

4. Sure and real is the grace,
     The manner be unknown;
   Only meet us in Thy ways,
     And perfect us in one.
   Let us taste the heavenly powers;
     Lord, we ask for nothing more:
   Thine to bless, 'tis only ours
     To wonder and adore.

## No. 72

1. Come, Holy Ghost, Thine influence shed,
     And realize the sign;
   Thy life infuse into the bread,
     Thy power into the wine.

2. Effectual let the tokens prove,
   And made, by heavenly art,
Fit channels to convey Thy love
   To every faithful heart.

*No. 93*

1. Come, let us join with one accord
   Who share the supper of the Lord,
      Our Lord and Master's praise to sing;
   Nourish'd on earth with living bread,
   We now are at His table fed,
      But wait to see our heavenly King;
   To see the great Invisible
   Without a sacramental veil,
      With all His robes of glory on,
   In rapturous joy and love and praise
   Him to behold with open face,
      High on his everlasting throne!

*No. 116*

1. Victim Divine, Thy grace we claim
      While thus Thy precious death we show;
   Once offer'd up, a spotless Lamb,
      In Thy great temple here below,
   Thou didst for all mankind atone,
   And standest now before the throne.

2. Thou standest in the holiest place,
      As now for guilty sinners slain;
   Thy blood of sprinkling speaks, and prays,
      All-prevalent for helpless man;
   Thy blood is still our ransom found,
   And spreads salvation all around.

**H. The American frontier recovers weekly communion for all
and, in accord with Jacksonian democracy, institutes liturgical
democracy.**
27. Alexander Campbell, "Breaking the Loaf," *The Christian System,*
2nd ed. (1839; New York: Arno Press and New York Times, 1969), pp.
305, 311, 325, 327, 329–331.

**Prop. IV.**—*All Christians are members of the house or family of God, are called and constituted a holy and royal priesthood, and may, therefore, bless God for the Lord's table, its loaf, and cup—approach it without fear, and partake of it with joy as often as they please, in remembrance of the death of their Lord and Saviour. . . .*

**Prop. VII.**—*The breaking of the one loaf, and the joint participation of the cup of the Lord, in commemoration of the Lord's death, usually called "the Lord's Supper," is an instituted part of the worship and edification of all Christian congregations in all their stated meetings. . . .*

A cloud of witnesses to the plainness and evidence of the New Testament on the subject of the weekly celebration of the Lord's supper might be adduced. . . .

Thus our seventh proposition is sustained by the explicit declarations of the New Testament, by the reasonableness of the thing itself when suggested by the Apostles, by analogy, by the conclusions of the most eminent reformers, and by the concurrent voice of all Christian antiquity. But on the plain sayings of the Lord and his Apostles, we rely for authority and instruction upon *this* and *every other* Christian institution. . . .

The model which we have in our eye of good order and Christian decency in celebrating this institution [is a small church of undisclosed location]. . . .

They had appointed two senior members, of a very grave deportment, to preside in their meetings. These persons were not competent to labor in the word and teaching; but they were qualified to rule well, and to preside with Christian dignity. One of them presided at each meeting. . . .

Thus having spoken, he took a small loaf from the table, and in one or two periods gave thanks for it. After thanksgiving, he raised it in his hand, and significantly brake it, and handed it to the disciples on each side of him, who passed the broken loaf from one to another, until they all partook of it. There was no stiffness, no formality, no pageantry; all was easy, familiar, solemn, cheerful. He then took the cup in a similar manner, and returned thanks for it, and handed it to the disciple sitting next to him, who passed it round; each one waiting upon his brother, until all were served. The thanksgiving before the breaking of the loaf, and the distributing of the cup, were as brief and pertinent to the occasion, as the thanks usually presented at a common table for the ordinary blessings of God's bounty. . . .

Nothing appeared to be done in a formal or ceremonious manner. . . . The joy, the affection, and the reverence which appeared in this little assembly was the strongest argument in favor of their order, and the best comment on the excellency of the Christian institution.

## IV. MODERN INTERPRETATIONS
### A. New Approaches to the eucharist dawn.
28. *Constitution on the Sacred Liturgy* (Collegeville, Minn.: Liturgical Press, 1963), pp. 7, 9, 33.

7. To accomplish so great a work, Christ is always present in his Church, especially in her liturgical celebrations. He is present in the sacrifice of the Mass, not only in the person of his minister, "the same now offering, through the ministry of priests, who formerly offered himself on the cross, but especially under the eucharistic species. By his power, he is present in the sacraments, so that when a man baptizes it is really Christ himself who baptizes. He is present in his word, since it is he himself who speaks when the holy scriptures are read in the Church. He is present, lastly, when the Church prays and sings, for he promised: "Where two or three are gathered together in my name, there am I in the midst of them" [Matt. 18:20]. . . .

54. In Masses which are celebrated with the people, a suitable place may be allotted to their mother tongue. . . .

55. The dogmatic principles which were laid down by the Council of Trent remaining intact, communion under both kinds may be granted when the bishops think fit, not only to clerics and religious, but also to the laity, in cases to be determined by the Apostolic See.

## B. A consensus is developing.
29. *Baptism, Eucharist and Ministry* (Geneva: World Council of Churches, 1982), p. 10.

> II. 2. The eucharist is essentially the sacrament of the gift which God makes to us in Christ through the power of the Holy Spirit. Every Christian receives this gift of salvation through communion in the body and blood of Christ. In the eucharistic meal, in the eating and drinking of the bread and wine, Christ grants communion with himself. God himself acts, giving life to the body of Christ and renewing each member. In accordance with Christ's promise, each baptized member of the body of Christ receives in the eucharist the assurance of the forgiveness of sins (Matt. 26:28) and the pledge of eternal life (John 6:51–58). Although the eucharist is essentially one complete act, it will be considered here under the following aspects: thanksgiving to the Father, memorial of Christ, invocation of the Spirit, communion of the faithful, meal of the Kingdom.

## Select Bibliography on the Eucharist

Bouyer, Louis. *Eucharist.* Notre Dame. University of Notre Dame Press, 1968.

Cabié, Robert. *The Church at Prayer*, vol. 2: *The Eucharist.* Collegeville, Minn.: Liturgical Press, 1986.

Delorme, H., et al. *The Eucharist in the New Testament.* Baltimore: Helicon Press, 1964.

Jasper, R. C. D., and Geoffrey Cuming. *Prayers of the Eucharist.* 3rd ed. New York: Pueblo Publishing Co., 1987.

Jungmann, Joseph. *The Mass of the Roman Rite.* 2 vols. New York: Benziger Brothers, 1951–1955.

Klauser, Theodor. *A Short History of the Western Liturgy.* London: Oxford University Press, 1969.

McKenna, John H. *Eucharist and Holy Spirit.* London: Alcuin Club, 1975.

Rordorf, Willy, et al. *The Eucharist of the Early Christians.* New York: Pueblo Publishing Co., 1978.

Schmemann, Alexander. *The Eucharist: Sacrament of the Kingdom.* Crestwood, N.Y.: St. Vladimir's Press, 1988.

Senn, Frank, ed. *New Eucharistic Prayers.* New York: Paulist Press, 1987.

Wainwright, Geoffrey. *Eucharist and Eschatology.* London: Epworth Press, 1971.

Watkins, Keith. *The Feast of Joy.* St. Louis: Bethany Press, 1977.

# CHAPTER IX

# Occasional Services

## I. RECONCILIATION (PENANCE, CONFESSION)
### A. Early practice is communal and only for serious offenders.
1. Scripture.

*a.* Matthew 18:15–18 (see also Luke 17:3–4; 1 Cor. 6:1–7; Gal. 6:1; James 5:19–20).

> If another member of the church sins against you, go and point out the fault when the two of you are alone. If the member listens to you, you have regained that one. But if you are not listened to,

take one or two others along with you, so that every word may be confirmed by the evidence of two or three witnesses. If the member refuses to listen to them, tell it to the church; and if the offender refuses to listen even to the church, let such a one be to you as a Gentile and a tax collector. Truly I tell you, whatever you bind on earth will be bound in heaven, and whatever you loose on earth will be loosed in heaven.

*b.* John 20:22–23.

When he had said this, he breathed on them and said to them, "Receive the Holy Spirit. If you forgive the sins of any, they are forgiven them; if you retain the sins of any, they are retained.

2. Tertullian, *On Penance* (203). Trans. S. Thelwall, ANF, III, 659–665.

4. To all sins, then, committed whether by flesh or spirit, whether by deed or will, the same *God* who has destined penalty by means of judgment, has withal engaged to grant pardon by means of repentance, saying to the people, "Repent thee, and I will save thee;" and again, "I live, saith the Lord, and I will (have) repentance rather than death." Repentance, then, is "life," since it is preferred to "death." That repentance, O sinner, like myself (nay, rather, less than myself, for pre-eminence in sins I acknowledge to be mine), do you so hasten to, so embrace, as a shipwrecked man the protection of some plank. This will draw you forth when sunk in the waves of sins, and will bear you forward into the port of the divine clemency. . . .

6. That *baptismal* washing is a sealing of faith, which faith is begun and is commended by the faith of repentance. We are not washed *in order that* we *may* cease sinning, but *because* we *have* ceased, since in *heart* we have *been* bathed already. For the *first* baptism of a learner is *this*, a perfect fear; thenceforward, in so far as you have understanding of the Lord, faith *is* sound, the conscience having once for all embraced repentance. . . .

7. It is irksome to append mention of a *second*—nay, in that case, the *last*—hope; lest, by treating of a remedial repenting yet in reserve, we seem to be pointing to a yet further space for sinning. Far be it that any one so interpret our meaning, as if, because there is an opening for repenting, there were even now, on that account,

an opening for sinning; and *as if* the redundance of celestial clemency constituted a license for human temerity. Let no one be less good because God is more so, by repeating his sin as often as he is forgiven. Otherwise be sure he will find an end of *escaping*, when he shall not find one of *sinning*. We have escaped *once*: thus far *and no farther* let us commit ourselves to perils, even if we seem likely to escape a second time. Men in general, after escaping shipwreck, thenceforward declare divorce with ship and sea; and by *cherishing* the memory of the danger, honour the benefit conferred by God,—their deliverance, namely. . . .

9. The narrower, then, the sphere of action of this second and only (remaining) repentance, the more laborious is its probation; in order that it may not be exhibited in the conscience alone, but may likewise be carried out in some (external) act. This act, which is more usually expressed and commonly spoken of under a Greek name, is *exomologēsis* [confession] whereby we confess our sins to the Lord, not indeed as if He were ignorant of them, but inasmuch as by confession satisfaction is settled, of confession repentance is born; by repentance God is appeased. And thus *exomologēsis* is a discipline for man's prostration and humiliation, enjoining a demeanor calculated to move mercy. With regard also to the very dress and food, it commands (the penitent) to lie in sackcloth and ashes, to cover his body in mourning, to lay his spirit low in sorrows, to exchange for severe treatment the sins which he has committed; moreover, to know no food and drink but such as is plain,—not for the stomach's sake, to wit, but the soul's; for the most part, however, to feed prayers on fastings, to groan, to weep and make outcries unto the Lord your God; to bow before the feet of the presbyters, and kneel to God's dear ones; to enjoin on all the brethren to be ambassadors to bear his deprecatory supplication (before God). All this *exomologēsis* (does), that it may enhance repentance; may honour God by its fear of the (incurred) danger; may, by itself pronouncing against the sinner, stand in the stead of God's indignation, and by temporal mortification ( I will not say frustrate, but) expunge eternal punishments. Therefore, while it abases the man, it raises him; while it covers him with squalor, it renders him more clean; while it accuses, it excuses; while it condemns, it absolves. The less quarter you give yourself, the more (believe me) will God give you. . . .

10. Are the judgment of men and the knowledge of God so put upon a par? Is it better to be damned in secret than absolved in public? *But you say,* "It is a miserable thing thus to come to *exomologēsis:*" Yes, for evil does bring to misery; but where repentance is to be made, the misery ceases, because it is turned into something salutary. Miserable it is to be cut, and cauterized, and racked with the pungency of some (medicinal) powder: still, the things which heal by unpleasant means do, by the benefit of the cure, excuse their own offensiveness, and make present injury bearable for the sake of the advantage to supervene.

## B. The Irish church develops a pattern of tariff penance celebrated privately and repeatedly.

3. Finnian of Clonard, *The Penitential of Finnian* (c. 540). Trans. John T. McNeill and Helena M. Gamer, *Medieval Handbooks of Penance* (New York: Columbia University Press, 1938), pp. 88, 91.

6. If anyone has started a quarrel and plotted in his heart to strike or kill his neighbor, if [the offender] is a cleric, he shall do penance for half a year with an allowance of bread and water and for a whole year abstain from wine and meats, and thus he will be reconciled to the altar.

7. But if he is a layman, he shall do penance for a week, since he is a man of this world and his guilt is lighter in this world and his reward less in the world to come. . . .

23. If any cleric commits murder and kills his neighbor and he is dead, he must become an exile for ten years and do penance seven years in another region . . . and having thus completed the ten years, if he has done well and is approved by testimonial of the abbot or priest, he shall be received into his own country.

4. *An Old Irish Table of Commutations* (eighth century). Ibid., p. 143.

5. Now every penance, both for severity and length of time in which one is at it, depends on the greatness of the sin and on the space of time which one perseveres in it, and on the reason for which it is done, and on the zeal with which one departs from it afterwards. For there are certain sins which do not deserve any remission of penance, however long the time that shall be asked

for them, unless God Himself shortens it through death or a message of sickness; or the greatness of the work which a person lays on himself; such as are parricides and manslaughters and man-stealings, and such as brigandage and druidism and satirising [defamatory verses], and such as adultery and lewdness and lying and heresy and transgression of order. For there are certain sins for which half-penances with half-*arrea* [substitutions] atone. There are others for which an *arreum* only atones.

5. Peter Lombard, *Four Books of Sentences,* IV (c. 1152). Trans. Elizabeth Frances Rogers, *Peter Lombard and the Sacramental System* (Merrick, N.Y.: Richwood Publishing Company, 1976), pp. 151, 158, 171.

**Distinction XIV.** I. Next we must discuss penance. Penance is needful to those who are far from God, that they may come near. For it is, as Jerome says, "the second plank after shipwreck"; because if anyone by sinning sullies the robe of innocence received in baptism, he can restore it by the remedy of penance. . . . A man is allowed to do penance often, but not be baptized often. Baptism is called only a sacrament, but penance is called both a sacrament and virtue of the mind. For there is an inner penance and an outer: the outer is the sacrament, the inner is the virtue of the mind; and both are for the sake of salvation and justification. . . .

IV. From these and from many other testimonies it is clearly shown, that by penance not only once, but often, we rise from our sins, and that true penance may be done repeatedly. . . .

**Distinction XVI.** I. Moreover in the perfection of penance three steps are to be observed, that is compunction of the heart, confession of the mouth, satisfaction in deed. Wherefore John the golden-mouthed [Chrysostom]: "Perfect penance compels the sinner to bear all things cheerfully; in his heart contrition, in his mouth confession, in deed all humility. This is fruitful penance; that just as we offend God in three ways, that is, with the heart, the mouth, and the deed, so in three ways we make satisfaction."

6. "Decree for the Armenians" (1439). Trans. from *Enchiridion Symbolorum Definitionum et Declarationum,* ed. Henry Denzinger and Adolf Schönmetzer, 33rd ed. (Freiburg: Herder, 1965), pp. 335–336.

The fourth sacrament is penance. The matter is the acts of peni-
tence which are distinguished in three parts. The first is contrition
of the heart, to which belongs grief at sin committed with the
resolution of not sinning further. The second is confession of the
mouth; to which pertains that the sinner confesses all sins to his
priest of which he has memory. The third is satisfaction for sins
according to the guidance of a priest; which principally may be
through prayers, fasting and charity. The form of this sacrament is
the words of absolution, which the priest pronounces when he
says: "I absolve you." The minister of this sacrament is a priest
having authority of absolving, either ordinarily or by commission
of a superior. The effect of this sacrament is the absolution from
sins.

## C. The Reformation takes positions both conservative and radical on penance.
7. Martin Luther, *The Babylonian Captivity of the Church* (1520). Trans.
A. T. W. Steinhäuser, Frederick C. Ahrens, and Abdel Ross Wentz, LW,
XXXVI, 86–88.

As to the current practice of private confession, I am heartily in
favor of it, even though it cannot be proved from the Scriptures. It
is useful, even necessary, and I would not have it abolished. Indeed, I rejoice that it exists in the Church of Christ, for it is a cure
without equal for distressed consciences. For when we have laid
bare our conscience to our brother and privately made known to
him the evil that lurked within, we receive from our brother's lips
the word of comfort spoken by God himself. And if we accept this
in faith, we find peace in the mercy of God speaking to us through
our brother. There is just one thing about it that I abominate, and
that is the fact that this kind of confession has been subjected to
the despotism and extortion of the pontiffs. . . .

In the first place, Christ speaks in Matt. 18: [15–17] of public sins
and says that if our brother hears us, when we tell him his fault,
we have saved the soul of our brother, and that he is to be brought
before the church only if he refuses to hear us, so that his sin can
be corrected among brethren. . . .

Hence, I have no doubt but that every one is absolved from his
secret sins when he has made confession, privately before any

brother, either of his own accord or after being rebuked, and has sought pardon and amended his ways, no matter how much the violence of the pontiffs may rage against it. For Christ has given to every one of his believers the power to absolve even open sins. . . . Let them, moreover, permit all brothers and sisters most freely to hear the confession of secret sins, so that the sinner may make his sins known to whomever he will and seek pardon and comfort, that is, the word of Christ, by the mouth of his neighbor.

8. *The Schleitheim Confession* (1527). Trans. Walter Klaassen, *Anabaptism in Outline* (Scottdale, Pa.: Herald Press, 1981), p. 215.

II. We have been united as follows concerning the ban. The ban shall be employed with all those who have given themselves over to the Lord, to walk after [him] in his commandments, those who have been baptized into the one body of Christ, and let themselves be called brothers or sisters, and still somehow slip and fall into error and sin, being inadvertently overtaken. The same [shall] be warned twice privately and the third time be publicly admonished before the entire congregation according to the command of Christ (Matt. 18). But this shall be done according to the ordering of the Spirit of God before the breaking of bread, so that we may all in one spirit and in one love break and eat from one bread and drink from one cup.

9. Menno Simons, *A Kind Admonition on Church Discipline* (1541). Trans. Leonard Verduin, *The Complete Writings of Menno Simons* (Scottdale, Pa.: Herald Press, 1974), p. 413.

But we do not want to expel any, but rather to receive, not to amputate, but rather to heal; not to discard, but rather to win back; not to grieve but rather to comfort; not to condemn, but rather to save.

10. Peter Riedeman, *Account* (1542). Trans. Walter Klaassen, *Anabaptism in Outline* (Scottdale, Pa.: Herald Press, 1981), p. 221.

But as in the beginning one is received into the church by means of a sign (that is baptism), so also after he fell and was separated from the church he must likewise be received by a sign, that is through the laying on of hands, which must be done by a servant of the gospel. This indicates that he once more has part and is rooted in the grace of God. When this has taken place he is accepted again in full love.

## D. Trent continues the Western medieval arrangements.

11. *The Canons and Decrees of the Council of Trent* (1551). Trans. Philip Schaff, *Creeds of Christendom* (Grand Rapids: Baker Book House, n.d.), II, 151, 165–166.

*Fourteenth Session, held November 25, 1551*

**Chapter VI.** But, as regards the minister of this sacrament, the holy Synod declares all those doctrines to be false, and utterly alien from the truth of the Gospel, which perniciously extend the ministry of the keys to any others soever besides bishops and priests. . . .

**Canon VI.**—If any one denieth, either that sacramental confession was instituted, or is necessary to salvation, of divine right; or saith, that the manner of confessing to salvation, of divine right; or saith, that the manner of confessing secretly to a priest alone, which the Church hath ever observed from the beginning, and doth observe, is alien from the institution and command of Christ, and is a human invention: let him be anathema.

## II. HEALING OF THE SICK
## A. Healing of soul and of body have a long and close affinity.
12. Scripture.

*a.* Mark 16:18c.
["They will lay their hands on the sick, and they will recover."]

*b.* James 5:14–16.
Are any among you sick? They should call for the elders of the church and have them pray over them, anointing them with oil in the name of the Lord. The prayer of faith will save the sick, and the Lord will raise them up; and anyone who has committed sins will be forgiven. Therefore confess your sins to one another, and pray for one another, so that you may be healed. The prayer of the righteous is powerful and effective.

13. Sarapion of Thmuis, *Prayer-Book* (c. 350). Trans. John Wordsworth, *Bishop Sarapion's Prayer-Book* (Hamden, Conn.: Archon Books, 1964), pp. 77–78.

> 17. We invoke thee who has all authority and power, the Saviour of all men, father of our Lord and Saviour Jesus Christ, and pray thee to send healing power of the only-begotten from heaven upon this oil, that it may become to those who are being anointed (with it) or are partaking of these thy creatures, for a throwing off of every sickness and every infirmity, for a charm against every demon, for a separation of every unclean spirit, for an expulsion of every evil spirit, for a driving out of all fever and ague and every infirmity, for good grace and remission of sins, for a medicine of life and salvation, for health and soundness of soul, body, spirit, for perfect strengthening.
>
> O Master, let every Satanic energy, every plague, every scourge, every pain, every labour or stroke or shaking or evil shadowing, fear thy holy name which we have now invoked and the name of the only-begotten; and let them depart from the inward [and] outward parts of these thy servants, that his name may be glorified who for us was crucified and rose again, who took up our sicknesses and our infirmities, (even) Jesus Christ and who is coming to judge [the] quick and dead. Because through him to thee (is) the glory and the strength in holy Spirit both now and to all the ages of the ages. Amen.

## B. The medieval development makes anointing a sacrament for the dying, extreme unction.

14. Peter Lombard, *Four Books of Sentences*, IV (c. 1152). Trans. Elizabeth Frances Rogers, *Peter Lombard and the Sacramental System* (Merrick, N.Y.: Richwood Publishing Co., 1976), pp. 221–223.

**Distinction XXIII.** 1. Beside the preceding, there is another sacrament, that is, the unction of the sick, which is administered at the end of life, with oil consecrated by the bishop. . . .

3. The sacrament was instituted for a double purpose, namely for the remission of sins, and for the relief of bodily infirmity. Wherefore it is plain that he who receives this unction faithfully and devoutly, is relieved both in body and in soul, provided it is expedient that he be

relieved in both. But if perhaps it is not expedient for him to have bodily health, he acquires in this sacrament that health which is of the soul. . . .

4. But if you apply it to the receiving of the "sacrament," it is true of some that they are not repeated or frequently received, but it is not true of others, because they are frequently received like this sacrament of unction, which is often repeated in almost every Church.

15. Thomas Aquinas, *Summa Theologica*, Suppl. XXX (c. 1271). Trans. Fathers of the English Dominican Province (New York: Benziger Brothers, 1948), III, 2671–2672.

> *Article I. Whether Extreme Unction Avails for the Remission of Sins? . . .*
> I answer that, Each sacrament was instituted for the purpose of one principal effect, though it may, in consequence, produce other effects besides. And since a sacrament causes what it signifies, the principal effect of a sacrament must be gathered from its signification. Now this sacrament is conferred by way of a kind of medicament, even just as Baptism is conferred by way of a washing, and the purpose of a medicament is to expel sickness. Hence the chief object of the institution of this sacrament is to cure the sickness of sin. . . .
>
> Consequently we must say that the principal effect of this sacrament is the remission of sin as to its remnants, and consequently, even as to its guilt, if it find it.

## C. The Reformers take vigorous exception to these changes.

16. John Calvin, *Institutes of the Christian Religion*, IV (1559). Trans. Ford Lewis Battles, LCC, XXI, 1467–1469.

> 18. But that gift of healing, like the rest of the miracles, which the Lord willed to be brought forth for a time, has vanished away in order to make the new preaching of the gospel marvelous forever. Therefore, even if we grant to the full that anointing was a sacrament of those powers which were then administered by the hands of the apostles, it now has nothing to do with us, to whom the administering of such powers has not been committed. . . .

21. James wishes all sick persons to be anointed [James 5:14]; these fellows smear with their grease not the sick but half dead corpses when they are already drawing their last breath, or (as they say), *in extremis.* If in their sacrament they have a powerful medicine with which to alleviate the agony of diseases, or at least to bring some comfort to the soul, it is cruel of them never to heal in time. . . . The prayers of believers, with which the afflicted brother has been commended to God, will not be in vain. . . . Pope Innocent [I], who presided over the church at Rome in Augustine's day, established the practice that not only presbyters but also all Christians should use oil for anointing when they or their dependents should need it.

17. Council of Trent, *Canons and Decrees of the Council of Trent* (1551). Trans. Philip Schaff, *The Creeds of Christendom* (Grand Rapids: Baker Book House, n.d.), II, 170.

### Fourteenth Session, held November 25, 1551

**Canon IV.**—If any one saith, that the presbyters [*presbyteros*] of the Church, whom the blessed James exhorts to be brought to anoint the sick, are not the priests who have been ordained by a bishop, but the elders [*seniores*] in each community, and that for this cause a priest alone is not the proper minister of Extreme Unction: let him be anathema.

### D. Vatican II points to new orientations.

18. *Constitution on the Sacred Liturgy* (Collegeville, Minn.: Liturgical Press, 1963), p. 41.

73. "Extreme unction," which may also and more fittingly be called "anointing of the sick," is not a sacrament for those only who are at the point of death. Hence, as soon as any one of the faithful begins to be in danger of death from sickness or old age, the fitting time for him to receive this sacrament has certainly already arrived.

74. In addition to the separate rites for anointing of the sick and for viaticum, a continuous rite shall be prepared according to which the sick man is anointed after he has made his confession and before he receives viaticum.

75. The number of anointings is to be adapted to the occasion, and the prayers which belong to the rite of anointing are to be revised so as to correspond with the varying conditions of the sick who receive the sacrament.

## III. CHRISTIAN MARRIAGE
### A. Marriage rites reflect local cultures.
19. Scripture.

*a.* Matthew 19:4–6 (see also Gen. 1:27; 2:24; Mark 10:1–12).
He answered, "Have you not read that the one who made them at the beginning 'made them male and female,' and said, 'For this reason a man shall leave his father and mother and be joined to his wife, and the two shall become one flesh'? So they are no longer two, but one flesh. Therefore what God has joined together, let no one separate."

*b.* John 2:1–2.
On the third day there was a wedding in Cana of Galilee, and the mother of Jesus was there. Jesus and his disciples had also been invited to the wedding.

*c.* Ephesians 5:31–32.
"For this reason a man will leave his father and mother and be joined to his wife, and the two will become one flesh." This is a great mystery [*mystērion*], and I am applying it to Christ and the church.

20. Ignatius of Antioch, *Letter to Polycarp*, V, 2 (c. 115). Trans. Cyril C. Richardson, LCC, I, 119.

It is right for men and women who marry to be united with the bishop's approval. In that way their marriage will follow God's will and not the promptings of lust. Let everything be done so as to advance God's honor.

### B. Marriage barely makes it onto the list of seven sacraments.
21. Peter Lombard, *Four Books of Sentences*, IV (c. 1152). Trans. Elizabeth Frances Rogers, *Peter Lombard and the Sacramental System* (Merrick, N.Y.: Richwood Publishing Co., 1976), p. 243.

**Distinction XXVI.** 1. "Although the other sacraments took their rise after sin and on account of sin, we read that the sacrament of marriage was instituted by the Lord before sin, yet not as a remedy, but as a duty." . . .

2. Now the institution of marriage is two-fold: one was instituted before sin in paradise as a duty, that there might be a blameless couch and honorable nuptials; as a result of which they might conceive without passion and bring forth without pain; the other was instituted after sin outside paradise for a remedy, to prevent unlawful desires; the first that nature might be multiplied; the second, that nature might be protected, and sin repressed. For even before sin God said: "Increase and multiply" and again after sin, when most men had been destroyed by the deluge. But Augustine testified that before sin marriage was instituted for a duty, and after sin allowed for a remedy, when he says: "What is a duty for the sound is a remedy for the sick." For the infirmity of incontinence which exists in the flesh that is dead through sin, is protected by honorable marriage lest it fall into the ruin of vice. If the first men had not sinned, they and their descendants would have united without the incentive of the flesh and the heat of passion; and as any good deed deserves reward, so their union would have been good and worthy of reward. But because on account of sin the law of deadly concupiscence has beset our members, without which there is no carnal union, an evil union is reprehensible unless it be excused by the blessings of marriage. . . .

6. Since therefore marriage is a sacrament, it is also a sacred sign and of a sacred thing, namely, of the union of Christ and the Church, as the Apostle says: It is written, he says: "A man shall leave father and mother and shall cling to his wife, and they shall be two in one flesh. This is a great sacrament, but I speak of Christ and of the Church" [Eph. 5:31–32].

22. Marriage vows in the vernacular, *Manual of York Use* (fourteenth century). University Library, Cambridge, England (MS Ee.iv.19), pp. 23, 23B, 24 (spelling and punctuation modernized).

[Name] will you have this woman to your wife, and love her, and worship her and keep her in health and in sickness, and in all other degrees, be to her as a husband should be to his wife, and all other forsake, and hold you only to her to your life's end? . . . I will. . . .

[Name] will you have this man to your husband, and to be buxom to him, love him, obey to him, and worship him, serve him, and keep him in health and in sickness, and in all other degrees, be to him as a wife should be to her husband, and all other to forsake for him, and hold you only to him till your life's end? . . . I will. . . .

Here I take you [name] to my wedded wife, to hold and to have at bed and at board, for fairer for [fouler], for better for worse, in sickness and in health, till death us do part, if holy Church it will ordain, and thereto I plight you my troth. . . .

Here I take you [name] to my wedded husband, to hold and to have at bed and at board, for fairer for [fouler], for better for worse, in sickness and in health, till death us do part, if holy Church it will ordain, and thereto I plight you my troth. . . .

With this ring I wed you, and with this gold and silver I honor you, and with this gift I endow you.

23. John Calvin, *Institutes of the Christian Religion*, IV (1559). Trans. Ford Lewis Battles, LCC, XXI, 1480–1483.

34. The last one is marriage. All men admit that it was instituted by God [Gen. 2:21–24; Matt. 19:4ff.]; but no man ever saw it administered as a sacrament until the time of Gregory [VII]. And what sober man would ever have thought it such? Marriage is a good and holy ordinance of God; and farming, building, cobbling, and barbering are lawful ordinances of God, and yet are not sacraments. For it is required that a sacrament be not only a work of God but an outward ceremony appointed by God to confirm a promise. Even children can discern that there is no such thing in matrimony.

36. The term "sacrament" deceived them. But was it right that the whole church should suffer the punishment of their ignorance? Paul had said "mystery." The translator [of the Latin version]

could have left this word, as one not unfamiliar to Latin ears, or rendered it as "secret." He preferred to use the word "sacrament" [Eph. 5:32, Vulgate], but in the same sense that the word "mystery" had been used by Paul.

24. Council of Trent, *Canons and Decrees of the Council of Trent* (1563). Trans. Philip Schaff, *The Creeds of Christendom* (Grand Rapids: Baker Book House, n.d.), II, 197.

*Twenty-Fourth Session, held November 11, 1563.*

**Canon X.**—If any one saith, that the marriage state is to be placed above the state of virginity, or of celibacy, and that it is not better and more blessed to remain in virginity, or in celibacy, than to be united in matrimony: let him be anathema.

## C. The purposes of marriage enunciated in medieval documents survive the Reformation.

25. *The Booke of the Common Prayer*, "The Forme of Solemnizacion of Matrimonie" (1549). *The First and Second Prayer Books of Edward VI* (London: J. M. Dent & Sons, 1910), p. 252 (spelling modernized).

Dearly beloved friends, we are gathered together here in the sight of God, and in the face of his congregation, to join together this man and this woman in holy matrimony, which is an honorable estate instituted of God in paradise, in the time of man's innocency, signifying unto us the mystical union that is betwixt Christ and his Church: which holy estate, Christ adorned and beautified with his presence, and first miracle that he wrought in Cana of Galilee, and is commended of Saint Paul to be honorable among all men; and therefore is not to be enterprised, nor taken in hand inadvisedly, lightly, or wantonly, to satisfy men's carnal lusts and appetites, like brute beasts that have no understanding: but reverently, discreetly, advisedly, soberly, and in the fear of God. Duly considering the causes for the which matrimony was ordained. One cause was the procreation of children, to be brought up in the fear and nurture of the Lord, and praise of God. Secondly it was ordained for a remedy against sin, and to avoid fornication, that such persons as be married, might live chastely in matrimony, and keep themselves undefiled members of Christ's body. Thirdly for the mutual society, help, and comfort, that the one ought to have of the other, both in prosperity and adversity. Into the which holy estate these two persons present: come now to be joined. Therefore if any man can show any just cause why they may not lawfully be joined so together: Let him now speak, or else hereafter for ever hold his peace.

## IV. ORDINATION
### A. Early patterns show a variety of ministries.
26. Scripture.

*a.* Acts 6:2b–6.

"It is not right that we should neglect the word of God in order to wait on tables. Therefore, friends, select from among yourselves seven men of good standing, full of the Spirit and of wisdom, whom we may appoint to this task, while we, for our part, will devote ourselves to prayer and to serving the word." . . . They had these men stand before the apostles, who prayed and laid their hands on them.

*b.* Acts 20:17; 28.

From Miletus he [Paul] sent a message to Ephesus, asking the elders [*presbyterous*] of the church to meet him. . . .

"Keep watch over yourselves and over all the flock, of which the Holy Spirit has made you overseers [*episkopous*], to shepherd the church of God that he obtained with the blood of his own Son."

27. Ignatius of Antioch, *Letter to the Magnesians,* VI (c. 115). Trans. Cyril C. Richardson, LCC, I, 95.

Let the bishop preside in God's place, and the presbyters take the place of the apostolic council, and let the deacons (my special favorites) be entrusted with the ministry of Jesus Christ who was with the Father from eternity and appeared at the end [of the world].

28. *The Didache,* X (late first or early second century). Trans. Cyril C. Richardson, LCC, I, 176.

In the case of prophets, however, you should let them give thanks in their own way.

29.  Hippolytus, *Apostolic Tradition*, II, VII–IX (c. 217). Trans. Geoffrey J. Cuming, *Hippolytus: A Text for Students* (Bramcote, Notts.: Grove Books, 1976), pp. 8–14.

### Of Bishops

2. Let him be ordained bishop who has been chosen by all the people; and when he has been named and accepted by all, let the people assemble, together with the presbytery and those bishops who are present, on the Lord's day. When all give consent, they shall lay hands on him, and the presbytery shall stand by and be still. And all shall keep silence, praying in their hearts for the descent of the Spirit; after which one of the bishops present, being asked by all, shall lay his hand on him who is being ordained bishop, and pray, saying thus: . . . .

### Of Presbyters

7. And when a presbyter is ordained, the bishop shall lay his hand on his head, the presbyters also touching him; and he shall say according to what was said above, as we said before about the bishop, praying and saying: . . . .

### Of Deacons

8. And when a deacon is ordained, let him be chosen according to what was said above, the bishop alone laying on hands, in the same way as we also directed above. In the ordination of a deacon, the bishop alone shall lay on hands, because he is not being ordained to the priesthood, but to the service of the bishop, to do what is ordered by him. For he does not share in the counsel of the presbyterate, but administers and informs the bishop of what is fitting; he does not receive the common spirit of seniority in which the presbyters share, but that which is entrusted to him under the bishop's authority. For this reason the bishop alone shall ordain a deacon; but on a presbyter the presbyters alone shall lay hands, because of the common and like spirit of their order. For a presbyter has authority only to receive; he has not authority to give. For this reason he does not ordain the clergy, but at the ordination of a presbyter he seals, while the bishop ordains.

Over a deacon, then, (the bishop) shall say thus: . . . .

*Of Confessors*
9. But a confessor, if he was in chains for the name of the Lord shall not have hands laid on him for the diaconate or the presbyterate, for he has the honour of the presbyterate by his confession. But if he is appointed bishop, hands shall be laid on him.

But if there is a confessor who was not brought before the authorities, nor punished with chains, nor shut up in prison, nor condemned to any other penalty, but has only been derided on occasion for the name of our Lord and punished with a domestic punishment: if he confessed, let hands be laid on him for any order of which he is worthy.

And the bishop shall give thanks according to what we said above. It is not at all necessary for him to utter the same words as we said above, as though reciting them from memory, when giving thanks to God; but let each pray according to his ability. If indeed anyone has the ability to pray at length and with a solemn prayer, it is good. But if anyone, when he prays, utters a brief prayer, do not prevent him. Only, he must pray what is sound and orthodox [*orthodoxia*].

30. Peter Lombard, *Four Books of Sentences*, IV (c. 1152). Trans. Elizabeth Frances Rogers, *Peter Lombard and the Sacramental System* (Merrick, N.Y.: Richwood Publishing Co., 1976), p. 224.

**Distinction XXIV.** 1. Now we come to the consideration of holy ordination. There are seven grades or orders of spiritual office, as is clearly taught us in the words of the holy Fathers, and as is shown by the example of our head, that is Jesus Christ, who performed in his own person the duties of them all, and left the same orders to be observed in his body which is the Church.

2. And there are seven on account of the sevenfold grace of the holy Spirit, and those who do not participate in this grace, enter the ecclesiastical grades unworthily. But when men in whose minds the sevenfold grace of the holy Spirit is diffused, enter the

ecclesiastical orders, they are believed to receive a fuller grace in the very promotion to the spiritual rank.

3. (See Chapter VI, document 3*f–h*, pp. 124f. above).

31. "Decree for the Armenians" (1439). Trans. from *Enchiridion Symbolorum Definitionum et Declarationum*, ed. Henry Denzinger and Adolf Schönmetzer, 33rd ed. (Freiburg: Herder, 1965), p. 336.

> The sixth sacrament is ordination. The matter is according to the order which is conferred: for a presbyter it is passed on through a chalice with wine and a paten with bread; for a deacon through the giving of books of the Gospels; for a subdeacon through an empty chalice placed on an empty paten; and likewise for the others the things pertaining to the assignments of their ministries. The form for a priest is: "Receive the power for the offering of sacrifice in the Church for the living and the dead, in the name of the Father and of the Son and of the Holy Spirit." And thus for the other forms of order, according as they are contained in the Roman Pontifical. The ordinary minister of this sacrament is a bishop. The effect is the increase of grace, that whoever is ordained may be a fit minister.

**B. The Reformation challenges ministry as power and calls for equality on the basis of baptism.**
32. Martin Luther, *To the Christian Nobility of the German Nation Concerning the Reform of the Christian Estate* (1520). Trans. Charles M. Jacobs and James Atkinson, LW, XLIV, 128, 129.

> Suppose a group of earnest Christian laymen were taken prisoner and set down in a desert without an episcopally ordained priest among them. And suppose they were to come to a common mind there and then in the desert and elect one of their number, whether he were married or not, and charge him to baptize, say mass, pronounce absolution, and preach the gospel. Such a man would be as truly a priest as though he had been ordained by all the bishops and popes in the world. . . .

> For whoever comes out of the water of baptism can boast that he is already a consecrated priest, bishop and pope, although of course it is not seemly that just anybody should exercise such office. Be-

cause we are priests of equal standing, no one must push himself forward and take it upon himself, without our consent and election, to do that for which we all have equal authority. For no one dare take upon himself what is common to all without the authority and consent of the community. And should it happen that a person chosen for such office were deposed for abuse of trust, he would then be exactly what he was before. Therefore a priest in Christendom is nothing else but an office-holder. . . .

There is no true, basic difference between laymen and priests, princes and bishops, between religious and secular, except for the sake of office and work, but not for the sake of status. They are all of the spiritual estate, all are truly priests, bishops, and popes. But they do not all have the same work to do.

33. Martin Bucer, *Sermon on the Good Shepherd* (c. 1550). Trans. E. C. Whitaker, *Martin Bucer and the Book of Common Prayer* (Great Wakering: Mayhew-McCrimmon, 1974), ACC, LV, 178–180.

Brethren, you have heard both in your canonical examination and now in the sermon and in the sacred lessons which have been read from the Apostles and the gospels, how great is the dignity and the responsibility of this office to which you have been called and are now in the name of our Lord Jesus Christ to be solemnly instituted. . . . Consider now how great is the treasure which is committed to you: for the sheep are Christ's, and he has bought them for himself at the price of his own life: the church to which you are to administer even to eternal life is his bride, his body.

## V. CHRISTIAN BURIAL
### A. Hope gives way to fear with a return to hope encouraged.
34. Augustine, *Confessions*, IX (c. 400). Trans. Albert C. Outler, LCC, VII, 197.

32. So, when the body [of Monica, his mother] was carried forth, we both went and returned without tears. For neither in those prayers which we poured forth to thee, when the sacrifice of our redemption was offered up to thee for her—with the body placed by the side of the grave as the custom is there, before it is lowered down into it—neither in those prayers did I weep. But I was most

grievously sad in secret all the day, and with a troubled mind en-
treated thee, as I could, to heal my sorrow; but thou didst not.

35. Thomas of Celano (possibly), *Dies Irae* (13th century). Trans. William J. Irons and Isaac Williams, in *The Hymnal 1940* (New York: Church
Pension Fund, 1940), 468.

> Day of wrath! O day of mourning!
> See fulfilled the prophets' warning,
> Heav'n and earth in ashes burning!
>
> O what fear man's bosom rendeth,
> When from heav'n the Judge descendeth,
> On whose sentence all dependeth!
>
> Wondrous sound the trumpet flingeth,
> Through earth's sepulchres it ringeth,
> All before the throne it bringeth!

. . . . . . . . . . . . . . . . . . . . . . . . . . . .

> Worthless are my prayers and sighing,
> Yet, good Lord, in grace complying,
> Rescue me from fires undying!
>
> With thy favored sheep, O place me!
> Nor among the goats abase me;
> But to thy right hand upraise me.
>
> While the wicked are confounded,
> Doomed to flames of woe unbounded,
> Call me with thy saints surrounded.
>
> Low I kneel, with heart submission;
> See, like ashes, my contrition;
> Help me, in my last condition.
>
> Ah that day of tears and mourning!
> From the dust of earth returning,
> Man for judgment must prepare him;

Spare, O God, in mercy spare him!
Lord, all pitying, Jesus blest,
Grant them thine eternal rest!

36. Martin Luther, *Preface to the Burial Hymns* (1542). Trans. Paul Zeller Strodach and Ulrich S. Leupold, LW, LIII, 326–327.

> Nor do we sing any dirges or doleful songs over our dead and at the grave, but comforting hymns of the forgiveness of sins, of rest, sleep, life, and of the resurrection of departed Christians so that our faith may be strengthened and the people be moved to true devotion.

> For it is meet and right that we should conduct these funerals with proper decorum in order to honor and praise that joyous article of our faith, namely, the resurrection of the dead, and in order to defy Death, that terrible foe who so shamefully and in so many horrible ways goes on to devour us. . . .

> All this is done so that the article of the resurrection may be firmly implanted in us. For it is our lasting, blessed, and eternal comfort and joy against death, hell, devil, and every woe.

37. John Knox, *The Forme of Prayers* (1556). Ed. William D. Maxwell, *The Liturgical Portions of the Genevan Service Book* (London: Faith Press, 1965), p. 161 (spelling modernized).

> ### Of Burial
> The corpse is reverently brought to the grave, accompanied with the congregation, without any further ceremonies, which being buried, the minister goes to the church, if it be not far off, and makes some comfortable exhortation to the people, touching death, and resurrection.

38. John Wesley, *Journal* (1738). *The Works of John Wesley: Journal and Diaries*, ed. W. Reginald Ward and Richard P. Heitzenrater (Nashville: Abingdon Press, 1988), XVIII, 269.

> [Herrnhut] Tue. 8. [August 1738] A child was buried. The burying ground (called by them *Gottes Acker*, i.e. God's ground) lies a few hundred yards out of the town, under the side of a little wood.

There are distinct squares in it for married men and unmarried; for married and unmarried women; for male and female children, and for widows. The corpse was carried from the chapel, the children walking first; next the "orphan-father" (so they call him who has the chief care of the orphan-house) with the minister of Berthelsdorf; then four children bearing the corpse, and after them, Martin Dober and the father of the child. Then followed the men, and last the women and girls. They all sung as they went. Being come into the square where the male children are buried, the men stood on two sides of it, the boys on the third, and the women and girls on the fourth. There they sung again; after which the minister used (I think, read) a short prayer, and concluded with that blessing, "Unto God's gracious mercy and protection I commit you."

Seeing the father (a plain man, a tailor by trade) looking at the grave, I asked, "How do you find yourself?" He said, "Praised be the Lord, never better. He has taken the soul of my child to himself. I have seen, according to my desire, his body committed to holy ground. And I know that when it is raised again, both he and I shall be ever with the Lord."

39. *Constitution on the Sacred Liturgy* (Collegeville, Minn.: Liturgical Press, 1963), p. 43.

81. The rite for the burial of the dead should express more clearly the paschal character of Christian death, and should correspond more closely to the circumstances and traditions found in various regions. This holds good also for the liturgical color to be used.

## Select Bibliography on Occasional Services

Bradshaw, Paul F. *Ordination Rites of the Ancient Churches: East and West.* New York: Pueblo Publishing Co., 1990.

Cooke, Bernard J. *Ministry to Word and Sacraments: History and Theology.* Philadelphia: Fortress Press, 1980.

Dallen, James. *The Reconciling Community: The Rite of Penance.* New York: Pueblo Publishing Co., 1986.

Empereur, James L. *Prophetic Anointing.* Wilmington, Del.: Michael Glazier, 1982.

Gusmer, Charles W. *And You Visited Me: Sacramental Ministry to the Sick and Dying.* New York: Pueblo Publishing Co., 1984.

Kelsey, Morton. *Healing and Christianity.* New York: Harper & Row, 1973.

McNeill, John T. *A History of the Cure of Souls.* New York: Harper & Row, 1977.

Rowell, Geoffrey. *The Liturgy of Christian Burial.* London: Alcuin/SPCK, 1982.

Rutherford, Richard, and Tony Barr. *The Death of a Christian: The Order of Christian Funerals.* Rev. ed. Collegeville, Minn.: Liturgical Press, 1990.

Stevenson, Kenneth. *Nuptial Blessing.* London: Alcuin/SPCK, 1982.

Vos, Wiebe, and Geoffrey Wainwright, eds. *Ordination Rites.* Rotterdam: Liturgical Ecumenical Trust, 1980.

Willimon, William. *Worship as Pastoral Care.* Nashville: Abingdon Press, 1979.

# Glossary

*a cappella* (singing) without instrumental accompaniment.

**altar** table on which the Lord's Supper is celebrated; the term is also used for the communion rail (Protestant) or space about the altar (Roman Catholic).

**altar call** an invitation for those newly converted or wishing to renew their commitment to Jesus Christ to come forward to kneel at the communion rail.

**altar prayers** prayers in which individuals come forward to kneel at the communion rail in silent prayer.

**Annunciation** March 25, the feast commemorating the visit of the angel Gabriel to the Virgin Mary and the conception of Christ (Luke 1:26–38).

**ante-communion** the first part of the Lord's Supper, service of the Word, fore-mass, synaxis, pro-anaphora.

**anthems** choral music, often with scriptural texts, usually of greater technical difficulty than congregational song.

**Athanasian Creed** a lengthy creedal statement of unknown origin but likely from the late fourth or early fifth century, occasionally used in worship in the West.

*Ausbund* the selection of hymns used by some Anabaptists since the sixteenth century.

*Ave Maria* "Hail Mary," a short prayer dating from the eleventh century and coming into wide use in the sixteenth century, based on Luke 1:28, 42.

*Baptism, Eucharist and Ministry*   an attempt to find ecumenical agreement on these three matters, produced by the World Council of Churches in 1982 after many years of preparation.

**baptistery**   building or space within a building housing the pool or font that contains the water used for baptism.

**breviary**   the book containing the texts for the daily services of prayer and praise, a compilation of several previous books.

**canon**   liturgically the main portion of the eucharistic prayer, the great thanksgiving, or anaphora, in the Lord's Supper.

**canticles**   various hymnic materials from both Testaments, other than the psalms, often said or sung, e.g., the Magnificat (Luke 1:46–55).

**catechism**   the basic doctrines of Christian faith for the study of young or new Christians, often in question and answer form.

**chancel**   the portion of a church building designed for the use of the persons presiding, usually clergy or singers.

**chantry chapels**   chapels erected for saying memorial masses for deceased benefactors, becoming numerous in parish churches and cathedrals from the fourteenth century.

**chasuble**   long garment worn by priests at the Lord's Supper, dating from the secular poncho worn by Romans of both sexes.

**Collect for Illumination**   prayer of invocation for the Holy Spirit to act through the reading of scripture and preaching.

*Collectio Rituum*   a ritual, i.e., collection of pastoral services: marriage, baptism, etc.

**compline**   the last of the daily services of prayer and praise said before retiring in the late evening.

**confessional documents**   statements of the faith of a specific tradition such as the Augsburg Confession of 1530 (Lutheran) or the Westminster Confession of 1646 (Presbyterian).

**Congregation of Rites** from 1588 the official Roman Catholic bureau in charge of the standardization of worship and of canonization of saints.

**congregationalism** the principle that each local Christian community is self-governing and hence competent to order worship for itself.

**consecration** the setting apart of a thing or person for holy uses; this can refer to the bread and wine in the Lord's Supper, religious workers, buildings, or furnishings.

*Consensus Tigurinus* "Zurich Agreement" on the doctrine of the Lord's Supper, agreed to by Swiss Protestants in 1549.

**cope** cloak worn by clergy on important ceremonial occasions other than the Lord's Supper.

**cultus** a general term for all the forms and practices of worship of a specific tradition at a given time.

**daily office** a daily cycle of services of prayer and praise; the number of services varies according to the church concerned; the contents are basically psalmody, scripture, hymns, and prayers.

*Deutsche Evangelische Messe* German Evangelical Mass published by Balthasar Hübmaier in 1527.

*Deutsche Messe* Luther's second revision of the mass, published in German in 1526, including detailed instruction about the order of service and music.

*Didache* "The Teaching of the Twelve Apostles," a church order dating from the late first or early second century.

**dominical injunctions** commands from Jesus Christ to "do this in remembrance of me" (1 Cor. 11:24–25) and "make disciples . . . baptizing" (Matt. 28:19), interpreted as warrants for sacraments.

**elevation** the lifting of the consecrated bread and wine in the Lord's Supper after the words of institution, as offering and for adoration.

*Ephphatha*   word of Jesus (Mark 7:34) meaning "be opened," at various times reenacted in baptismal rites.

*epiclesis*   prayer of invocation for the Father to send the Holy Spirit to the people and upon the gifts present in the eucharist; part of the eucharistic prayer.

**Epiphany**   January 6, the feast variously commemorating the birth of Christ, the visit of the Magi, or the first sign at Cana (John 2:11).

**epistle**   the lesson read in the Sunday service and other occasions, often today as the second lesson, from the New Testament epistles, Acts, or (occasionally) Revelation.

**extreme unction**   a sacrament among Roman Catholics, originally and most recently of healing, but long regarded as preparation for death.

*Formula Missae*   Luther's first revision of the mass, published in Latin in 1523, generally conservative.

**fraction**   the act of breaking of the bread in the Lord's Supper (Matt. 26:26).

**Gallic liturgies**   the liturgies other than the Roman rite in use in the West in the early middle ages, largely replaced from the ninth century onward but known for variety and poetical expression.

**Gallicanism**   the relative independence of the Roman Catholic Church in France from interference from Rome, particularly from the seventeenth to the nineteenth centuries, although with earlier precedents.

*Gloria in excelsis*   a musical part of the eucharist, beginning with the words, "Glory to God in the highest," the Great Doxology as contrasted to the Lesser Doxology, the *Gloria Patri*, "Glory Be to the Father."

**Gospel**   the lesson read from the canonical Gospels in public worship, usually read last and sometimes with ceremony.

**Hampton Court Conference**   conference in 1604 between Puritan leaders and the new King James I of England, resulting in the King James Bible (1611).

**homily**   a sermon, particularly one published and read as a sermon.

**iconoclasm**   the destruction of images because of concern that they may detract from the true worship of God, violate the second commandment, or teach false doctrine.

**iconostasis**   screen containing icons, which separates nave from chancel in Orthodox churches.

**images**   representations by painting, sculpture, or glazing, of members of the Trinity and holy persons from all ages, sometimes venerated.

**incense**   a smoke from burning gum or wood that produces a fragrant odor, recognized as symbolic of prayer ascending (Ps. 141:2).

**inclusive language**   the language of worship structured so as not to detract from the full human worth of all persons by sexual, racial, ethnic, or handicapping differentiations; linguistic manifestation of equality; God language that is not gender specific.

**introit**   essentially a sung entrance hymn at the beginning of the Lord's Supper, usually based on a psalm.

**invitatories**   verses at the beginning of a prayer service, usually leading to Psalm 95.

**kirk**   the Scottish term for church, often used for the Church of Scotland.

**lauds**   the ancient morning service of prayer and praise, part of the daily cycle.

**libation**   the act of pouring the wine in the Lord's Supper from a flagon into a chalice or chalices.

**litany**   a form of public prayer in which a refrain is repeated by the congregation in response to a series of petitions or thanksgivings spoken by an individual.

**matins**   originally a nighttime service but since the Reformation the morning service of prayer and praise often said or sung daily; morning prayer.

*Mediator Dei*   encyclical letter of Pope Pius XII issued in 1947 with a view to regulating the developing liturgical movement.

**Mennonites**   the largest body of Anabaptists, which grew rapidly in the Netherlands in the sixteenth century and is now worldwide.

**missal**   the book containing the texts and rubrics for saying mass, a compilation of several books previously in use.

**modern devotion**   a renewed spiritual life that spread from the Netherlands after the late fourteenth century.

**motet**   a choral piece of music sung in various parts, often unaccompanied, usually based on a sacred text.

**nave**   the portion of a church building usually occupied by the congregation, i.e., the main portion.

**offertory**   the moment in worship when offerings of gifts such as money, bread and wine, or music are offered for holy use.

**ordinary time**   a term used by Roman Catholics since 1969 for the seasons after Epiphany and Pentecost.

**ordination**   the rite of setting aside certain persons for distinctive functions in the Christian community as lay officers or as clergy.

*ordo, ordines*   liturgical book or books from Rome containing directions for ceremonies in the mass and other sacraments.

*Pascha*   the Christian Passover, originally commemorating both Good Friday and Easter but in the fourth century becoming simply a commemoration of the resurrection.

**penance**   a sacrament among Roman Catholics for the forgiveness of sins and reconciliation of repentant Christians with God and each other.

**pontifical**   the book containing services performed by a bishop such as ordinations and consecrations of persons, buildings, and objects.

**postils**  books of sermons, often published to help other preachers.

*Preces Privatae*  collection of private prayers by the saintly Anglican bishop Lancelot Andrewes (1555–1626), published after his death.

**predestination**  the belief that God has predetermined the identity of all to be saved or damned (Rom. 8:28–30).

**prime**  a short daily service at the first hour of the day, mostly obsolete.

**private pews**  church pews owned and occupied by private individuals; in the eighteenth and nineteenth centuries, selling pews often financed church building; now almost universally repudiated as a practice.

**prone**  an unofficial service, often added to the mass in the late medieval period before, during, or after mass, usually in the vernacular and including a sermon.

**propers**  texts in worship that change from date to date as contrasted to those that do not; includes prayers, hymns, lessons, and psalms.

**psalmody**  the psalms of the Old Testament used in worship, whether said or sung.

**relics**  sacred objects, especially parts of the bodies of holy persons or items in close contact with their bodies.

**reliquaries**  vessels to contain and (sometimes) display relics.

**requiem mass**  a celebration of the eucharist in commemoration of the life of someone deceased.

**responsories**  short dialogical verses and responses, usually between the leader of worship and the congregation.

**ritual**  the handbook of services such as marriage, burial, and baptismal rites performed by a pastor, hence, pastorale or manual.

**roodscreen**  a screen in medieval churches separating the nave from the chancel with a cross (rood) over it.

**rubric**   directions as to what to do in a service, often printed in red.

**rubricism**   the mentality that worship must be carried out strictly according to prescribed rules (rubrics).

*Sanctus*   part of the eucharistic prayer, "Holy, holy, holy," usually sung.

**Sarum use**   the late medieval version of Roman Catholic rites in general use throughout the southern province of England, from Salisbury Cathedral.

**Savoy Conference**   meeting of Puritans and Anglicans in 1661 as a last attempt to reconcile liturgical agenda; it proved fruitless.

*Small Catechism*   Luther's small book, published in 1529, for the instruction of Christians in the basics of the faith.

**Thirty-Nine Articles**   the original official doctrinal statement of the Church of England, issued first in 1563.

**transubstantiation**   doctrine that the substance (but not the appearances, the "accidents") of bread and wine become the body and blood of Christ in the eucharist; official teaching of Roman Catholics since 1215.

**Trent, Council of**   council for the reform of the Roman Catholic Church, convened in three periods between 1545 and 1563.

**Vatican Council II**   Roman Catholic council from 1962–1965, instrumental in opening Roman Catholicism to much of the thought and practices of the modern world.

**vespers**   the evening daily office of prayer and praise, also known as evening prayer or evensong.

**vestments**   garb worn by clergy for the eucharist and other services, originating as secular clothing but long hallowed by ecclesiastical custom.

**viaticum**   communion given to a dying person.

**vigils** (matins, nocturns)   nighttime services of prayer and praise, eventually becoming part of the daily cycle of services.

**Westminster** *Directory*   Puritan document replacing the *Book of Common Prayer* in the Church of England from 1645 to 1660 with detailed instructions for the ordering of worship.

# Acknowledgments

Grateful acknowledgment is made to the following.

Augsburg Fortress, for material from:

*Book of Concord,* by T. G. Tappert, copyright © 1959 Fortress Press.

*Luther's Works:* Vol. 35, edited by E. Theodore Bachmann, copyright © 1960 Muhlenberg Press; Vol. 36, edited by Abdel Ross Wentz, copyright © 1959 Fortress Press; Vol. 38, edited by Martin E. Lehmann, copyright © 1971 Fortress Press; Vol. 44, edited by James Atkinson, copyright © 1966 Fortress Press; Vol. 53, edited by Ulrich S. Leupold, copyright © 1965 Fortress Press.

Catholic University of America Press, for material from Hugh M. Riley, *Christian Initiation,* 1974.

Glencoe Publishing Co., for material from *The Summa Theologica of St. Thomas Aquinas,* translated by Fathers of the English Dominican Province. Copyright © 1947, 1948 by Benziger Brothers.

Herald Press, for material from *The Complete Writings of Menno Simons,* translated by Leonard Verduin. Copyright 1956.

Open Court Publishing Company, for material from *Religion Within the Limits of Reason Alone,* by Immanuel Kant, translated by T. M. Greene and H. H. Hudson. Copyright 1934.

SPCK, London, for material from *Egeria's Travels,* translated by John Wilkinson, 1971; from *St. Cyril of Jerusalem's Lectures on the Christian Sacraments,* edited by F. L. Cross, 1960; and from *Tertullian's Homily on Baptism,* translated by Ernest Evans, 1964.

Kenneth Stevenson, for material from Geoffrey Cuming's translation of

Hippolytus, from *Hippolytus: A Text for Students*, copyright Geoffrey Cuming, 1976.

Westminster/John Knox Press, for material from volumes of The Library of Christian Classics, published simultaneously in Great Britain and the U.S.A. by SCM Press Ltd., London, and The Westminster Press, Philadelphia:

Vol. I, *Early Christian Fathers*, translated and edited by Cyril C. Richardson. First published MCMLIII.

Vol. II, *Alexandrian Christianity*, edited by John Ernest Oulton and Henry Chadwick. First published MCMLIV.

Vol. IV, *Cyril of Jerusalem and Nemesius of Emesa*, translated and edited by W. Telfer. First published MCMLV.

Vol. VII, *Augustine: Confessions and Enchiridion*, translated and edited by Albert C. Outler. First published MCMLV.

Vol. IX, *Early Medieval Theology*, translated and edited by George E. McCracken. First published MCMLVI.

Vols. XX and XXI, *Calvin: Institutes of the Christian Religion*, edited by John T. McNeill and translated by Ford Lewis Battles. Copyright © MCMLX W. L. Jenkins.

Vol. XXII, *Calvin: Theological Treatises*, translated with Introductions and Notes by J. K. S. Reid. First published MCMLIV.

Vol. XXIV, *Zwingli and Bullinger*, translated with Introductions and Notes by G. W. Bromiley. First published MCMLIII.

Vol. XXV, *Spiritual and Anabaptist Writers*, edited by George Huston Williams and Angel M. Mergal. First published MCMLVII.

Yale University Press, for material from *The First Urban Christians*, by Wayne A. Meeks. Copyright © 1983 by Yale University. All rights reserved.

# Index of Authors
# and Documents

African American spiritual, 113–114

Ambrose, *On the Sacraments*, 159, 189–190

*Apostolic Constitutions*, 20, 28, 31, 83–84, 163

*Apostolic Tradition*, 25–26, 79–81, 82–83, 151–156, 186–188, 230–231

Aquinas, Thomas, *Summa Theologica*, 125–128, 195–196, 223

*Articles of Religion*, 137–138, 174, 207–208

Augustine
  *Against Faustus*, 120
  *City of God*, 192–193
  *Commentary on Psalms*, 120
  *Confessions*, 233–234
  *Enchiridion*, 163–164
  *Letter 55*, 25, 28
  *On Baptism*, 121
  *Questions on the Heptateuch*, 120
  *Sermon 272*, 192
  *Treatise on the Gospel of John*, 119–120, 191

Bach, J. S., *Order of Divine Service*, 111

*Baptism, Eucharist and Ministry*, 213

Barclay, Robert, *Apology*, 139–140

*Barnabas, Epistle of*, 19

Barth, Karl, *Teaching of the Church Regarding Baptism*, 176–177

Basil, *Long Rules*, 89–90

Benedict, *Rule*, 90–91

Berengarius, *Recantation*, 194

Bishops' Committee on the Liturgy, *Environment and Art in Catholic Worship*, 73–74

*Book of Common Prayer* (1549), 35–36, 94–95, 106–107, 173–174, 228–229; (1552), 35–36, 95–96

*Book of Discipline*, 36–37

Bucer, Martin, *Censura*, 174
  *Sermon on the Good Shepherd*, 233

Calvin, John
  *Articles Concerning Organization*, 105–106
  *Draft Ecclesiastical Ordinances*, 173
  *Institutes*, 132–135, 171–173, 203–205, 223–224, 227–228

Calvin, John (cont.)
  Short Treatise on the Holy
    Supper, 202–203
Campbell, Alexander, Christian
  System, 210–212
Cassian
  Conferences, 30
  Institutes, 88–89
Chrysostom, John
  Baptismal Instructions, 84–85,
    159–160
  Sermons, 30, 31, 82
Clement of Alexandria
  Miscellanies, 30, 78
  Teacher, 148
Codex Justinianus, 19
Constitution on the Sacred Liturgy,
  117, 212, 224, 236
Crosby, Fanny J., "Blessed
  Assurance," 116–117
Cyprian
  Letters, 188–189
  On the Lord's Prayer, 82
Cyril of Jerusalem, Catechetical
  Lectures, 26, 156–158, 190–191

Decree for the Armenians,
  128–129, 164–166, 196–197,
  218–219, 232
Didache, 18, 20, 78, 147,
  182–183, 229–230
Didascalia Apostolorum, 23, 156
Directory for Family-Worship,
  96–97
Directory for the Public Worship of
  God. See Westminster Directory
Doctrines and Discipline
  (Methodist), 115–116

Egeria, Travels, 24–25, 85–88,
  162–163

England, Church of. See Articles
  of Religion; Book of Common
  Prayer
Eusebius of Caesarea
  Commentary on Psalm 64, 83
  History of the Church, 23
  Life of Constantine, 28

Finney, Charles G., Lectures on
  Revivals, 97–98, 114–115
Finnian of Clonard, Penitential,
  217
Fourth Lateran Council, 194

Gerber, Christian, Historie der
  Kirchen, 93
Gorham, B. W., Camp Meeting
  Manual, 66, 111–112

Hippolytus. See Apostolic
  Tradition
Hoadly, Benjamin, Plain Account,
  208
Hübmaier, Balthasar, Summa of
  the Entire Christian Life,
  201–202
Hugh of St. Victor, On the
  Sacraments, 121

Ignatius of Antioch, Letters, 19,
  184, 225, 229
Innocent III, Concerning the Holy
  Mystery, 32–34
Irenaeus, Against the Heresies,
  148

Justin Martyr, First Apology, 19,
  101, 147–148, 184–186

Kant, Immanuel, Religion Within
  the Limits of Reason Alone,
  140–141

Knox, John
  Forme of Prayers, 236
  History of the Reformation,
    36–37

Liturgy of the Hours, 98
Lombard, Peter, Sentences,
  121–125, 218, 222–223,
  225–226, 231–232
Luther, Martin
  Babylonian Captivity of the
    Church, 129–131, 167,
    197–199, 219–220
  Christian Nobility, To the,
    232–233
  Formula Missae, 34, 91–92,
    103–105
  German Mass, 34–35, 92–93
  Holy and Blessed Sacrament of
    Baptism, 166–167
  Large Catechism, 131, 168, 199
  Marburg Colloquy, 202
  Order of Baptism, 167–168
  Preface to Burial Hymns, 235

Manual of York Use, 226–227
Martyrdom of Polycarp, 31–32
Methodism. See Wesley, John;
  Doctrines and Discipline
Millenary Petition, 107–108

Nicaea, Council of, 26

Old Irish Table of Commutations,
  217–218
Ordo Romanus Primus, 101–103
Origen, On Prayer, 81

Paschasius Radbertus, Lord's Body
  and Blood, 193

Philocalian Martyrology, 31
Pliny the Younger, Letter to
  Trajan, 18, 183–184
Pugin, A. W. N., Contrasts, 72–73
Puritans. See Millenary Petition;
  Westminster Confession of Faith;
  Westminster Directory

Quiñones, Francisco de,
  Breviarium, 93

Ratramnus of Corbie, Christ's
  Body and Blood, 193–194
Riedeman, Peter, Account,
  220–221
Rite of Christian Initiation of
  Adults, 177–178

Saragossa, Council of, 31
Sarapion, Prayer-Book, 222
Sattler, Michael, Trial and
  Martyrdom, 201
Schillebeeckx, Edward, Christ the
  Sacrament, 142–143
Schleitheim Confession, 168, 220
Scotch Confession of Faith, 137
Scotland, Church of. See Book of
  Discipline; Directory for Family-
  Worship; Scotch Confession of
  Faith
scripture, 17–18, 20–21, 26–27,
  29, 75–76, 100–101, 145–146,
  180–181, 214–215, 221, 225,
  229
Simons, Menno
  Foundation of Christian
    Doctrine, 168–170
  Kind Admonition, 220
Suger, Abbot, De Administratione,
  71

Tertullian
  *Of the Crown,* 27, 150
  *On Baptism,* 21, 27, 149
  *On Fasting,* 78–79
  *On Penance,* 215–217
  *On Prayer,* 20, 79
*Testament of Our Lord,* 38
Theodore of Mopsuestia,
  *Instructions,* 160–161
Thomas of Celano, *Dies Irae,*
  234–235
Trent, Council of, *Canons and
  Decrees,* 125–136, 205–207,
  221, 224, 228

Wesley, Charles, *Hymns on the
  Lord's Supper,* 208–210
Wesley, John
  *Hymns on the Lord's Supper,*
  208–210

*Journal,* 235–236
*New Birth,* 175–176
*Sunday Service,* 38, 97,
  137–138, 175, 207–208
*Wesleyan Camp Meeting
  Hymnbook,* 112–113
*Westminster Confession of Faith,*
  138–139
Westminster *Directory,* 37,
  108–110, 175
Wren, Christopher, *Letter,*
  71–72

Zwingli, Ulrich
  *Commentary on True and False
    Religion,* 132
  *Of Baptism,* 170–171
  *On the Lord's Supper,* 199, 201

# Index of Subjects

abbey churches, 54
absolution, 219
Advent, 31
altar-tables, 48–49
Anabaptists, 168–171, 220–221
anointing, baptismal, 149,
    154–155, 158, 161, 163, 166
Aquinas, Thomas, 128
Armenians, 128, 164, 218–219,
    232
Ascension, 28–29
assembly, 73, 108, 139
auditory churches, 71–72
Augustine, 122–124, 133, 226

Bach, J. S., 93, 111
baptism, 25–26, 123, 126, 128,
    140, 141, 145–179, 215, 232
baptisteries, 45–46
bishop, 165–166, 184, 186, 229,
    230–231, 232
Bucer, Martin, 170, 202
burial, Christian, 232–237

camp meeting, 66, 111–113
catechumens, 152–153, 162–163,
    178
cathedral office, 82–88
ceremonial, 107–108
character, 126, 129, 136
Christian year, 21–40
Christmas, 31
Chrysostom, John, 218

circumcision, 123, 170
Clement VII, 94
colors, liturgical, 32–34
Common Calendar, 39
concelebration, 186
confirmation, 126, 128, 129–130,
    165–166, 174
consecration, 189–191, 193–196,
    201, 207
Constantine, 19
conversion, 175–176, 177–178
Cranmer, Thomas, 93–96
creed, 155, 162–163

day, liturgical, 17
deacon, 156, 185–186, 229, 230
deaconess, 156, 184
dedication, infant, 171
disciples, making of, 1–2
Discipline (Methodist), 115–116

Easter, 21, 23–25, 150
elect, 153, 162, 178
England, Church of, 35–36, 137,
    173–174, 207
Enlightenment, 140–142, 208
Epiphany, 29–30
eucharist, 124, 127–128, 140,
    141, 180–213
    as memorial, 201–202
    in both kinds, 197, 206, 208,
    212

eucharistic prayer, 182–183,
    186–187, 211–212
exorcism, 25, 153–154, 160, 162
extreme unction, 124, 130–131,
    222–223

faith, 127, 130, 132, 133, 135,
    169
family worship, 96–97
fasting, 20, 27, 37, 147, 150, 163
footwashing, 159

*Gloria in excelsis,* 103–104
gothic revival, 72–73
grace, 124, 126, 136, 138,
    140–141
Grado, baptistery, 56
Gratian, 125

healing of the sick, 221–225. *See
    also* extreme unction
hearers of the word, 151–152
Holy Spirit, 133, 149, 159, 166,
    173, 191, 204
Holy Week, 24–25, 35
hours of prayer, 75–99
Hugh of St. Victor, 122, 123

immersion, 166
infant baptism, 149–150,
    168–171, 172, 174–177
intercession, 117
Ireland, 217–218
Isidore of Seville, 125

Jerome, 218
Jerusalem, 24–25, 85–88
Jewish calendar, 22

*Kyrie eleison,* 103–104

laying on of hands, 146
lections, 34–36, 38
Leipzig, 111
Lent, 25–26, 157, 162
Lincoln Cathedral, 53
liturgical arrangements, 50–70
liturgical families, classical, 6, 8
liturgical theology, 2–3
liturgy, history of, 2–3
Lord's Prayer, 78, 110
Lucernare, 86–87
Luther, Martin, 169, 205

Magdalene College, 55
marriage, 123, 130, 225–229
Methodism, 38, 97, 137–138,
    175, 207–208, 208–210,
    235–236
minor orders, 124, 231–232
monastic office, 88–91
monks, 85–91
Moravians, 235–236
mystagogical catechesis, 156–161

new measures, 114–115

observation, 3–4
ordination, 124–125, 126, 128,
    130, 134, 229–233
original sin, 164, 165
Orthodoxy, architecture of, 52

Pascha. *See* Easter
pastoral liturgy, 3–4
pedagogy, liturgical, 1–5
penance. *See* reconciliation
Pentecost, 26–29, 150
Polycarp, 31–32
prayer
    extempore, 110
    public, 75–99

prayer meetings, 97–98
Presbyterians, 37–38, 96–97,
    107–110, 137–139, 175
presbyters, 229, 230
presence, eucharistic, 201–205,
    209–210, 212
presider's chair, 49–50
prophets, 183, 230
Protestant traditions, 7, 9, 58–68
psalms, 85, 88–89, 91, 95,
    105–106
pulpits, 46–47
Puritans, 37–38, 107–110,
    138–139

Quakers, 139–140
Quartodecimans, 23

reading, scripture, 104–105, 109,
    117
reconciliation, 128, 131, 214–215
regeneration, 173–176
Reinhold, H. A., xi
renunciation, 154, 158, 159
Riley, Hugh M., 61

Sabbath, 20–23
sacraments
    definitions, 119–128
    number, 121, 123, 127,
        129–131, 132, 135, 137–138
    of old law, 120, 123, 126, 128,
        134, 135, 139
    primordial, 142–143
    validity, 129

sacrifice, 183, 192–193, 198–199,
    206, 208, 210
St.-Denis (Paris), 71
St. Lawrence (Rome), 51
saints' days, 31–32, 34, 35–36,
    37
Scotland, 26–27, 96–97, 137
scripture reading, 104–105, 109,
    117
sermon, 109–110, 115, 117
signs, 134, 138, 170, 172, 203
space, liturgical
    altar-table, 44
    baptismal, 44
    choir, 43
    congregational, 43
    gathering, 42
    movement, 42
Sunday, 18–19, 37
synagogue, 100–101

thanksgiving, days of, 37
transubstantiation, 195–196,
    197–198, 206, 207
Trinitarian formula, 146, 147,
    149, 160, 163, 165

vernacular, 103–104, 207
vocabulary, 3
vows, marriage, 226–227

water and wine, 188–189,
    196–197, 207
women, 97–98, 156, 184
words of institution, 181